The Complete Idiot's Reference Card

tear here

Waschka's Wealth Levels

Wealth Level 1

You are able to maintain your standard of living and at the same time save enough money to achieve your Target Savings Goal (TSG), the annual amount you need to save to meet your needs at retirement.

Wealth Level 2

Your portfolio is large enough to produce, on its own, a total return each year equal to your TSG as well as keep up with inflation.

Wealth Level 3

Your portfolio produces a total return large enough to cover your desired lifestyle and inflation.

Wealth Level 4

You have accumulated enough assets to produce a total return sufficient enough to substantially increase your current and future lifestyle while at the same time keeping up with inflation.

Wealth Level 5

You have accumulated enough assets to produce a total return well beyond what you would ever spend. You now have the option not to work, raise your standard of living, and bestow large charitable gifts.

The Habits of Very Wealthy People

❑ Save every month
❑ Avoid debt
❑ Shop before you buy
❑ Delay purchases of items you don't need
❑ Buy used when you can
❑ Take care of what you own
❑ Maintain a basic understanding of the stock and bond markets
❑ Take time to plan, research, and systematically measure your results

Characteristics of Wealthy People

❑ A passion for what you do
❑ The ability to make decisions
❑ Discipline
❑ Patience

alpha
books

Wealth Builder Worksheet

1. What is your current yearly income?_____

2. What are your monthly and annual expenses?

   Enter your monthly expenses and multiply by 12:

   _____ × 12 = _____

   (Monthly expenses) × 12 = Yearly expenses

   Don't forget to add any additional expenses you see coming in the next year.

3. Estimate income needed to cover your expenses in before-tax dollars.

   Calculate the inverse of your total average tax rate by subtracting your average tax rate from one:

   1.00 − _____=_____

   1.00 − (Total average federal and provincial income tax rate percentage) = Inverse rate

   Convert yearly expenses into a before-tax amount by dividing your yearly expenses by the inverse rate.

   _____ ÷_____ = _____

   (Total yearly expenses) ÷ (Inverse rate) = Pre-tax yearly expenses

4. Project the effect of inflation on expenses.

   _____ × _____ = _____

   (Pre-tax yearly expenses) × (1.00 + Inflation estimate) = Yearly inflated expenses

   Continue this calculation for every year until retirement to get the amount of money you will need each year to cover expenses at retirement.

5. Estimate Your Target Portfolio Goal (TPG).

   _____ ÷ _____ = _____

   (Yearly inflated expenses) ÷ (Estimated net rate of return) = Target Portfolio Goal

6. Estimate yearly and monthly TSGs.

   Your yearly TSG calculation is calculated by dividing your TPG by the Future Value Factor, which can be found in the Future Value of Annuity Factors Table in Chapter 4:

   _____ ÷ _____ = _____

   (Target Portfolio Goal) ÷ (Future Value Factor) = Yearly TSG

   Your monthly TSG calculation can be found by dividing your yearly TSG by 12:

   _____ ÷ 12 = _____

   (Yearly TSG) ÷12 = Monthly TSG

7. Now that you know your TSG, it's time to make it happen.

8. Once you've made it happen, and you've achieved Wealth Stage 1, just do all you can to maintain your savings amount. If you get confused, check out Chapter 4 for more details on this worksheet.

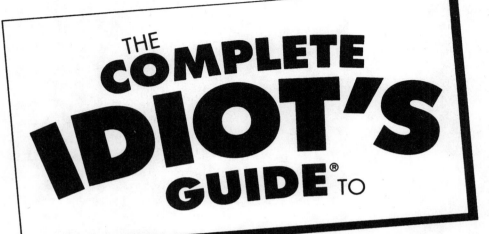

Getting Rich
for Canadians✴

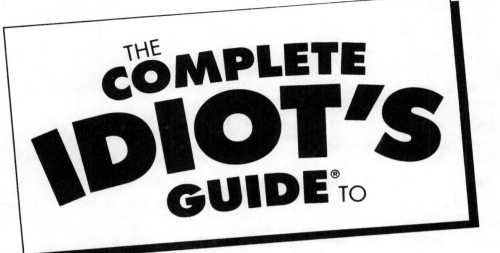

THE COMPLETE IDIOT'S GUIDE® TO

Getting Rich for Canadians✸

*by Mark J. Heinzl
and Larry Waschka*

Prentice
Hall
Canada

A Pearson Company
Toronto

alpha
books

Canadian Cataloguing in Publication Data

Heinzl, Mark, 1967-
  The complete idiot's guide to getting rich for Canadians

Includes index.
ISBN 0-13-086725-X

1. Finance, Personal - Canada. 2. Investments - Canada. I. Waschka, Larry. Complete idiot's guide to getting rich in Canada. II. Title.

HG179.W373 2000   332.024'01   C00-930172-0

©2000 Pearson Education Canada Inc.
Toronto, Ontario

Adapted from The Complete Idiot's Guide to Getting Rich © 1999 by Larry Waschka

ISBN 0-13-086725-X

Editorial Director, Trade Division: Andrea Crozier
Acquisitions Editor: Paul Woods
Copy Editor: Nancy Carroll
Production Editor: Lori McLellan
Art Direction: Mary Opper
Cover Image: 1998 GSO Images/The Image Bank
Interior Design: Scott Cook and Amy Adams of DesignLab
Production Manager: Kathrine Pummell
Page Layout: B.J. Weckerle
Illustrator: Jody P. Schaeffer

1 2 3 4 5 WC 04 03 02 01 00

Printed and bound in Canada.

THE COMPLETE IDIOT'S GUIDE TO and Design are registered trademarks of Macmillan USA, Inc.

Visit the Prentice Hall Canada Web site! Send us your comments, browse our catalogues, and more. **www.phcanada.com**.

Prentice Hall Canada

A Pearson Company

alpha books

Contents at a Glance

Part 1:   **The Basics: Wealth Levels 1 and 2**   **1**

  1   Who's Really Rich and Do You Have What It
Takes to Be Rich?   3
How to define what wealth means to you.

  2   Ten Key Concepts of Building Wealth   15
*Some of the basic concepts you should know on your
journey toward wealth.*

  3   The Five Levels of Wealth   25
A way to measure your relative level of wealth.

  4   The Eight Steps Toward Achieving Wealth Level 1   33
How to get started on the way to wealth.

  5   The Habits and Characteristics Needed to Reach
Wealth Level 2   55
The next step on the journey.

  6   Building Wealth as an Employee   67
How your job can help you reach your goals.

Part 2:   **Achieving Wealth Level 3 by Taming the
Portfolio Beast**   **79**

  7   Portfolio Tools You Need to Avoid   81
The best of what NOT to buy.

  8   Portfolio Tools That Work   93
The best types of investments.

  9   Five Things You Must Know Before You Hire
Professional Help   111
What to ask and who to ask.

  10   Getting Your Feet Wet with the First Decision   127
Take the plunge with your first investment.

  11   The Investment Management Cycle   137
Portfolio theory made easy.

  12   Six Things You Must Have to be a Successful
Portfolio Manager   151
Best traits of great money managers.

  13   My 10 Favourite Portfolio Management Tactics   161
How to play the market like a pro.

14 The Laws of Successful Portfolio Management   175
    Years' worth of experience in one easy chapter.

15 The Most Common Mistakes Made by Investors   185
    *No matter what the level of experience, investors still
    make the same common mistakes.*

**Part 3:   Achieving Wealth Levels 4 and 5 with
            Your Own Business   193**

16 Can You Supplement Your Income with
    Your Hobby?   195
    Laying the groundwork for your own business.

17 Working for the Perfect Boss—Yourself!   207
    Growing a successful business.

18 Your Accountant is Your Friend   217
    All the great things a good accountant can do for you.

19 Your Banker is Your Friend   227
    The no-sweat way to apply for a loan.

20 Hire the Best and Delegate   237
    Your most important business decision—who you hire.

21 Maximizing Profits and Selling Your Business   247
    Grow it well and then sell.

Part 4:   Rich People Have Rich Habits   263

22 Reducing Your Tax Bite   265
    Some basics on minimizing your taxes.

23 The Wealth Paradigms, and Why People Fail
    to Get Rich   273
    Getting your mind right is half the battle.

24 Planning Secrets That Will Build Wealth Faster   283
    How to get organized and jump-start your journey.

Appendix A—Glossary   295

Appendix B—List of Web Sites   301

Index   305

Contents

Foreword   **xvii**

Introduction   **xix**

How to Use This Book   **xxi**

Part 1: The Basics: Wealth Levels 1 and 2   **1**

1   Who's Really Rich and Do You Have What It Takes to Be Rich?   **3**

Who's Really Rich? 4

Invisible Rags-to-Riches Wealth 5

Even the Postman Can Build Wealth 6

You Don't Need a University Education 7

You'd Never Think These People Had Any Money 8

The Wealth Test 8

Why Do So Few Make It? 10

Wealth Deception 12

It's Not Impossible 12

This Is a Journey, Not a Destination 12

The Least You Need to Know 13

2   Ten Key Concepts of Building Wealth   **15**

How Do You Define Wealth? 15

Portfolio 16

Time 17

Standard of Living Expenses 19

Total Return 20

Risk 20

Inflation 21

Taxes 21

Compound Growth 22

Actual Savings Amount 23

Target Savings Goal (TSG) 23

The Least You Need to Know 24

3   The Five Levels of Wealth   **25**

Wealth Level 1 26

Focus 26

Stages 27

Shortcuts 27
Wealth Level 2 27
   Focus 28
   Stages 28
   Shortcuts 29
Wealth Level 3 29
   Focus 29
Wealth Level 4 29
   Focus 30
Wealth Level 5 30
   Focus 31
The Least You Need to Know 31

4 The Eight Steps Toward Achieving Wealth Level 1   **33**

Getting Ready for the Journey 33
Step 1: Analyse Your Current Income 35
Step 2: Analyse Your Current Spending Habits 37
Step 3: Estimate Income Needed to Cover Your Expenses
    in Before-Tax Dollars 42
Step 4: Project the Effect of Inflation on Expenses 42
Step 5: Estimate Your Target Portfolio Amount 43
Step 6: Estimate Yearly and Monthly TSGs 45
Step 7: Achieve Your Target Savings Goal 50
Step 8: Maintain Your Plan 52
The Least You Need to Know 53

5 The Habits and Characteristics Needed to Reach Wealth Level 2   **55**

1. Save Every Month 56
2. Avoid Debt 57
3. Shop Before You Buy 57
4. Buy Used When You Can 58
5. Take Care of What You Own 60
6. Maintain a Basic Understanding of the Stock and
   Bond Markets 61
7. Take Time to Plan, Research, and Systematically
   Measure Your Results 62
Characteristics of Wealthy People 63
   A Passion for What You Do 63
   Decision-Making Ability 64
   Discipline 65

Patience 65
The Least You Need to Know 65

6   Building Wealth as an Employee   67

How to Get Your Dream Job 68
Three Questions Revisited 68
Do You Enjoy What You Do Now? 68
The Perfect Day at Work 69
Looking at Your Options 69
Find a Role Model 70
The Job Proposal 71
How to Maximize Income while Working for Others 72
How to Maximize Savings while Working for Others 74
Maximize Contributions to Your Retirement Savings Plan—
   The Last Tax Shelter 74
Get into Another Qualified Defined-Contribution Plan 75
Maximize Savings in Your Investment Account 75
Buy Stock in the Company For Which You Work 76
The Least You Need to Know 77

**Part 2: Achieving Wealth Level 3 by Taming
            the Portfolio Beast   79**

7   Portfolio Tools You Need to Avoid   81

Reasons Why People Use the Wrong Tools 82
They Don't Do Their Homework 82
They Take Advice from Commission-Based Salespeople 82
They Don't Check for Bias and Conflicts of Interest 83
The Results of Using the Wrong Investment Tools 84
Unsuitability of the Investment 84
Unknown Expenses 85
Mediocrity 85
The Tools to Stay Away From 85
Proprietary Investment Products 85
High-Cost Mutual Funds 86
Limited Partnerships 87
Initial Public Offerings of Closed-End Funds 88
Options 89
Futures 89
Penny Stocks 89
Rumours and Hot Tips 90
Insurance Products 90
The Least You Need to Know 92

8   Portfolio Tools That Work   93

Five Questions to Ask Before You Buy Any Investment . . .   93
The Fixed-Income Tools   95
  Money-Market Funds *96*
  Guaranteed Investment Certificates *97*
  Government Bonds and Treasury Bills *97*
  Corporate Bonds *98*
  Hybrid Fixed-Income Securities *99*
The Equity Tools: Stocks and Such   99
  Domestic Stocks *101*
  Foreign Stocks *101*
The Mutual Fund Tools   102
  Mutual Funds Are No Longer Just for Small Accounts *102*
  Which Mutual Funds Are Best? *103*
  Actively Managed Funds *106*
  Closed-End Funds *107*
  A Little Secret about Bond Funds *107*
The Best Tools of Wealth   108
  The Best Tool: Your Own Business *108*
  A No-Load Mutual Fund Portfolio *108*
  The Perfect Portfolio *109*
  The Tools to Help You Invest *109*
The Least You Need to Know   110

**9   Five Things You Must Know Before You Hire
     Professional Help   111**

Will All the Great Advisors Please Stand Up?   112
  Full-Service Investment Brokers *113*
  Financial Planners and Advisors *114*
The Four Cs: Compatibility Questions You Should Ask
  Your Advisor   114
  Credentials *115*
  Compensation *116*
  Characteristics *118*
  Customer Service *119*
Client References   123
Background Check   124
The Least You Need to Know   125

10 Getting Your Feet Wet with the First Decision   127

Don't Be a Sucker   128
What Should Your First Investment Look Like?   129
  You Have to Meet the Minimums *129*

Narrowing the List 130
Risk and Return 130
  "To Thine Own Self Be True" 130
  What Kind of Return Do You Expect? 131
Investment Ideas for the Confused and Bewildered 131
  Individual Stocks 131
  Real Estate 132
  Mutual Funds 132
Don't Spend Too Much Time Monitoring Your
Investment 132
  The Tortoise and the Hare 133
  Invest Automatically 133
Where to Put the First Investment 133
Graduating to More Than One Fund 134
  Graduating to Two Funds 135
  Graduating to Three Funds 135
The Least You Need to Know 136

11 The Investment Management Cycle   **137**
Asset Allocation 139
  Throw Away Your Asset Allocation Software 139
  Don't Base It on Your Age 139
  Base Your Asset Allocation Upon the Hockey Puck Theory ... 140
Investment Selection 142
  Buy and Hold 143
  Market Timing 143
  Sector Rotation 144
  The Flower Portfolio 146
Maintenance and Review 147
  Measurement of Results 147
  The Most Important Investment Strategy: Micro-Delegation . 148
  Zero-Based Thinking 149
The Least You Need to Know 149

**12 Six Things You Must Have to Be a Successful
Portfolio Manager**   **151**
You've Got to Know the Markets and World Economy ... 152
  Inflation and Interest Rates 152
  Earnings Growth: The Key to Making Money in Stocks 152
Information: The Key to Wealth 153
  A Chart is Worth 1,000 Words 153
The Time Commitment 154
A Little Discipline Goes a Long Way 154

Take the Time to Research 155
Sell When It's Time to Sell 155
Buy When It's Time to Buy 155
Stick with Your Decision 156
Imagination Is More Important than You Think 156
You Have to Be a Little Unreasonable to Be Any Good 156
You Have to Be Able to Think Creatively 157
Desire and Passion Will Make You Very Wealthy 158
The Least You Need to Know 159

13 My 10 Favourite Portfolio Management Tactics   **161**

Interest Rate Tactic 162
Panic Cycle Tactic 164
Industry and Country Growth Tactic 166
Economic Cycle Tactic 166
Market Cycle Tactic 168
Demographic Tactic 169
Information Gap Tactic 169
Technology Gap Tactic 170
Inefficient Market Gap Tactic 171
The Weekly Top-10 Tactic 173
The Least You Need to Know 174

14 The Laws of Successful Portfolio Management   **175**

Waschka's Laws of Investing 176
Know When You're Being Sold 176
Stand on the Shoulders of Giants 176
What You Don't Know Can Really Hurt You 176
If It Sounds Too Good to Be True, It Probably Is 176
Accept Risk, but Learn How to Manage It 177
Always Be Prepared for the Stock Market to Go Down 177
Be Proactive 177
Know the Difference between Rumour and Reality 177
Recognise Conflicts of Interest When You See Them 177
Focus First on Value, Then on Costs 177
Focus on What You Can Control 178
Don't Sell in a Quick Correction 178
Avoid Custodian Fees 179
Buy Closed-End Funds that Sell at a Discount 179
Avoid Limited Partnerships 179
Avoid Buying on Margin for Extended Periods 180
Never, Never, Never Invest Just for the Tax Savings 180

Don't Buy from Strangers *180*
Take Advantage of Breakpoints *180*
Other Investment Laws Revisited 180
There's Always a Bull Market Somewhere *181*
The Market Is Full of Inefficiency *181*
Be an Unreasonable Investor *181*
Your First Investment Must Do It All *181*
Understand No-Load Mutual Funds vs. Load Funds *181*
Consolidate Accounts *181*
Start an RRSP *182*
Never Use Life Insurance for Investment *182*
Be Careful Purchasing Mutual Funds in December *182*
Check Twice for All Fees and Commissions *182*
Educate Yourself with Free or Low-Cost Resources *182*
If Interest Rates Are Rising, Don't Buy Long-Term Bonds *182*
Don't Buy Proprietary Products *182*
Don't Be a Trader *183*
Use "No Transaction Fee" Programs (NTF) *183*
Don't Buy Individual Foreign Stocks or Bonds *183*
Ask for a Discount *183*
Eliminate as Many Barriers or Limitations as You Can *183*
Demand Liquidity *183*
Make Portfolio Management Your Passion *183*
The Least You Need to Know 184

15 The Most Common Mistakes Made by Investors 185
Common Mistakes Made by Beginning Investors 186
Common Mistakes Made by Intermediate Investors 187
Common Mistakes Made by Advanced Investors 190
The Least You Need to Know 192

**Part 3: Achieving Wealth Levels 4 and 5 with
          Your Own Business   193**

**16 Can You Supplement Your Income with
      Your Hobby?   195**
Why Do People Start Their Own Businesses? 196
Businesses Can Reduce Taxes 196
What Business Will You Start? 197
How to Write a Winning Business Plan 199
Business Plan Software *202*
Pro-Forma Financial Statements *202*

Taking on a Partner 204
A Last-Minute Checklist 204
Supplement Your Existing Income 205
How Do You Know When You've Made It? 205
The Least You Need to Know 206

17 Working For the Perfect Boss—Yourself! **207**

Wearing All the Hats 208
Design Systems and Written Procedures 209
Focus on Marketing 211
   10 Marketing Questions You Need to Ask Yourself *212*
What If Things Go Wrong? 212
Taking Time Off 213
The 22 Most Common Mistakes Business Owners
   Make—Why Businesses Fail 214
The Least You Need to Know 215

18 Your Accountant Is Your Friend **217**

Finding the Perfect Accountant 218
Measuring Your Way to Wealth 220
Having Someone Who Knows You When Revenue
   Canada Calls 221
Problem Solving 222
Goal Setting 222
Basic Personal Financial Planning 223
Second Opinions 223
Referrals to Other Professionals 224
Helping You with Your Banker 224
Setting Up Your Corporate Documents 225
Getting the Most from Your Accountant 225
The Least You Need to Know 225

19 Your Banker Is Your Friend **227**

Establishing Good Credit 228
How to Find the Right Banker for You 229
The Perfect Loan Proposal 230
Questions to Ask When Interviewing Bankers 232
What If Your Loan Is Denied? 233
What If You Can't Make Your Payments? 234
The Least You Need to Know 235

20 Hire the Best and Delegate **237**

Getting Help—Don't Be So Quick to Hire 238
Keeping Payroll at 25 Percent 238

How to Find and Attract the Best Employees 238
   Ask Key People You Know in Your Industry 239
   Look for Those Who Are Disgruntled or Seem
      to Want More 239
Pay Employees a Little More than They Expect 239
Establish a Net Bonus Program 240
You Have to Delegate 241
Match Responsibilities with Personality 242
Meet with Your Employees Individually 243
Conduct Regular Team Meetings 243
Develop Your Vision and Let Your Employees Help 244
Consider an ESOP Plan 244
The Least You Need to Know 245

21 Maximizing Profits and Selling Your Business   **247**
23 Business Strategies that Will Make You Rich 248
Why Sell? 253
What's Your Business Worth? 253
   The Asset Method 254
   The Market Comparison Method 254
   The Discount Method 255
   The Industry-Specific Method 255
Finding a Buyer 255
Building a Business Profile 257
Making the Sale 258
   What Do You Want from the Sale? 258
   How to Negotiate the Right Way 258
   How to Make the Sale Go Smoothly 259
Taking Your Company Public—The Initial
   Public Offering 260
Other Books that Can Help 261
The Least You Need to Know 261

Part 4: Rich People Have Rich Habits   **263**

22 Reducing Your Tax Bite   **265**
The Last of the Great Tax Shelters 266
   Contribute to an RRSP 266
The Most Common Tax-Related Mistakes 267
   Believing Tax Savings Are Priority Number One 267
   Making Silly Mathematical Errors 267
   Keeping Poor Records 267
   Trying to Do It All Yourself 268

Overlooking Deductions 268
Withholding Too Much or Too Little 268
Not Taking Advantage of a Registered Retirement Plan 269
Not Realizing You Can't Take It with You 269
What Exactly Is Estate Planning? 269
The Tools of Estate Planning 270
Getting Started 271
The Least You Need to Know 272

23 The Wealth Paradigms, and Why People Fail to Get Rich   **273**

11 Reasons People Fail to Get Rich 273
The Study of Paradigms 274
The Wealth Paradigms 277
Past Performance versus Hockey Puck Paradigms 277
Fear versus Contrarian Paradigms 279
Greed versus Philanthropic Paradigms 279
One Final Note on Paradigms 280
The Least You Need to Know 281

24 Planning Secrets That Will Build Wealth Faster   **283**

The Power of Your Mind 284
Time- and Life-Planning Tools 285
Yearly Planning 285
Mission Statement Work 285
Conventional Brainstorming 286
Mind-Mapping 286
Monthly Planning 288
Prioritize Goals 288
Plan Projects 288
Build a Project Notebook 289
Reorganize 289
Weekly Planning 290
Daily Planning 290
Planning Tips 291
Get Fired Up 291
Make Better Decisions 292
Keep a Communications Book 292
The Least You Need to Know 293

Appendix A—Glossary   **295**

Appendix B—List of Web Sites   **301**

Index   **305**

Foreword

The way I see it, there are three ways to get rich.

One is the old-fashioned way, by inheriting the money from your parents. Nothing beats this for sheer simplicity, although there is the complication of requiring rich parents. The second way to get rich is a lot trendier—just start up an Internet dot-com and then take it public. The beauty of this technique is that you can watch your money grow as your share price rises (the reverse is also true, of course). The third way? The details are in this book. It isn't a glamorous process, nor is it easy. But it does have the potential to work for most anyone who is motivated.

As you'll see, getting rich requires a plan, as well as discipline and perseverance. If you're looking for easy formulas, forget it. It's not simply a matter of just putting the right percentage of your salary away every paycheque, bulk-buying your groceries at Costco or driving a used car instead of a new set of wheels. Really, it's a matter of all these things and more.

What I like about this book is that it takes you through all the steps, gently. Early on, you'll read about the seven habits for building wealth. Saving every month is on the list, as is avoiding debt and shopping around when buying things. Maybe you're already doing some of these things. If so, great. All you have to do is stretch yourself to pick up the other habits and then press on to the next stage of the book's battle plan.

That would be investing. This book doesn't tell you anything you can't find in the zillions of other investing books out there, but it does cut to the chase in a way you don't often find. Here, you'll encounter all the investing knowledge needed to build a portfolio sensibly. No, it's not recommended that you jump into the next dot-com IPO. Think you'll need help managing your investments? There's good advice in this book on how to tackle the very important task of choosing a financial advisor.

If you're like most people, you'll probably need a pep talk somewhere along the road to wealth. This book has one at the end and it includes a list of 11 reasons why people fail to get rich. The reasons are all interesting, but they basically amount to the same thing: You won't get rich if you don't try.

Wait, I just thought of another way to become wealthy. You could buy lottery tickets every week in the hope that you'll hit the jackpot. If imagining yourself as rich is enough for you, then get to those lottery tickets. If not, then read this book.

Rob Carrick
Personal Finance columnist for *The Globe and Mail* and co-author of *E-Investing: How to Choose and Use a Discount Broker.*

Introduction

"Save every nickel," my grandfather was fond of saying.

It's simple advice, but amazing how many people don't follow it. After all, many people find saving money, rather than spending it, rather boring. What some of these people don't realize is that over the long term, failing to save enough money is no fun at all.

Even if you have a modest income, you can turn your little piggy bank into a tidy nest egg over time by following some basic rules and behavioural guidelines.

Primary among these is the ability to save and invest money regularly. The younger you are when you start, the better. But it's never too late to start putting money aside on a monthly basis, and let the power of compound growth make it grow.

Many who long to be rich believe it's about making the big score, like winning the lottery or buying the right stock. Who can blame them, especially with all kinds of millionaires and billionaires created in the 1990s with soaring Internet stocks and shares of other high-tech companies. In reality, becoming financially well-off doesn't usually happen that quickly or easily. Building wealth is a long-term, painfully slow process, with many setbacks along the way.

While reading this book doesn't ensure you will become wealthy, it does give you a game plan, which is something that so many people who desire wealth are lacking.

I remember practising baseball one day with some friends in high school. No matter what pitch I threw, the batter was able to connect on it or let it pass for a ball. I realized that I was throwing pitches without any forethought, often deciding what kind of pitch to throw even as I was in the middle of my delivery. The catcher saw what was going on and walked up to the mound for a discussion. "We need a game plan," he said. "From now on," he said, "I'll position my catcher's mitt in different spots around the strike zone, and you aim your pitches at it."

It worked. The batter fanned on all the next pitches as I worked him around the strike zone with deliberate pitches, and he struck out repeatedly. It worked because my psychology was vastly improved, only because I knew where I was going to throw the next pitch. I had a game plan.

That's what you will get from this book—a game plan. It's not practical to expect you'll be able to stick with it every step of the way, since life is full of curveballs. But by trying to stick to a game plan, you will develop the right psychology to become a money saver and a builder of wealth, rather than haphazardly wandering through life where your finances are concerned.

One attribute wealth builders must have is patience. Time is the friend of average income earners seeking to become wealthy. Of course, sacrifices must be made along the way. My idea of a fancy restaurant is the pizza joint down the street. The Mazda wagon

I drive was built in 1987, during Brian Mulroney's first term as Prime Minister, when the Edmonton Oilers were the champions of NHL hockey. My wife and I moved away from a high-priced part of Toronto to buy our first home in a more affordable, less conveniently located area.

I remember the day I finally paid off my student loan, thinking how impossible it would be to ever sock away a lot of money. Several months after starting my first full-time job, I invested $3,000 as my first RRSP contribution, and made similar contributions every year afterward. Those first years were excruciatingly slow, and I sometimes wondered why I didn't just spend the money on things I'd enjoy. But somehow, after nine years, the RRSP has grown 25-fold over my first contribution.

And where has all this frugal living and investing gotten me? Am I rich? Not yet, but at the rate I'm going, I'll do nicely. We expect to have the house paid off by my late 30s, which means much of our subsequent income will be gravy (unless we move back downtown). Even if I don't add another dime to my RRSP, a 10 percent annual return will turn it into well over $1 million by the time I'm 60.

The original author of this book, U.S. financial advisor Larry Waschka, has a more impressive story. As the author of a guide to getting rich, he is sometimes asked if he is rich. He replies that at the age of 34 he had a net worth of US$2 million, which is easily enough money to quit working if he chose to. That kind of wealth at that age requires more than a job with a decent salary. Larry got there by starting a business and running it successfully. It's a lot of hard work, but the payoff can be enormous.

Larry's voice permeates this book. I've updated it and tweaked it for 21st century Canadians, with my own thoughts on saving and low-cost investing.

May you prosper,

Mark Heinzl

How to Use This Book

This book is carefully organized to present the tools and techniques you can use to set and reach your goals for wealth. I've defined five levels of wealth to make it easier for you to plan your journey, and the book leads you through each level.

Part 1: The Basics: Wealth Levels 1 and 2 is all about the basics of getting rich. It breaks down the definition of wealth into five measurable levels and shows you how to design a plan to achieve the first two levels. This part covers the habits and characteristics of wealthy people, as well as explaining how to get rich as an employee.

Part 2: Achieving Wealth Level 3 by Taming the Portfolio Beast shows you how to become financially independent. It focuses on the investment tools and strategies you'll need to invest wisely.

Part 3: Achieving Wealth Levels 4 and 5 with Your Own Business will explain the basic details of starting, expanding, and selling your own business. It will show you how to achieve the top two levels of wealth using your own business.

Part 4: Rich People Have Rich Habits lists all the basic tax strategies, mental paradigms, and planning secrets you'll need to build your wealth. It will also teach you why so many people fail to achieve wealth.

A glossary of wealth-related terms and definitions will help you better understand the words of the wealthy. These terms will also help you keep up a conversation with any wealthy person.

Extras

The text in each chapter provides full coverage of each topic. However, while I wrote each chapter, certain related topics would come to mind that were just too good not to include. I've placed these extras in four different types of information boxes within each chapter:

That Reminds Me...

It seems that every significant lesson I've learned about building wealth has been the result of my own experience or the experiences of others. These boxes explain such lessons for you in the form of a story or observation so that you will better understand the concepts within this book.

Wealth Warning

If you know what to avoid in your financial life, you can significantly reduce your chances of experiencing problems. These warning boxes will help you do just that. Consider these the caution signs on your journey toward wealth. They are common errors and things to be aware of.

Words of the Wealthy

These **terms and definitions** are part of the language of the wealthy. If you know and understand these words, you are well on your way to building wealth. These terms will also help you have more meaningful discussions with your financial advisors.

Treasure Tip

These are helpful little hints to make life easier. If you prefer the "path of least resistance," be sure to read them.

Part 1
The Basics: Wealth Levels 1 and 2

Wouldn't it be nice to get paid all of your future income in a single lump sum? Just the thought of it might seem nice, but if you really examine how your income is paid, you'll probably be surprised. For example, you'd receive your payout minus federal and provincial taxes, based on your life expectancy. Now it's not all that attractive.

The opposite is true with building wealth. I have found that once you really examine the truth about building wealth, it's not only more attractive, but also a lot easier to achieve than you may think. You just have to break it up into different levels and design a plan to achieve the first level first, then the second, and so on. That's exactly what I've done for you in this part of the book. All you have to do is read and implement the steps, habits, and characteristics needed—and you will be on your way to building wealth.

Chapter 1

Who's Really Rich and Do You Have What It Takes to Be Rich?

In This Chapter

➤ Stories of self-made wealthy people who are under 30

➤ Rags-to-riches stories about real people who built their wealth from simple means

➤ A test to see if you have what it takes to be wealthy

➤ Why is it so difficult to get rich?

➤ Wealth is a journey, not a destination

It's easy to find stories of wealthy people. Occasionally you'll find such individuals featured in magazines or on television. However, the wealthy people that I'm the most proud to know are those who built their wealth with their own hands. This is self-made wealth. It's not inherited, acquired through marriage, or won in the lottery. It's built with hard work, determination, and passion.

What is difficult to understand is that this kind of wealth is often invisible. You don't see it or recognize it because it's owned by people who don't flaunt or talk about it. You can learn a lot from these people, but they aren't featured in magazines or on television. They may live next door to you and have an incredible knowledge about building wealth, but you'd never know to ask.

This chapter is about these people. I'm going to discuss a few wealthy people featured in magazines, but most of this chapter focuses on the invisible wealthy people. I dedicate this book to them because they taught me the secrets of building wealth. The second part of this chapter will enable you to find out if you have what it takes to be wealthy.

Who's Really Rich?

In recent years, the Internet has spawned countless young millionaires, and even many billionaires. In the late 1990s, investors were falling all over themselves to buy into brand new companies with Web-based businesses, high-tech communications technology, or new software and operating systems. Shares of these technology companies skyrocketed, mostly on the U.S. Nasdaq Stock Market, in an unprecedented bull market (rising stock market).

Based on stock market valuations, these companies were worth many millions or billions of dollars even though many were just a few years or months old, employed just 100 or so people, and were without a saleable product on the market. The trend got going in 1996 when software designer, Marc Andreessen, at the age of 24, saw the value of his stake in Netscape Communications, an Internet browser company that he started, rocket to about US$131 million. Countless other examples of instant multimillionaires followed in the ensuing years.

Words of the Wealthy

Wealth is defined by the *Canadian Oxford Dictionary* as "riches; abundant possessions," and the word **wealthy** is defined as "having an abundance, esp. of money." But the definition of **affluent** sounds even better: "an abundant supply of money, commodities, etc.; wealth."

For example, Robert Young, originally from Hamilton, Ontario, started a company called Red Hat Inc., which sells products for the Linux computer operating system. At the end of 1999, his stake in the company was valued at more than US$2 billion (that's 2,000 million), yet the company had no earnings, only a promising future. By the end of 1999, Microsoft Corp. founder Bill Gates was worth about US$91 billion, greater than the gross domestic product of Ireland.

Toronto-based DocSpace Co. was bought out in late 1999 by a San Francisco company for US$530 million, making multimillionaires out of Evan Chrapko and other founders of the two-year-old company, which few people had ever heard of at the time.

There is a long list of business success stories like these. Of course, there are plenty of skeptics who say that the astronomical valuations of startup technology companies in recent years is based on nothing more than excitement and hope, and the market for these stocks will surely crash. But even if they do, these people will remain quite wealthy.

Of course, the success stories aren't limited to technology companies. Canadian industrial companies such as Magna International Inc. and Royal Group Technologies Inc. made multimillionaires of their hard-working founders, who started with almost nothing.

The point of these examples is that most truly rich people made it by starting their own businesses. That doesn't mean that if you start your own business you will get rich; in fact, most new businesses fail after a few years. But starting your own business does give you the opportunity to make really big money.

Still, as you will see, you don't have to start a business to become wealthy.

Invisible Rags-to-Riches Wealth

The stories that give us all hope are the stories of real people who built fortunes out of almost nothing. I'm talking about wealthy people who earned every dime they made. Most of them don't wear flashy clothes or drive fancy cars. They don't live in mansions or travel to Paris for a vacation. They live next door to you, and you may not even know their names. Many of my clients fit this description. Some of these people drive old trucks with worn-out tires. If I pointed them out to you on the street you would never believe they had any money. They earned every dime and they're darn proud of it.

Frank Lalli wrote an article about Anne Scheiver in *Money* magazine ("How She Turned $5,000 into $22 million," January 1996, p. 64, copyright 1996 Time, Inc.) that I found to be priceless. It read, "In the depths of the depression, when she was already 38 years old and earning only a little more than $3,000 a year, Anne invested a major portion of her life savings in stocks. She entrusted the money to the youngest of her four brothers, Bernard, who was getting started at 22 as a Wall Street broker. He did well picking issues for her as the market drifted upward in 1933 and '34; but his firm did not. It went bust suddenly, and Anne lost all her money. In 1944, 10 years after her big loss, she started fresh with a $5,000 account at Merrill Lynch Pierce Fenner & Bean and slowly built the nest egg up to $20 million by the time she died last January, loveless and alone at 101. It's now worth $22 million."

The article stated that her performance of 17.5 percent per year exceeded some of the best known investment professionals in the world, including John Neff and Ben Graham. In 51 years, this incredible lady built a fortune using simple strategies that anyone can follow. Those who knew her said she lived a terrible existence as a recluse who never enjoyed her money. My bet is that investing was her passion, her love, and her life. I'm also willing to bet that this woman enjoyed her money more than most people ever will. She enjoyed managing it, not spending it. As a result, she turned near disaster into an almost unbelievable fortune with nothing more than patience, interest in the market, research, and a little planning. So what if she didn't take vacations or eat out? This woman left a legacy behind that all of us can learn from. She was able to outperform trained professionals in their own field for more than 50 years! The story of Anne's life is what I call an invisible rags-to-riches story.

Even the Postman Can Build Wealth

My favourite story is about a couple who attended my investment workshop back in 1993. This is a true story from which everyone can learn something—I know I did. This couple, let's call them Mr. and Mrs. Post, met with me after the workshop to discuss some specific questions they had regarding their no-load fund portfolio. As usual, I asked some questions and found that Mr. Post had worked all his life for the post office and was considering retirement the next year. His wife had raised their children and had never earned any additional income. Mr. Post told me that the most they had ever made in one year was $30,000. They were conservatively dressed, simple in their ways, and almost shy about talking to me.

Words of the Wealthy

No-load funds are mutual funds that can be purchased, sold, and owned without any commission charges (or loads). The only charges involved are yearly management fees. Most brokers and financial advisers would never offer to sell you a no-load fund because there is no commission for them.

Wealth Warning

Two other common ways to become wealthy include inheritance and marriage. Most people who achieve wealth in that manner do not become good stewards of their money.

They wanted me to review their no-load mutual fund portfolio to see if I thought anything needed to be sold. As Mr. Post began to show me his portfolio, I put my pen down and got ready to take a look. I was prepared to see a small portfolio of funds.

Wrong! Their portfolio had more than 35 different no-load mutual funds worth more than $800,000! To say the least, I was dumbfounded. How could this couple have so much money? Well, of course, I made all kinds of assumptions. First, I asked if any of the money was inherited. They replied quickly and firmly, "No, not one dime." I asked if they owned any real estate other than their home. They replied, "No." I was impressed.

They quickly told me that they had also purchased homes for each of their two daughters as wedding presents. They, of course, paid cash. They had also pre-funded their four grandchildren's college education.

I gave up and asked how they did it. They had come to me for advice, but I turned the appointment around and asked for theirs. What I learned from them that day, I will never forget. Their story (see Chapter 5) immediately made me want to write a book so I could share what I learned. By the way, you are holding that book in your hands, and I hope it helps you achieve the wealth you dream of. This couple told me later in the most humble tone, "If we can do it, anybody can." They, too, were invisibly wealthy.

That Reminds Me...

I've learned over the last 10 years that most of the really wealthy people do not own fancy cars, jet planes, or huge mansions. Most of the wealthy people I know are more like Sam Walton, the founder of Wal-Mart stores. They drive older cars or trucks, fly coach seats on commercial airlines, and wear very simple clothes. To my surprise, most of them live well within their means in simple homes. They tend to avoid anything flashy, and they avoid large mortgages and car payments by often paying cash. My point is that you would never think these people had any more money than the average citizen. As a matter of fact, they keep their wealth confidential.

You Don't Need a University Education

What may surprise you is that many wealthy people never finished university. My second favourite story about wealthy people is about a man who built a $10-million net worth from the ground up without a university education. He decided to retire in his early 50s. He worked hard and earned his wealth.

When he was 18, he decided to skip university and work in a soft drink distribution company. He was dedicated and worked harder than anyone in the company. In fact, he worked so hard that a truck driver at the company told him, "Don't work so hard. You'll make all of us look bad." This didn't even faze him. He soon became a truck driver, and then a supervisor for all the truck drivers. After four years, a national soft drink company saw what he had done for his employer and asked him to be a division manager. This position gave him the opportunity to help other soft drink distributors in several provinces. In only a few years, one of his distributors offered him 20 percent of the company to manage his distributorship. He agreed. Soon they bought other distributorships and added other brands to their line. The original owner wanted to retire, so he offered the remaining stock to my client. The transaction involved a lot of money for my client at that time, so he took on a partner to make the transaction. Soon they bought other distributorships.

The business became larger than my client ever dreamed. I asked him to sum up in a few sentences how he built his wealth. He said, "Dedication, hard work, and going that extra mile." I asked him where he got his motivation to work so hard. He replied, "Believe it or not, it had a lot to do with the fact that I didn't have a college education. I felt like everyone else did, and I had this complex about not finishing college."

I really believe that a university education is a great idea, but it certainly is not a requirement for building wealth. My client proved that some things are much more important than a university education. By the way, the truck driver who told him not to work so hard is still a truck driver! I bet my client's wealth isn't invisible to *him*.

You'd Never Think These People Had Any Money

One day, a retired couple in their 60s came to my office for some help. They were a tiny couple, both about five feet tall, and wore clothes that had to be 10 years old. You couldn't ask for a nicer couple. They asked almost bashfully if I would take a look at their "little" portfolio and make some suggestions. They both apologized for the "small" size of their holdings. The husband said, "I know that you are accustomed to dealing with much larger amounts, but would you please just give us some advice?" I explained that size didn't matter and that I would be glad to help them in any way I could.

I nearly fell out of my chair when I opened the portfolio to find more than $1 million in stocks, bonds, and mutual funds. You would never think that these people had any money. It never ceases to amaze me how people like this can be so humble and simple, yet be completely sophisticated with their investment knowledge.

I asked them a little about their background. They said that the most they ever made in income in one year was $27,000 and they hadn't inherited anything. I just love these people! They are another example of invisible wealth.

The Wealth Test

Words of the Wealthy

Hodad is word used to describe people who are generally fake or phoney. They may look like they're rich, they might smell like they're rich, but if you take a close look, you'll find they owe lots of money and lease everything they have.

Just because someone makes a lot of money doesn't mean he's wealthy. If his expenses equal or exceed his income, he doesn't qualify as wealthy. Just because someone works hard, earns a great salary, and has nice things, doesn't make him wealthy. The person may look like wealth and smell like wealth, but it's all a big show. In Texas, they call these people "hodads." They're all hat and no cattle. They wear fancy hats and talk the talk, but they don't even have a pasture or a cow to put in it.

Somewhere along the way, these seemingly wealthy people didn't learn the habits and characteristics necessary to build real wealth. No one taught them the concept of saving for a rainy day, much less for retirement. They don't have what it takes to be wealthy.

I know you're saying, "So how do I become wealthy? Most everyone I know would like to be rich. They may not all be willing to admit it, but it's the truth. If this is the case, then why do so few people get rich? What do these people do to become so wealthy? Why can't I do that?" We are going to discuss the answers to all these questions throughout this book, but first we must ask the most important one:

Do you have what it takes to be rich?

That Reminds Me...

I knew a business owner once who didn't have any capital, so he leased every single thing in his business. He leased his car, his condo, his office furniture, his office equipment, his office, and all his manufacturing equipment. Leases typically are ridiculously expensive, and therefore he didn't make enough money for his business to survive. So he gave it all back and moved out of that industry and went to another province. For a while he looked like a rich young man. He looked rich, but after a closer look, you could tell he was a hodad.

I have designed a test based solely on my own experience and the experiences of wealthy people I have met. There are certain habits and characteristics that almost all of them share. This test is not scientifically perfect, but the scoring levels measure your probability of achieving wealth.

The purpose of the wealth test is to get a picture of yourself today based upon what you have learned in the past and what you are doing now to achieve wealth. If you answer honestly, you will see what your chances would have been if you hadn't purchased this book and made the necessary adjustments. You don't have to show your results to anyone. Remember, your chances

Treasure Tip

No matter what your education or resources, the key to building financial wealth is to put together and follow a plan of action you design to meet your specific needs and goals. Your plan should identify and combat your weaknesses.

will increase once you've finished the book and implemented what you've learned. For now, let's focus on the "old you," and after the test we'll focus on the "new you."

Even if you scored low on the test, don't worry. Regardless of your score, you can achieve wealth. Your score just identifies your weak points. Take a moment and look at the questions to which you answered "no." By identifying these areas now, you will recognize the solutions as you study this book.

Why Do So Few Make It?

Why is it so difficult to get rich? It might be that most people don't have any of the characteristics noted in the last section. These people don't have the discipline or patience it takes to keep trying. Brian Tracy, in his famous cassette-tape series *The Psychology of Achievement*, mentioned a study that was done several years ago involving a group of people who were worth more than $1 million before the age of 30. They were all asked, "How many different businesses were you involved in before you became a millionaire?" The average answer was 18! Can you imagine? What does this tell you? It tells me that achieving wealth takes a lot of tenacity and patience. You have to be willing to stick to this goal and be willing to fail more than once. I speak from experience. When I don't enjoy what I'm doing, the chances are good that I'm going to give up after failing the first few times. My money management firm lost money during the first three years of business. But this didn't get me down. I had a passion for building my firm that would never let me quit. Now my profit margin exceeds 50 percent.

That Reminds Me...

It seems that so much motivation and accomplishment can come from adversity. This has certainly been true for me. My first job out of college was not what I expected. I was a southern boy travelling the northeastern states, I was all alone, and my company was taking advantage of me. They were not paying me the bonuses that I had earned. It was a miserable nightmare. To make things worse, when I quit, my boss followed me out the door yelling, "You're a quitter, a loser. You'll never get a job anywhere. You're finished. You'll never achieve anything." He had no idea how much this motivated me. All I could think about at that time was making enough money to buy the company one day and have him work for me! Thank goodness I quit. It enabled me to go into the investment industry, which is where I wanted to be in the first place.

The Wealth Test

1.	Do you enjoy your work?	Yes	No
2.	Do you often visualize yourself achieving something bigger than what you are currently doing?	Yes	No
3.	Do you save money almost every month?	Yes	No
4.	Do you invest at least some of your money directly in the stock market either through individual stocks or mutual funds?	Yes	No
5.	Do you shop before you buy most of the time, especially for big-ticket items?	Yes	No
6.	Do you take care of your home or apartment, performing regular maintenance as well as repairs?	Yes	No
7.	Do you perform regular maintenance on your car and other expensive items?	Yes	No
8.	Do you pay off the full balance on your credit cards each month?	Yes	No
9.	Are you comfortable buying used big-ticket items such as cars and appliances?	Yes	No
10.	Have you ever started your own business? (Even a lemonade stand counts.)	Yes	No
11.	Have you ever estimated how much money you would need in a portfolio to produce enough income to cover your current living expenses?	Yes	No
12.	Do you measure the performance results of your portfolio at least each quarter?	Yes	No
13.	Do you maximize your personal contribution to your RRSP?	Yes	No
14.	Is your mortgage payment less than 20 percent of your total gross household income? (If you do not own a home, is your rent less than 20 percent of your total gross household income?)	Yes	No
15.	Do you spend less than you make?	Yes	No
16.	Have you ever read a book about building wealth or an autobiography about someone who was wealthy?	Yes	No
17.	Do you have your own business now that produces a positive net income?	Yes	No
18.	Have you ever worked all night or more than 24 hours on a project?	Yes	No

For each question to which you answered "yes," give yourself one point.

Total these points, then compare the result to the scale below to check the probability of your becoming wealthy.

Score	Probability of Becoming Rich
1–5	Low
6–10	Average
10–15	Very likely
16–18	You are on your way!

Wealth Deception

Now that I've seen both sides of the story, I've learned that there are many misconceptions regarding wealth. People simply misunderstand what wealth is and how you get it. It may sound simple, but it's the truth. I've seen it all my life. I remember as a child hearing people make hundreds of comments about their concepts of wealth. These misconceptions, which many may believe, hold these people back from wealth for the rest of their lives. If you believe any of what I call the fallacies of wealth, one of the things you should do immediately is stop using them as an excuse not to build your wealth:

Wealth Warning

In spite of the fact that the chances of winning the lottery are usually worse than a million to one, it seems that most Canadians use lottery tickets to plan for their retirement. The irony is that a large percentage of people who win the lottery end up in serious financial trouble, if not dead broke.

➤ If I just had a little more money, I'd be happy.

➤ If I were wealthy, I could buy anything I wanted.

➤ I wish I were wealthy, so I wouldn't have to worry about money anymore.

➤ I'm young, I've got plenty of time to become wealthy. Why save money now?

➤ I'm too old to start saving money.

➤ I wish I'd saved more money when I was younger.

➤ There's no chance of me ever becoming wealthy. I only make $20,000 per year.

➤ The only way to get rich is to inherit, win the lottery, own commercial real estate, or start a business.

➤ If I were really wealthy, I wouldn't care how much I paid in taxes.

It's Not Impossible

I think most people aren't willing to make the decisions or sacrifices it takes to become wealthy. The whole process seems too overwhelming to them. Admittedly, if you are starting with very little or no money, this process of building wealth might seem daunting. *But it's not impossible!* If you think becoming wealthy is impossible, well, you can bet it will be. You'll never make it. Someone once said, "Argue your limitations...and they're yours."

This Is a Journey, Not a Destination

Occasionally you'll have setbacks. You can plan for most of these in advance. However, if you do fall back, all you have to do is retrace your steps and continue your journey. Remember that wealth is a journey and not a destination. When you make the *decision* to seek wealth, you have taken the first step on this lifelong journey. Let's get started.

The Least You Need to Know

➤ Wealth can be built by anyone at any age who is willing to learn and develop the habits and characteristics necessary.

➤ The habits and characteristics are simple to understand, easy to implement, but overlooked by many people.

➤ Avoid becoming a "hodad"—someone living in a fancy home or driving a fancy car who doesn't have a dime in the bank or an investment account.

➤ Start identifying the common misconceptions of wealth and don't let these hold you back from achieving your fortune.

➤ Wealth is a journey that requires a high level of tenacity and determination to overcome the occasional setbacks.

➤ To build real wealth, you have to believe that it can be done.

Chapter 2

Ten Key Concepts of Building Wealth

In This Chapter

➤ The definition of liquid and illiquid wealth

➤ How time affects your portfolio

➤ How your standard of living affects your portfolio

➤ When the amount of money you save is more important than your portfolio performance

➤ Why compound growth is so powerful

Every industry has its own unique language, which consists of jargon and concepts used every day. Since almost everyone deals with at least some financial issues, most of the terms should already be familiar. Even so, it is important to make sure that we are all using the same language for our discussions. In this chapter, we'll review some of the basics.

How Do You Define Wealth?

Everyone's definition of financial wealth is different. So, to make things simple, I've defined five specific, measurable levels of wealth, which we'll discuss in the next chapter. These levels of wealth reduce the confusion surrounding the concept of wealth by breaking down the definition into easy-to-understand pieces.

Before discussing the five wealth levels, let's go over 10 concepts that are very important to understand. If you don't understand these concepts, you will have trouble understanding the logic of the five wealth levels.

➤ Portfolio

➤ Time

➤ Standard of Living Expenses

➤ Total Return

➤ Risk

➤ Inflation

➤ Taxes

➤ Compound Growth

➤ Actual Savings Amount

➤ Target Savings Goal (TSG

Words of the Wealthy

An **asset** can be liquid or illiquid property that can be sold for cash. This can include stocks, bonds, and real estate.

Words of the Wealthy

A **privately held company** is one whose shares are not publicly trad-ed. Privately held stock is issued to a small number of shareholders, and the value or price of the stock is usually determined by comparisons with other similar companies using factors such as company earnings and gross income.

Portfolio

For the purpose of this book, the term *portfolio* primarily refers to a collection of liquid assets (an asset being something you own) that are traded in a regulated market such as the banking or stock markets. An asset is considered liquid if it can be easily sold for cash within an established financial market: stocks, bonds, guaranteed investment certificates (GICs), mutual funds, and foreign securities. The most common liquid assets are checking and savings accounts. You can sell or liquidate these assets and get your money within 24 hours.

A portfolio could also include illiquid assets such as privately held securities or commercial real estate. These assets are not easily sold for cash because you have to go out and find a buyer yourself. For the most part, there is nothing wrong with illiquid assets. For example, the most commonly held illiquid asset is a home. It can be sold and converted to cash, but it could take some time. Another example of an illiquid asset would be privately held stock (not listed on an exchange such as the Toronto Stock Exchange.)

What's the problem with owning illiquid assets? Establishing a price tag. Illiquid assets are not always easy to value. Therefore, they must be evaluated by an expert to establish a fair market value.

Many wealthy people have built their fortunes using illiquid assets such as land, commercial buildings, and privately held company stock. However, these people understood the characteristics and risks unique to each particular illiquid asset. Do not attempt to get involved with illiquid assets without doing some serious homework. If you understand what you own and the market in which you participate, you can make money by investing in illiquid assets.

Time

Time is a very powerful tool. If you are in your 20s or 30s, you have an advantage over someone who is in her 40s or 50s. When I think of the time component, I think of an old expression, "Give me a lever long enough and I can move the world." Time works the same way with wealth. Give me enough time and I can build a fortune. The opposite is also true. The less time you have, the less likely it is that you will build any significant wealth. It's not impossible, though. Remember Anne Scheiver in the first chapter who began saving at the age of 50 and died with a $22-million portfolio. If she can do it, so can you. Let's take a closer look at how important time is in the accumulation of wealth by using the following illustration.

Words of the Wealthy

Liquid assets include assets that can be instantly converted into cash. **Illiquid assets** are just the opposite; they are not easily converted into cash.

The Early Saver versus The Late Saver

| Age | Early start | | | Late start | | |
---	Savings per Year	Total Annual Return 9%	Total Portfolio	Savings per Year	Total Annual Return 9%	Portfolio
22	$2,000	$180	$2,180	$0	$0	$0
23	$2,000	$376	$4,556	$0	$0	$0
24	$2,000	$590	$7,146	$0	$0	$0
25	$2,000	$823	$9,969	$0	$0	$0
26	$2,000	$1,077	$13,047	$0	$0	$0
27	$2,000	$1,354	$16,401	$0	$0	$0
28	$2,000	$1,656	$20,057	$0	$0	$0

continued

The Early Saver versus The Late Saver (continued)

Age	Early start			Late start		
	Savings per Year	Total Annual Return 9%	Total Portfolio	Savings per Year	Total Annual Return 9%	Portfolio
29	$2,000	$1,985	$24,042	$0	$0	$0
30	$2,000	$2,344	$28,386	$0	$0	$0
31	$0	$2,555	$30,941	$2,000	$180	$2,180
32	$0	$2,785	$33,725	$2,000	$376	$4,556
33	$0	$3,035	$36,761	$2,000	$590	$7,146
34	$0	$3,308	$40,069	$2,000	$823	$9,969
35	$0	$3,606	$43,675	$2,000	$1,077	$13,047
36	$0	$3,931	$47,606	$2,000	$1,354	$16,401
37	$0	$4,285	$51,890	$2,000	$1,656	$20,057
38	$0	$4,670	$56,561	$2,000	$1,985	$24,042
39	$0	$5,090	$61,651	$2,000	$2,344	$28,386
40	$0	$5,549	$67,200	$2,000	$2,735	$33,121
41	$0	$6,048	$73,248	$2,000	$3,161	$38,281
42	$0	$6,592	$79,840	$2,000	$3,625	$43,907
43	$0	$7,186	$87,025	$2,000	$4,132	$50,038
44	$0	$7,832	$94,858	$2,000	$4,683	$56,722
45	$0	$8,537	$103,395	$2,000	$5,285	$64,007
46	$0	$9,306	$112,701	$2,000	$5,941	$71,947
47	$0	$10,143	$122,844	$2,000	$6,655	$80,603
48	$0	$11,056	$133,900	$2,000	$7,434	$90,037
49	$0	$12,051	$145,950	$2,000	$8,283	$100,320
50	$0	$13,136	$159,086	$2,000	$9,209	$111,529
51	$0	$14,318	$173,404	$2,000	$10,218	$123,747
52	$0	$15,606	$189,010	$2,000	$11,317	$137,064
53	$0	$17,011	$206,021	$2,000	$12,516	$151,580
54	$0	$18,542	$224,563	$2,000	$13,822	$167,402
55	$0	$20,211	$244,774	$2,000	$15,246	$184,648
56	$0	$22,030	$266,803	$2,000	$16,798	$203,446
57	$0	$24,012	$290,815	$2,000	$18,490	$223,936
58	$0	$26,173	$316,989	$2,000	$20,334	$246,271
59	$0	$28,529	$345,518	$2,000	$22,344	$270,615
60	$0	$31,097	$376,614	$2,000	$24,535	$297,150
61	$0	$33,895	$410,510	$2,000	$26,924	$326,074
62	$0	$36,946	$447,456	$2,000	$29,527	$357,601
63	$0	$40,271	$487,727	$2,000	$32,364	$391,965
64	$0	$43,895	$531,622	$2,000	$35,457	$429,422
65	$0	$47,846	$579,468	$2,000	$38,828	$470,249
	$18,000			$70,000		

*Please note that this illustration is for comparison purposes only.
*Taxes are not calculated into the equation.

The first investor deposits $18,000 between the ages of 22 and 30 and ends up with a $579,468 account. The second investor gets a later start and deposits $70,000 between the ages of 31 and 65, which is almost four times as much money, but his account grows to only $470,249. That's a difference of $109,219! How is this possible? The first investor simply had the advantage of more time to compound the growth. Notice that by the time the second investor began saving money, the first investor's gain exceeded the second investor's deposit. This is powerful stuff and is, ironically, often completely overlooked by investors. The message: use the power of time.

Standard of Living Expenses

There are many different categories of expenses. There are variable expenses such as entertainment, clothing, and travel. And there are fixed expenses such as rent or mortgage payments. This might seem like a relatively boring subject, but most people don't understand just how important the expense component can be in building wealth. When you are just beginning to build your portfolio, the amount you spend monthly for expenses directly affects the speed of your journey to wealth. If you are accustomed to a high standard of living with no willingness to be flexible, your chances of saving money in the early years are quite small.

I truly believe that the main reason why people don't save money is that they are unwilling to limit their standard of living. I see this in young couples mostly, but also in older retired couples. In the later years, especially during retirement, if you spend more than your portfolio produces, you deplete your capital source or principal. I now have a client who started with a $100,000 retirement account. For the past two years, this client has lived beyond his means and the account is now worth only $33,000. His portfolio grew faster than the world stock market index, but didn't grow fast enough to keep up with his spending habits. This scenario is a nightmare that didn't have to happen. The client did not measure spending habits, ignored his resources, and now has a very big problem. Don't let this happen to you. It's important to understand that systematic measurement of your monthly expenses is vital to the wealth building process. I'll show you how to do this in Chapter 3.

Wealth Warning

The tool of time can also work in reverse. The longer you wait to start your portfolio, the harder it is to build any significant wealth. A good place to start your investment portfolio is a registered retirement savings plan (RRSP), which can grow tax-deferred until all the money is drawn out during retirement. This account allows you to combine the tools of time, compound growth, and tax deferral.

Wealth Warning

You must be willing to make some sacrifices now to build wealth in the future.

Wealth Warning

Ignoring your spending habits relative to your income will get you into hot water fast.

Words of the Wealthy

Harvesting is a term I came up with to describe a more unconventional method of deriving income from a portfolio that includes not only dividends and interest, but also the harvesting of capital gains. These capital gains can be easily obtained by occasionally selling (harvesting) pieces of a portfolio that have appreciated.

Total Return

The next concept is the total return on your capital. Total return consists of dividends, interest, and capital gains. A capital gain is the price appreciation realized from the sale of an asset. If you invest in real estate, your portfolio might also produce rental income. Total return is also known as portfolio gains, portfolio performance, and portfolio growth.

The most confusing thing about total return involves the concept of taking regular monthly income from your portfolio, which is most commonly needed once retirement begins. When it comes time to take income from a liquid portfolio for living expenses, most investors look only at dividends and interest (cash flow). They pay little, if any, attention to capital gain because they claim it's not reliable. This is conventional thinking.

In the long run, capital gains can be reliable given a properly diversified portfolio. Whether you are building wealth in the early years or maintaining wealth in the later years, you should not ignore capital gains. You should harvest them over time and consider them part of the "cash flow." This concept of harvesting might be new to you, and therefore, a bit unconventional. That's okay. To build and maintain the levels of wealth this book discusses, you're going to have to think unconventionally.

Risk

There are many different types of risk, which I will discuss in more detail later. Risk, for now, can be defined as the volatility (potential to rise or fall quickly) of the total portfolio value. Some investors are willing to accept higher levels of volatility for potentially higher rates of return. Return is your reward for your willingness to assume risk. In general, risk can increase your potential for return, but it can also lead to more potential for loss. Setting proper return goals involves determining your acceptable level of risk.

Inflation

I'll spare you the economics lesson that explains what causes inflation. Think of it simply as an increase in the price of goods and services. The most important thing to remember about inflation is that it will affect your future living expenses. What costs $1 today may cost $5 in the future. You must take this into account when making projections about the future. The easy way to measure and project inflation is to use the Consumer Price Index (CPI) growth rate. This is the yearly growth rate of the total price of a basket of consumer goods. All financial publications show this rate as the CPI. You will need to know the growth rate of this index in Chapter 3 when I show you how to project your future living expenses.

Wealth Warning

Risk tolerance is the degree to which an investor can withstand or live with the volatility of her portfolio. When asked, most investors tend to overestimate their tolerance for risk. However, only when confronted with significantly poor performance or losses from an investment do they fully understand their true tolerance.

Taxes

When I mention taxes, I am referring to federal and provincial income taxes. Specifically, in the next chapter you will need to know your average income tax rate. An easy way to calculate this is to add up the federal and provincial taxes you paid last year and divide the total by your gross income. This will give you your average income tax rate. If you need help calculating this, ask your accountant.

That Reminds Me...

The Consumer Price Index (CPI) is a price index, tabulated by the federal government, that measures the cost of a representative basket of consumer goods. The price of the basket is not important. The most important aspect of the CPI is the rate of change from one month to another. The amount of change from month to month in the cost of this basket of goods is stated as a percentage of the CPI for the previous month. This percentage is known as the rate of inflation and is usually quoted as an annualized percentage. This measurement can be found every month in the financial pages of the *National Post, The Globe and Mail,* and other such publications.

(Federal + Provincial taxes) ÷ Gross annual income = Your average income tax rate

For example, if you had a gross income of $30,000 with federal taxes of $3,540 and provincial taxes of $1,344, your average income tax rate would equal 16.28 percent.

Taxes can be avoided or deferred using certain investment vehicles, such as the RRSP. However, the most important goal of an investor should be to make money, not to avoid taxes. If you focus primarily on avoiding taxes, you might accomplish your goal, but I can promise you that you will not make much money in the process. Later in this book, I will discuss some ways you can defer taxes without sacrificing total return.

Compound Growth

Compound growth is different from compound interest. It is achieved when you invest in stocks (or anything that appreciates in value) over a long period, while allowing the capital gains and dividends to reinvest into the original investment.

Dr. Albert Einstein left Germany to come to the United States to escape potential conflict with Hitler. It's been said that a young reporter met Einstein when he arrived at the Port of New York and asked him what he believed was the eighth wonder of the world. Einstein replied, "I believe it is compound growth."

Treasure Tip

Compound growth over time allows even moderate rates of return to produce great wealth.

That Reminds Me...

The rule of 72 is a way to estimate how fast money can compound over time. You can divide the number 72 by the rate of return you expect to receive. The result is the number of years it will take for your money to double. If you were getting 6 percent, your money would double in 12 years. If you were getting 8 percent, your money would double in 9 years; if 10 percent, 7.2 years; if 12 percent, 6 years. As you can see, it also works in reverse. You can divide the number 72 by the number of years you have to invest. The result will be the percentage of total return you'll need to double the portfolio. I cannot explain how this phenomenon works, but it does. This equation measures pure compound growth without the effect of any taxes. Therefore, it works best in measuring the growth of tax-deferred accounts such as RRSPs.

Over the past seven years, I have spoken to more than 2,000 investors—both successful and unsuccessful. What seems to be common among those who are successful is really very simple: successful investors understand that compound growth is a powerful investment tool.

What makes compound growth so attractive is the added effect of price appreciation with reinvested interest or dividends.

Actual Savings Amount

Your actual savings amount is just what it says: the difference between your total household income and expenses. This surplus is what goes into your investment account. If there is money available for savings, you are living within your means and that's great. If you have a negative actual savings amount, you are living beyond your means, and that's not good at all.

This amount is very important in the early stages of your life. Therefore, your focus should be on saving and investing as much as you can when you are young. During the first years of saving when your portfolio is small, total return is relatively less important than the amount of money you save (deposits you make). The deposits you make at first will dwarf the amount of money you make on your investments (dividends and gains). Therefore, this is a great time to learn about investing. When you are new to the game of investing, you tend to make a lot of mistakes. If you can make those mistakes early, when the returns have relatively less effect on your overall portfolio, you will save your portfolio from harm later when your return really counts.

Target Savings Goal (TSG)

A very important concept for building wealth is your target savings goal (TSG). This is the amount of money you need to save every year in order to build a portfolio large enough to produce a total return by a certain date (usually retirement) that will sustain your standard of living plus keep up with inflation. I realize that this might be a mouthful, but don't worry. We'll take this step by step in the next chapter and make it easy for you.

The Least You Need to Know

➤ To understand the definition of wealth, you must first understand the concepts that make up that definition.

➤ The more time you allow your portfolio to compound its growth, the more potential you have to build significant wealth.

➤ If you are accustomed to a high standard of living and are unwilling to be flexible, your chances of saving money in the early years are quite small.

Chapter 3

The Five Levels of Wealth

> ## In This Chapter
> ➤ Defining the five levels of wealth
> ➤ Building wealth in stages
> ➤ Shortcuts to the higher levels
> ➤ When saving money becomes less important

The first thing you must realize in your search for a personal definition of wealth is that your definition will always be a relative term. Relative to what? A poor immigrant family might say that being rich would mean having an apartment with running water and a roof overhead. You might like to be wealthy relative to your neighbour or friend. I was guilty of this when I was a young man in my 20s. I found myself constantly in a battle to beat other people, which was silly and futile. I constantly met new people who were more wealthy than the last. The benchmark kept moving, and it always seemed out of reach.

Your definition of wealth should be defined relative to your desired standard of living—not your neighbour's or your friend's, but your own. Be realistic about this and focus on what income level makes you happy. Your life will be a lot easier and you will feel more fulfilled in the process.

To learn more about wealth, you must associate yourself with wealthy people. You can do this through clubs, nonprofit organizations, churches, and friends who can introduce you. An alternative would be to read books about wealthy people. You need to learn how they think, how they got there, and what is important to them—their values. One excellent book to consider reading is *Buffett—The Making of an American Capitalist*, by Roger Lowenstein. It's the story of one of the world's richest people, and reveals how persistence, patience, careful investing, and a frugal lifestyle can be extremely rewarding.

The most common way to define your current level of wealth is by measuring your net worth. When you go to a bank and apply for a loan, one of the first things they want is a *net-worth statement*. This statement lists both liquid and nonliquid assets, subtracts your liabilities (debts you owe, such as your mortgage) and results in a bottom-line, net-worth amount. Ask your local bank for a blank net-worth statement.

Now that you understand the 10 key wealth concepts from Chapter 2, let's discuss the five levels of wealth. Please understand these are *my* definitions. Each person has her own definition of wealth, which might or might not involve anything financial. Wealth to one person might be extensive wisdom. Wealth to another might be artistic ability. This book focuses on financial wealth.

Words of the Wealthy

Your **Target Savings Goal** (TSG) refers to the amount of money required each year to build a portfolio large enough to support your preferred standard of living at retirement, as calculated in Chapter 4.

Wealth Level 1

At this level of wealth, you can maintain your standard of living and save enough money to achieve your target savings goal. When you live within your means and your actual savings equal or exceed your TSG, you've made it to Wealth Level 1. It's the easiest level to achieve and can be your wealth safeguard if you fail at other levels.

Focus

To make it to Wealth Level 1, the most important thing to focus on is your actual savings amount. This will affect the portfolio much more than the total return on your portfolio. For now, total return is of secondary importance. The most common mistake made by neophyte investors is that they focus too much on total return. To achieve and maintain this level, you should focus on maximizing your actual savings amount as much as you possibly can.

During your journey toward Wealth Level 1, you should also learn as much as you can about investment management, and learn from your mistakes now. These mistakes, if made now, will not have nearly the effect that they will later, when your account is much larger and the mistakes are much harder to recover from. For example, a common mistake made by neophyte investors is using futures and options contracts. This is not a wise way to start out investing. I know, because I did it and lost a lot of money!

However, I'm glad I did this in the early part of my life. It taught me to stick with stocks, bonds, and mutual funds.

Stages

If this all seems too overwhelming, it may be easier to conquer this level in stages. For example, you could set your first target savings goal at 5 percent of your net monthly income. The second goal could be 10 percent; third, 15 percent; and so on. The last stage would be to save your true total TSG. If you save in slowly increasing amounts over time and continue this habit through life as your income increases, you will dramatically improve your chances of reaching Wealth Levels 2 through 5.

Wealth Warning

Canadians were once known as careful savers. But statistics in recent years show savings rates have plummeted to just a few percent of income, from above 10 percent or so in years past. Don't follow the crowd—be a saver!

Setting and sticking to a savings goal may sound easy, but few people follow through to meet their savings goals. Either they are unwilling to cut back their standard of living to save the 10 percent, or they are unwilling to try harder for more income. They procrastinate saving money, have too much pride to cut back their spending, borrow too much to keep up with the neighbours, or just never think about the future. Whatever the reason, they will never achieve the level of wealth they desire.

Shortcuts

You can skip this level completely if you are starting a business that you believe could substantially increase your income and net worth. This might get you to Level 3 or 4 faster. If you take this route, get ready for an exciting ride. There's much more risk of failure, and if the business fails, recovery time might be very slow depending upon the damage done. Therefore, you must be willing to accept failure and keep on going. Before skipping this level and starting your own business, you must be willing to accept the worst thing that can happen. I was willing to accept the risk years ago when I started my own business. I'm glad I did. Would I do it again? You bet I would—even if I couldn't manage money. As long as I had a vision and was excited about it, I would do it. Later in Part 3, I will discuss how you can develop your own vision and improve your chances of success in your own business.

Wealth Level 2

At the beginning of this wealth level, your portfolio is large enough to produce, on its own, a total return each year equal to your TSG. That means you have now, in essence, doubled your TSG: one part comes from your monthly TSG deposit, and the other part

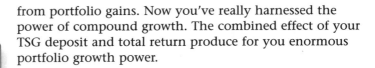

Wealth Warning

Total return, also known as port-folio performance, refers to the per-centage return of an investment or portfolio that includes dividends, interest, and capital gains. By the way, when the total return is reinvested into the investment or portfolio, the result is compound growth.

from portfolio gains. Now you've really harnessed the power of compound growth. The combined effect of your TSG deposit and total return produce for you enormous portfolio growth power.

Focus

Because at this level your actual savings amount and total return are equal, they become equally important. You must focus on both of these components. This is also the stage of wealth where knowledge of risk becomes vital to the remainder of the wealth-building process. Unfortunately, most people wait until this stage to begin learning about risks. Bad investment decisions made now in Wealth Level 2 are much more costly than they would have been in Level 1.

Stages

You haven't completed Wealth Level 2 when your portfolio's annual return equals your TSG. There are actually three stages to this level. Stage 2 continues as your portfolio produces a total return equal to two times your TSG. Therefore, your portfolio is growing by three times your TSG. One part is your actual TSG deposit, and the other two parts come from portfolio performance. The most important component now becomes total return. Your actual savings amount still helps speed the process, but total return now is much more important and powerful. If total return is twice the size of your actual savings amount, then your downside risk is also twice as big. This makes mistakes much more difficult to recover from. Making the right investment decisions becomes paramount, and risk management becomes vital.

Wealth Warning

Many Canadians expect programs such as the Canada Pension Plan will carry them through retirement. Don't count on it! Canada now spends more than 25 cents of every tax dollar just on interest payments for government debt. Such financial mismanagement means you must prepare for retirement on your own.

You've reached the third stage of Wealth Level 2 when your portfolio produces a total return equal to three times your TSG. The compounding effect is expanding your portfolio geometrically. Now the relative effect of an additional deposit equal to your TSG has very little influence on the growth of the portfolio. Total return is vital and investment management has never before been so important.

Shortcuts

This level can also be skipped if you start a business that substantially increases your income and net worth. But you must be willing to accept and manage the risks involved.

Wealth Level 3

If your portfolio produces a total return large enough to cover your desired lifestyle and inflation, then congratulations! You've made it to Wealth Level 3. Now employment is optional and your money is working hard for you. According to my research, only about 5 percent of the population achieve this level of wealth by retirement age. However, most of my clients have made it to this level. They enjoy life by doing what they love to do. Once they make the decision to retire, or at least slow down, their living expenses usually decrease. Maybe they take more vacations and spend more money, but they still live within their means. The habit is so ingrained that they actually feel uncomfortable spending more than normal, even if they can afford to do so.

Focus

If you are not relying upon your portfolio for income, the most important component is total return. The amount of money you're saving now is probably dwarfed by the effect of total return. Likewise, your potential downside is also significant, which reduces your ability to recover from a loss using additional deposits. This is especially true if you are no longer earning a salary. At this stage, proper diversification of your investments is crucial. You can't afford to be concentrated in too few stocks, or mutual funds, and part of your savings should be in other asset classes, such as bonds.

If you are relying upon your portfolio for income (such as to pay your living expenses after you retire), you have to focus on two components: total return and standard of living expenses. If you spend more than your portfolio produces, over the long run you'll erode your income-generating capital and drop back into Level 1 or 2 with no source of income to replace what you lost. The wealthy people I know in this level prevent this from happening by simply making it a habit to live well within their means. They always spend less than their total income.

Wealth Level 4

You have accumulated enough assets to produce a total return sufficient to substantially increase your desired lifestyle, while at the same time keep up with inflation. If you've made it beyond Level 3, and you've built your portfolio big enough to support your dream lifestyle, you've made it to Wealth Level 4. You now have the option not to work and, at the same time, to raise your standard of living. You might buy a bigger home, travel more, or just spend more money. You not only have enough total return to cover your desired lifestyle, you also have a little extra to build your portfolio further.

Only about 1 percent of the population make it to Wealth Level 4. Most people aren't willing to take the time to plan, make the sacrifices, or take the risk. That's right: this level involves planning, sacrifices, and risk! Oh no! There's that word *risk*, again! After reading this book you will understand more about risk and how to manage it properly.

Most of the individuals who make it to this level are business owners. Their wealth was built from net income, the sale of the business, or both.

That Reminds Me...

There have been dire warnings in recent years that there won't be enough money available for all of us to collect CPP benefits by the time baby boomers reach 65 and start devouring all the pension money. Even if the government is able to fund the program adequately when the baby boomers age, we might still have to pay for it through higher taxes, a higher retirement age, or cutbacks in government services. Either way, it's smart to plan for retirement without banking on much from the CPP.

Focus

Your two master components are total return and risk management. The portfolio now is very large and you want to reduce volatility. You can do this yourself, but it must be a hobby you enjoy. Some Wealth Level 4 people hire help in the investment management process.

Wealth Level 5

You have accumulated enough assets to produce a total return well beyond what you would ever spend. You now have the option not to work, to raise your standard of living, and to bestow large charitable gifts. Once you reach this level, you will need some serious estate-planning help, in order to minimize taxation as you pass on assets to loved ones and others.

If you want to make it to this level, you could become a famous movie star or corporate executive with lots of stock options. However, the most common way people make it to this level is through the sale of a large cash-generating asset such as a business or commercial real estate. You can also get there by building and selling a company. It happens all the time. Just look back at the stories in Chapter 1.

Focus

What do you think Wealth Level 5 people focus on with regard to their money? I can tell you from experience that the answer to this question is risk. The master component is risk and, more specifically, the management of risk. When you make it to this level, you tend to focus on protection of principal. It doesn't matter whether you make 5 percent or 15 percent on your portfolio. Your needs are covered either way. Therefore, you tend to focus on maintenance instead of total return. First, you want to reduce the possibility of a substantial loss. Second, you want to maintain an adequate rate of return.

Certainly it would be great to achieve this level of wealth, but most people would be content with Level 3 or 4. Therefore, this book will focus primarily on the first four levels.

The Least You Need to Know

➤ Your definition of wealth should be relative to your own desired standard of living and not your neighbour's.

➤ In your early years of building wealth, the actual amount you save is much more important than the performance of your portfolio.

➤ In your attempt to reach Wealth Level 1, learn the basics, go with your gut instinct, and learn from any investment mistakes.

➤ You can take a shortcut to the higher levels of wealth by starting your own business, but the risks can be greater.

Chapter 4

The Eight Steps Toward Achieving Wealth Level 1

In This Chapter

➤ Analysing your income and spending habits

➤ Estimating your future income needs

➤ Estimating your target portfolio goal

➤ Estimating your yearly and monthly Target Savings Goal

➤ Maintaining your wealth plan

Most people never achieve any significant wealth because they have no idea how to get started. There's no class or television show that really shows you how to do it. You might find a few books on the subject, but rarely do you find an actual formula that works. If you do find a formula, it is probably either too complicated or too ambiguous. Therefore, I sat down and designed an easy step-by-step plan that would help others get to Wealth Level 1. It's simple to complete and it should be the first step in your journey toward wealth. You'll learn about the plan in this chapter.

Getting Ready for the Journey

I've learned that wealth, when achieved over a long period, tends to be appreciated more; wealth acquired suddenly tends to be squandered. This is especially evident among lottery winners. An article in *The New York Times* (April 23, 1995) titled "Ticket To Trouble" stated, "There are no statistics on what happens to jackpot

Treasure Tip

The great wealth hunter Waschka says, "If you always hunt elephants, you may die of starvation. But if you focus on the easier little game like rabbits and birds, you'll be better prepared when the elephant comes along."

Treasure Tip

Looking back at all the wealthy people I've met in my life, it seems that the ones who built their own wealth slowly over time seem to appreciate and maintain it better than those who inherited or married it.

winners. But a growing body of evidence suggests that winning big often brings big, if not ruinous trouble." For example, William Post of Oil City, PA, won a $16.2-million jackpot in 1988. Five years later, he was completely broke and his brother was in jail charged with hiring a hit man to murder William and his wife for the lottery money.

Why do these lottery winners end up in so much trouble? Just think about it a minute. They win the lottery and suddenly they feel like they're rich. They begin spending money like never before, and they pay little attention to planning for the future. Who cares about the future when you're rich and have all this money coming in? Well, that's the problem. These winners see wealth as a destination, and they feel like they have definitely arrived. What they don't understand is that wealth is a journey, not a destination. You can't just get to Wealth Level 3 and go nuts. You have to continue to be a good steward of your money, which requires some responsibility.

If you want to achieve and maintain wealth throughout your lifetime, you must see wealth as a journey. As you saw in Chapter 3, this journey has many levels and transitions, and most people don't understand them. If you take the time to plan and prepare for each step or transition, you improve your chances of becoming and staying wealthy. It also helps to be patient along the way, especially at the beginning of your journey.

Let's begin your journey by focusing on accomplishing the first level of wealth. Here are the steps to follow:

1. Analyse your current income—and focus on maximizing it.

2. Analyse your current spending habits—and focus on minimizing spending.

3. Estimate how much you need to cover your future expenses (such as your living expenses after retirement) in before-tax dollars.

4. Project the effect of inflation on expenses.

5. Estimate your target portfolio amount (the amount of money you'll need in your portfolio to retire).

6. Estimate your yearly and monthly target savings goal.

7. Achieve your target savings goal.

8. Maintain your plan.

What you are about to embark on is a simple process of estimating income and expenses designed to give you an approximate target savings goal. You could get really serious here with this exercise and build a complex model of expense analysis and wealth projections. That's great if you want to take the time. I suggest using computer spreadsheets or personal finance software that will do all this for you. But to make things easy for now, let's establish some approximate goals so you can at least get started. The overall tool you'll use is the Wealth Builder Worksheet, shown next. The subsequent sections in this chapter walk you, in detail, through each of the steps in the Wealth Builder Worksheet, particularly those steps that require calculations. Read the chapter before using the worksheet, then make numerous copies of it so you can update it from year to year to review your progress toward your goals.

Step 1: Analyse Your Current Income

Write down on a piece of paper your current yearly salary or income before tax. Under that amount, write this question: "What can I do to increase my income now and in the future?" Find a peaceful place of solitude and complete 20 answers to this question. If you can't come up with 20 answers, ask a friend to help you. Here are a few ideas to get you started:

➤ Ask the boss for a raise.

➤ Offer to take on more responsibility for more pay.

➤ Start a small income-generating business on the side.

➤ Come up with an idea at work that will make the company more profitable.

➤ Find another job that will pay you what you're worth.

Afterwards, select the best answers and make an effort to implement them. If building wealth is really important to you, you'll take the time to complete this step. As I've mentioned in Chapter 1, your journey toward wealth doesn't require a huge salary. However, if you'll at least attempt to maximize your income, you might shorten the distance you have to travel. There are so many different ways to do this. If you're creative and proactive by nature, you'll have no problem doing this. In Chapter 6, I will discuss several techniques you can use to maximize your salary if you work for others. In Part 3, I'll discuss ways to maximize your net income if you're self-employed.

The ultimate goal in this step is to calculate the amount of yearly income you would like to make before taxes and retirement savings plan contributions. What amount of income would you need to be happy? Before you answer this question, you might want to complete step two regarding expenses.

Wealth Builder Worksheet

1. **Analyse your current yearly income.**_____

2. **Analyse your current spending habits.**
   Estimate your total yearly expenses:

   _____ x 12 = _____

   (Monthly expenses) _____ = x 12 (Yearly expenses) _____

   Project the growth of your monthly spending habits.

   _____ + _____ = _____

   (Yearly expenses) + (Estimated additions) = (Total yearly expenses)

3. **Estimate income needed to cover your expenses in before-tax dollars.**
   Calculate the inverse of your total average tax rate:

   1.00 – = _____

   1.00 – (Total average federal and provincial income tax rate) = (Inverse rate)

   Convert yearly expenses into a before-tax amount.

   _____ / _____ = _____

   (Total yearly expenses)/(Inverse rate) = (Pre-tax yearly expenses)

4. **Project the effect of inflation on expenses.**

   _____ x _____ = _____

   (Yearly expenses before tax) x (1.00 + inflation estimate) = Expenses
   Continue this calculation for the number of years until retirement.

5. **Estimate Your Target Portfolio Amount.**

   _____ / _____ = _____

   (Highest yearly expenses)/(Estimated net rate of return) = (Portfolio size needed)

6. **Estimate yearly and monthly TSGs.**
   Yearly TSG Calculation:

   _____ / _____ = _____

   Target Portfolio Goal/Future Value Factor= Yearly TSG

   Monthly TSG calculation:

   _____ /12 = _____

   Yearly TSG /12 = Monthly TSG

7. **Achieve your target savings goal.**

8. **Maintain your plan.**

Step 2: Analyse Your Current Spending Habits

What are your current yearly expenses? How much money do you spend each month? The best way to keep track of this is to keep a pen and paper with you for a month. This sounds like a lot of trouble, but remember, we're talking here about building your wealth. I always find that whatever is measured seems to improve. If you take the time to do this, you will learn a lot about yourself and quickly see where your money is going. Do this for one month and calculate your actual monthly expenditures. Then multiply this by 12. This should give you an approximate idea of your yearly expenses.

If you prefer a more structured approach, the Weekly Expense Worksheet (page 39) in this chapter is designed for you to copy four times, one for each week of the month. (Make five copies if the current month spans five weeks.) You may want to enlarge it to fit a full page. Take a sheet with you and begin recording now. Record every penny you spend for one month. This includes all cash, credit, and chequebook expenditures.

After you enter each monthly total, take a look at where you're spending money. Find the expenses that are unnecessary. What could you do without? In the second column of the Monthly Expense Worksheet, Next Month's Budget, record what you think your expenses should be. This will be your budget. If you want, do the same exercise again next month, record your actual expenses in the third column, and see how close you came. I have found that by simply measuring expenses, I tend to be more in control of my spending habits. The goal is to find additional money that you can save.

Using your monthly expense total, calculate a yearly total by multiplying by 12. You will need this yearly total for the next step. If you want more exact numbers, look back over the past year's expenses using your chequebook register and credit card statements. Set these up on a computer spreadsheet and see what your actual yearly expenses have been. The most effective way to do this is to use one of the personal financial software packages that are now available, such as Quicken. This program will help you do an expense analysis in great detail. For those who are computer illiterate, good old-fashioned notebook paper works just as well; it just takes longer.

But you're not finished yet. Do you foresee any change in these spending habits? Here are some common changes that affect spending habits: getting married, buying a home, having a child, or sending a child to college. Ask yourself what

Treasure Tip

All work and no play makes Jack a dull boy. Don't forget to budget some money for fun.

changes you expect to make in the next five years. Estimate the costs, and project how much your monthly spending will increase or decrease. Multiply this by 12 to get a yearly figure. The result should be the amount of money you will need per year for the added expense, and you should add it into the expense total you've just calculated.

Weekly Expense Worksheet

Expense Items	Mon	Tues	Wed	Thurs	Fri	Sat	Sun	Total
Auto: Gas								
Auto: Maintenance								
Children: Tuition/Child Care								
Food: Dining Out/Credit Card								
Food: Grocery								
Fun:								
Fun:								
Fun: Vacation/Entertainment								
Home: Furniture								
Home: Housekeeper								
Home: Pest Control								
Home: Rent								
Home: Repair/Maintenance								
Home: Security Monitoring								
Home: Yard Maintenance								
Insurance: Auto & Liability								
Insurance:								
Insurance: Disability								
Insurance: Health								
Insurance: Life								
Loan:								
Loan: Home Mortgage								
Membership: Athletic Club								
Membership:								
Membership Dues:								

Expense Items	Mon	Tues	Wed	Thurs	Fri	Sat	Sun	Total
Misc:								
Misc:								
Misc: Clothing								
Misc: Contributions/Gifts								
Misc: Laundry/Dry Cleaning								
Misc: Medical/Dental								
Misc: Parking								
Misc: Personal Care								
Misc: Transportation								
Taxes: Property								
Taxes: Income (out of paycheque)								
Taxes: Quarterly, Federal								
Taxes: Tax Account to pay April								
Utility: Electric								
Utility: Gas								
Utility: Phone								
Utility: Water								
Retirement Account								
Other								
Other								
Other								
Other								

At the end of each week, total each row. Once you have all four sheets, total the corresponding row entries. For example, total your four weeks' worth of expenses for Misc: Personal Care. Make copies of the Monthly Expense Worksheet, shown next in this book, and record the sum of the four weekly totals for each expense item. If you don't want to complete the Weekly Expense Worksheet now, you may just want to estimate your monthly expenses for each category so that you can get started. That's okay, but don't disregard the Weekly Expense Worksheet. If you do, you may be basing your entire financial future on incorrect data.

Monthly Expense Worksheet

Expense Items	This Month	Actual	Next Month's Budget
Auto: Gas			
Auto: Maintenance			
Children: Tuition/Child Care			
Food: Dining Out/Credit Card			
Food: Grocery			
Fun:			
Fun:			
Fun: Vacation/Entertainment			
Home: Furniture			
Home: Housekeeper			
Home: Pest Control			
Home: Rent			
Home: Repair/Maintenance			
Home: Security Monitoring			
Home: Yard Maintenance			
Insurance: Auto & Liability			
Insurance:			
Insurance: Disability			
Insurance: Health			
Insurance: Life			
Loan:			
Loan: Home Mortgage			
Membership: Athletic Club			
Membership:			

Expense Items	This Month	Actual	Next Month's Budget
Membership:			
Misc:			
Misc:			
Misc: Clothing			
Misc: Contributions/Gifts			
Misc: Laundry/Dry Cleaning			
Misc: Medical/Dental			
Misc: Parking			
Misc: Personal Care			
Misc: Transportation			
Taxes: Property			
Taxes: Income (out of paycheque)			
Taxes: Quarterly, Federal			
Taxes: Tax Account to pay April			
Utility: Electric			
Utility: Gas			
Utility: Phone			
Utility: Water			
Retirement Account			
Other			
Other			
Other			
Total			

Make sure that this is a conservative figure with some room for error. Pad the amount if you want, just to be sure you've covered all your expenses. Your goal should be to establish the lowest amount of expenses you'd be happy to live with now. If you are not satisfied with your current standard of living and you feel you would need additional money, then add it. Just remember that if you do so, your target savings goal will be higher and more difficult to achieve.

Step 3: Estimate Income Needed to Cover Your Expenses in Before-Tax Dollars

This step is easy. Estimate your total federal and provincial income tax rate. You may want to use your average income tax rate, which we calculated earlier in Chapter 2. You may want to call your accountant if you have one, or get a federal and provincial tax table from Revenue Canada. Once you have your estimated tax rate, subtract the percentage from 1 to calculate the inverse of your tax rate. For example, if your average income tax rate is 35 percent, then the equation would look like this:

$1 - .35 = .65$ .65 is the inverse of your tax rate

Then take your projected yearly expenses that you calculated in the preceding section and divide your expenses by this number. For example, if your estimated yearly expenses added up to $40,000, the equation would look like this:

$40,000 / .65 = 61,538$

Therefore, you are going to need $61,538 in income per year before tax in order to maintain your spending habits.

Words of the Wealthy

The **inverse** of a percentage number is easily calculated by subtracting the percentage number from 1.

Step 4: Project the Effect of Inflation on Expenses

The next step is to calculate the effect of *inflation* on your expenses in later years. If we continue the example you saw in the last section, we know you'll need $61,538 each year in today's dollars to cover your expenses—but what about when you retire? What will inflation do to prices by that time?

The only way to answer that question is to make an estimate of future inflation and calculate its effect on your yearly expense needs. This process involves a simple calculation. To calculate the one-year effect of inflation, just take the yearly expense total and multiply it by 1 plus your estimate of inflation.

(Yearly expenses before tax) x (1 + Estimate of inflation) = Next year's expense estimate

If we use a 3-percent estimate of the annual inflation rate, here is what the calculation would look like:

$61,538 x (1 + .03) = $63,384

This calculation shows that if the inflation rate is 3 percent, you will need $63,384 in income next year to cover the same amount of expenses.

Now that you understand the calculation, you can project further into the future. First you have to decide how many years you are willing to wait to achieve Level 3 wealth when your portfolio is producing enough income for you to retire. Let's say you're willing to wait 25 years. Just continue the calculation 24 more times. Using the same example, Table 4.1 shows what the result should look like (see page 44).

As you can see from Table 4.1, in 25 years, you will need approximately $128,847 in income to cover your yearly expense needs. Isn't it scary what inflation of only 3 percent can do to your standard of living?

Step 5: Estimate Your Target Portfolio Amount

You have to assume several variables before you can estimate how much money you'll need. You have to estimate your rate of return. Depending upon whom you ask, estimates of rate of return can vary widely. If you ask a very conservative investor, the answer could be as low as 5 percent. On the other hand, a very aggressive investor might say 15 percent. Your return obviously depends upon the level of risk you take and how your investments perform. For now, let's continue to assume a 10-percent rate of return, which is a little below the average return on the TSE 300 (the major Toronto Stock Exchange performance index) over the last 40 years.

Words of the Wealthy

Most people think that **inflation** is the simple rise in prices. The technical definition is an increase in the volume of money and credit relative to available goods, which results in a substantial and continuing rise in the general price level. The rate of inflation is measured by the month-to-month percentage change of the Consumer Price Index (CPI).

Wealth Warning

The Canada Pension Plan was started in 1966. You can start collecting CPP when you turn 60, but for every month of your age under 65, you lose 0.5 percent of your pension eligibility, to a maximum of 30 percent.

Table 4.1
Estimating Future Income Needs Based on Inflation

No. of Years	Year	Pre-tax Income Needed for Expenses (base of $61,538)	Estimated Inflation
1	2000	$ 63,384	3%
2	2001	$ 65,286	3%
3	2002	$ 67,244	3%
4	2003	$ 69,262	3%
5	2004	$ 71,339	3%
6	2005	$ 73,480	3%
7	2006	$ 75,684	3%
8	2007	$ 77,954	3%
9	2008	$ 80,293	3%
10	2009	$ 82,702	3%
11	2010	$ 85,183	3%
12	2011	$ 87,738	3%
13	2012	$ 90,371	3%
14	2013	$ 93,082	3%
15	2014	$ 95,874	3%
16	2015	$ 98,750	3%
17	2016	$101,713	3%
18	2017	$104,764	3%
19	2018	$107,907	3%
20	2019	$111,144	3%
21	2020	$114,479	3%
22	2021	$117,913	3%
23	2022	$121,451	3%
24	2023	$125,094	3%
25	2024	$128,847	3%

That Reminds Me...

To achieve real wealth, you must be open-minded enough to recognize and break down the self-imposed barriers that keep you in your current financial condition. These barriers are usually mental paradigms or mind-sets that need a little adjustment. Normally the adjustment requires a catalyst or disruption to get it started. The most common catalysts and disruptions come from reading and discussing ideas with others. First, take some time to understand your own paradigm barriers about building wealth. Then discuss them with others who have achieved the level of wealth you desire. How do these people think? How did they overcome the same barriers? Did they have similar barriers or different ones? This meeting might be just the catalyst you need.

Now divide your yearly before-tax income, adjusted for inflation, by your estimated net rate of return.

Yearly before-tax income adjusted for inflation / Estimated net rate of return = Target Portfolio Goal

For example, here is the calculation using the assumptions above:

$128,847 / .10 = $1,288,470

Therefore, in order to retire comfortably and to begin living off the return from your portfolio, you'll need a portfolio of assets totalling $1,288,470, producing a rate of return of 10 percent per year.

Isn't this great? Now you can measure exactly what you will need in assets to achieve Wealth Level 3! Don't be overwhelmed by the result. You're about to learn how to build this pool of assets.

Step 6: Estimate Yearly and Monthly TSGs

Using Table 4.2, Future Value of Annuity Due (page 47), you can find what your yearly target savings goal should be. Let's review the assumptions before we calculate:

Target portfolio goal	$1,288,470
Yearly before-tax income needed at retirement	$128,847
Estimated rate of return	10%
Number of years until retirement	25

In Tables 4.2 through 4.4 (pages 47–49), find the future value of annuity due factor that corresponds to your assumptions. Look at the top row and find your estimated Rate of Return of 10 percent. (If you want to use a different Rate of Return, select it from the table.) Look down the column until you find the factor for the number of years until you retire—in this case, 25 years.

Your factor for this example should be 108.1818, which we'll call the future value factor. Thus, the calculation to find your yearly TSG looks like this:

Target Portfolio Goal / Future Value Factor = Yearly TSG

Here are the actual numbers, for example:

$1,288,470 / 108.1818 = $11,910

Now to calculate your monthly TSG, just divide this number by 12.

$11,910 / 12 = $992.50

Please understand that this simple calculation does not take into consideration the effect of taxes on the total return of your investments. If this amount of money were saved in a retirement savings plan, the math is almost perfect. However, if you are saving in a taxable account (i.e., outside your RRSP) or the combination of a taxable account and a tax-deferred qualified plan, then you must consider the effect of taxes each year on your total return accumulation. Here are a few things to consider.

Let's assume your net tax liability on dividends, interest, and capital gains is 30 percent. If you make an average total return of 10 percent, then you could subtract 30 percent of the 10 percent return to get a net total return of 7 percent. This 7 percent can then be used to estimate your target portfolio return. (That is, you should choose a 7-percent Rate of Return factor from Table 4.2 rather than the 10-percent Rate of Return factor from Table 4.3 before making your calculation.) However, remember this is an estimate. Your capital gains may not all accrue each year, which means that there will be irregular capital gains taxes to pay each year depending upon when your investment transactions result in a capital gain.

Wealth Warning

This process is not difficult to complete, but can easily result in a mistake. Once you complete all the necessary steps and calculations, be sure to go back and check your math.

Table 4.2
Future Value of Annuity Factors (Annuity Due), Part 1

Years until You Retire	Rate of Return						
	1%	2%	3%	4%	5%	6%	7%
5	5.1520	5.3081	5.4684	5.6330	5.8019	5.9753	6.1533
6	6.2135	6.4343	6.6625	6.8983	7.1420	7.3938	7.6540
7	7.2857	7.5830	7.8923	8.2142	8.5491	8.8975	9.2598
8	8.3685	8.7546	9.1591	9.5828	10.0266	10.4913	10.9780
9	9.4622	9.9497	10.4639	11.0061	11.5779	12.1808	12.8164
10	10.5668	11.1687	11.8078	12.4864	13.2068	13.9716	14.7836
11	11.6825	12.4121	13.1920	14.0258	14.9171	15.8699	16.8885
12	12.8093	13.6803	14.6178	15.6268	16.7130	17.8821	19.1406
13	13.9474	14.9739	16.0863	17.2919	18.5986	20.0151	21.5505
14	15.0969	16.2934	17.5989	19.0236	20.5786	22.2760	24.1290
15	16.2579	17.6393	19.1569	20.8245	22.6575	24.6725	26.8881
16	17.4304	19.0121	20.7616	22.6975	24.8404	27.2129	29.8402
17	18.6147	20.4123	22.4144	24.6454	27.1324	29.9057	32.9990
18	19.8109	21.8406	24.1169	26.6712	29.5390	32.7600	36.3790
19	21.0190	23.2974	25.8704	28.7781	32.0660	35.7856	39.9955
20	22.2392	24.7833	27.6765	30.9692	34.7193	38.9927	43.8652
21	23.4716	26.2990	29.5368	33.2480	37.5052	42.3923	48.0057
22	24.7163	27.8450	31.4529	35.6179	40.4305	45.9958	52.4361
23	25.9735	29.4219	33.4265	38.0826	43.5020	49.8156	57.1767
24	27.2432	31.0303	35.4593	40.6459	46.7271	53.8645	62.2490
25	28.5256	32.6709	37.5530	43.3117	50.1135	58.1564	67.6765
26	29.8209	34.3443	39.7096	46.0842	53.6691	62.7058	73.4838
27	31.1291	36.0512	41.9309	48.9676	57.4026	67.5281	79.6977
28	32.4504	37.7922	44.2189	51.9663	61.3227	72.6398	86.3465
29	33.7849	39.5681	46.5754	55.0849	65.4388	78.0582	93.4608
30	35.1327	41.3794	49.0027	58.3283	69.7608	83.8017	101.0730
35	42.0769	50.9944	62.2759	76.5983	94.8363	118.1209	147.9135
40	49.3752	61.6100	77.6633	98.8265	126.8398	164.0477	213.6096
45	57.0459	73.3306	95.5015	125.8706	167.6852	225.5081	305.7518
50	65.1078	86.2710	116.1808	158.7738	219.8154	307.7561	434.9860

Table 4.3
Future Value of Annuity Factors (Annuity Due), Part 2

Years until You Retire	Rate of Return						
	8%	**9%**	**10%**	**11%**	**12%**	**13%**	**14%**
5	6.3359	6.5233	6.7156	6.9129	7.1152	7.3227	7.5355
6	7.9228	8.2004	8.4872	8.7833	9.0890	9.4047	9.7305
7	9.6366	10.0285	10.4359	10.8594	11.2997	11.7573	12.2328
8	11.4876	12.0210	12.5795	13.1640	13.7757	14.4157	15.0853
9	13.4866	14.1929	14.3974	15.7220	16.5487	17.4197	18.3373
10	15.6455	16.5603	17.5312	18.5614	19.6546	20.8143	22.0445
11	17.9771	19.1407	20.3843	21.7132	23.1331	24.6502	26.2707
12	20.4953	21.9534	23.5227	25.2116	27.0291	28.9847	31.0887
13	23.2149	25.0192	26.9750	29.0949	31.3926	33.8827	36.5811
14	26.1521	28.3609	30.7725	33.4054	36.2797	39.4175	42.8424
15	29.3243	32.0034	34.9497	38.1899	41.7533	45.6717	49.9804
16	32.7502	35.9737	39.5447	43.5008	47.8837	52.7391	58.1176
17	36.4502	40.3013	44.5992	49.3959	54.7497	60.7251	67.3941
18	40.4463	45.0185	50.1591	55.9395	62.4397	69.7494	77.9692
19	44.7620	50.1601	56.2750	63.2028	71.0524	79.9468	90.0249
20	49.4229	55.7645	63.0025	71.2651	80.6987	91.4699	103.7684
21	54.4568	61.8733	70.4027	80.2143	91.5026	104.4910	119.4360
22	59.8933	68.5319	78.5430	90.1479	103.6029	119.2048	137.2970
23	65.7648	75.7898	87.4973	101.1741	117.1552	135.8315	157.6586
24	72.1059	83.7009	97.3471	113.4133	132.3339	154.6196	180.8708
25	78.9544	92.3240	108.1818	126.9988	149.3339	175.8501	207.3327
26	86.3508	101.7231	120.0999	142.0786	168.3740	199.8406	237.4993
27	94.3388	111.9682	133.2099	158.8173	189.6989	226.9499	271.8892
28	102.9659	123.1354	147.6309	177.3972	213.5828	257.5834	311.0937
29	112.2832	135.3075	163.4940	198.0209	240.3327	292.1992	355.7868
30	122.3459	148.5752	180.9434	220.9132	270.2926	331.3151	406.7370
35	186.1021	235.1247	298.1268	379.1644	483.4631	617.7493	790.6729
40	279.7810	368.2919	486.8518	645.8269	859.1424	1145.4858	1529.9086
45	417.4261	573.1860	790.7953	1095.1688	1521.2176	2117.8060	2953.2439
50	619.6718	888.4411	1280.2994	1852.3359	2688.0204	3909.2430	5693.7543

Table 4.4
Future Value of Annuity Factors (Annuity Due), Part 3

Years until You Retire	Rate of Return				
	15%	**16%**	**17%**	**18%**	**19%**
5	7.7537	7.9775	8.2068	8.4420	8.6830
6	10.0668	10.4139	10.7720	11.1415	11.5227
7	12.7268	13.2401	13.7733	14.3270	14.9020
8	15.7858	16.5185	17.2847	18.0859	18.9234
9	19.3037	20.3215	21.3931	22.5213	23.7089
10	23.3493	24.7329	26.1999	27.7551	29.4035
11	28.0017	29.8502	31.8239	33.9311	36.1802
12	33.3519	35.7862	38.4040	41.2187	44.2445
13	39.5047	42.6720	46.1027	49.8180	53.8409
14	46.5804	50.6595	55.1101	59.9653	65.2607
15	54.7175	59.9250	65.6488	71.9390	78.8502
16	64.0751	70.6730	77.9792	86.0680	95.0218
17	74.8364	83.1407	92.4056	102.7403	114.2659
18	87.2118	97.6032	109.2846	122.4135	137.1664
19	101.4436	114.3739	129.0329	145.6280	164.4180
20	117.8101	133.8405	152.1385	173.0210	196.8474
21	136.6316	156.4150	179.1721	205.3448	235.4385
22	158.2764	182.6014	210.8013	243.4868	281.3618
23	183.1678	212.9776	247.8076	288.4945	336.0105
24	211.7930	248.2140	291.1049	341.6035	401.0425
25	244.7120	289.0883	341.7627	404.2721	478.4306
26	282.5688	336.5024	401.0323	478.2211	570.5224
27	326.1041	391.5028	470.3778	565.4809	680.1116
28	376.1697	455.3032	551.5121	668.4475	810.5228
29	433.7451	529.3117	646.4391	789.9480	965.7122
30	499.9569	615.1616	757.5038	933.3186	1150.3875
35	1013.3757	1300.0270	1668.9945	2143.6489	2753.9143
40	2045.9539	2738.4784	3667.3906	4912.5914	6580.4965
45	4122.8977	5759.7178	8048.7701	11247.2610	15712.0750
50	8300.3737	1210.5353	17654.7170	25739.4510	37503.2500

Step 7: Achieve Your Target Savings Goal

If you are overwhelmed by your target portfolio size, don't be concerned. Don't forget that this amount is based upon some assumptions you made that can be adjusted. First, you could decrease the assumed inflation rate used to project your future living expenses. Second, you could accept some more risk and increase your estimated total return assumption. Third, you could extend the number of years you are willing to wait before you reach Wealth Level 3.

If you want to achieve your target savings goal, you have to ask yourself what factors you have the most control over. You have the least control over things like inflation and total return. You have the most control over expenses. You have some control over income, but reducing expenses is usually easier than increasing income. It may not be as glamorous, but it is very effective in achieving a larger savings goal. The less you spend, the more you have available for savings. The following list of ideas is designed to reduce your expenses. This is a small list (the rest of the book presents more tips and ideas, but it's a start).

➤ **Lower expenses.** Remember that cutting back on expenses is just as effective as earning more money. In fact, it's better to not spend a dollar than to earn an extra dollar, since your extra dollar will be taxed. Many people can't be bothered to change their lives in simple ways that save a little bit of money at a time, or they're worried about looking like cheapskates. Forget about it. There are plenty of ways to cut back on your expenses that are easy and don't make you look cheap. Saving a bit here and a bit there quickly adds up to a lot of money. It's like the old saying—look after the pennies, and the dollars will take care of themselves.

➤ **Don't buy lottery tickets.** If you understood the odds of winning the lottery, you would never buy a ticket.

➤ **Maintain your home and automobile.** I just replaced my 15–year-old air-conditioning system with a new one. My electric bills are less and my home is much cooler when it's hot outside.

➤ **Don't use life insurance for investment purposes.** This is one of the most common mistakes investors make. The cost of the insurance and commissions drain your investment, which decreases the total return you get. A friend who is an insurance agent says, "But the investment grows tax-deferred." And my reply is, "I don't care! It costs too much and the policyholder is limited to only a handful of investment choices that usually are mediocre at best." My suggestion is to separate your investment money from your life insurance. Consider going to a less expensive term policy and depositing the savings in a low-cost mutual fund. WARNING: Do not drop your existing life insurance first. If you plan to change to the term policy, do it first. Once it is set up, then cancel your past insurance. You don't want to be uncovered. If you can't get a term policy because of a preexistent condition, you will have your existing policy to fall back on.

➤ **Save money when you travel.** Smart travellers know that airlines want to charge business travellers more money than they charge vacationers. They assume that business travellers can write off the travel and therefore are more willing to pay higher prices. By simply staying at your destination over a Saturday night, you can sometimes save 75 percent off your airline ticket. You can also book hotel rooms cheaper in large cities by using services that offer more inexpensive lodging by purchasing rooms in bulk.

➤ **Read the fine print on your bank account and save.** You can avoid service charges by maintaining the required minimum balance. Avoid automated banking charges by using only your bank's automated tellers.

Treasure Tip

Many wealthy people I know built part of their fortune using residual income, which is income derived over time from previous efforts or past accomplishments that continue to produce cash flow. This includes rental income and income from books, tapes, or other media that continue to sell with little additional effort.

➤ **Switch phone companies for cheaper long-distance, local, and Internet service.** Some companies offer evening and weekend calls across Canada for five cents a minute, and 10 cents for weekdays, with no strings attached. Most people are still with companies that charge much more.

➤ **Avoid eating and drinking out.** Restaurant food is expensive, and taxes and tips add another 25 percent or more. Make eating at home a pleasurable event. Even if you splurge on fine food and drink in a supermarket, you won't spend nearly as much as you would in a restaurant.

➤ **Open a deposit account that pays a high interest rate.** Savings and chequing accounts at Canada's big banks have very low interest rates, for the most part. Accounts such as ING Direct and President's Choice Financial offer far better rates. It's worthwhile to park your uninvested loose money in these accounts, or place it in a money-market fund.

➤ **Shop around for vehicle, home, and life insurance.** The insurance industry is extremely competitive. Simply by making a few phone calls to a few different insurers, you will likely find lower rates for your various insurance needs.

➤ **Use a credit card, not cash or a debit card, to make purchases.** ALWAYS pay off your bill before interest charges kick in. By doing this, you will defer payment on goods by several weeks, pocketing the interest for yourself.

➤ **If you need a car only occasionally, rent instead of owning.** The cost of owning, insuring, fueling, and maintaining a vehicle is enormous. If you need one only a few times a month, arrange for a regular rental—it's far cheaper. Use public transit and taxis for quick trips.

➤ **Exercise at home and outside.** Some people join an expensive fitness centre only to jog 25 laps around a boring track twice a month.

➤ **Save on home energy costs.** Turn the heat down while you sleep and before you go to work. Turn off lights when not needed, and run dishwashers, washing machines, and dryers with full loads.

➤ **Avoid buying brewed coffee or tea from cafes.** The markup is outrageous. Make your own at your workplace for a fraction of the cost. Bring other beverages and food to work instead of buying them at food stands.

➤ **Quit smoking.**

➤ **Say no to telephone or door-to-door sales pitches.** Buy things you really need, not things that people try to sell you.

Step 8: Maintain Your Plan

Wealth Warning

Try to associate with other people who share your ambitions and aspirations and who are willing to share ideas and support you in your efforts. Look for win–win relationships. Avoid people who pull you down and drain your enthusiasm.

The last step is to maintain your plan. Redo all the calculations for the Wealth Builder Worksheet and the other two worksheets in this chapter at least once a year. Your monthly expenses should be measured each month, if not quarterly. If you continue to measure your expenses, you will be better able to meet your goal. I guarantee that your plan will change over time. Some of these changes will be small and some large. Your success in maintaining your plan depends a great deal upon several things:

➤ **Flexibility and creativity.** You must be willing to respond to the inevitable changes that life brings.

➤ **Organizational skills.** You must keep current with all of the elements of your plan.

➤ **Willingness to work on your plan.** Your journey toward wealth will take some time, but the payoff will be worth it!

The Least You Need to Know

➤ In order to save enough money to retire, you have to regularly measure your expenses, compare them to your income, and maximize your savings.

➤ The effect of taxes and inflation are staggering and always need to be part of your wealth-building equation.

➤ If you calculate your target savings goal every year, you will always know what you need to save each month.

➤ If you can let your assets grow tax-deferred in a tax-sheltered plan (RRSP), and then roll them over to an RRIF when you retire, your portfolio will grow faster and the end result will be more money when you need it.

Chapter 5

The Habits and Characteristics Needed to Reach Wealth Level 2

In This Chapter

➤ Save money systematically each month

➤ Avoid debt and pay cash for items

➤ Make it a habit to shop around

➤ Make wealth and passion work together

Remember the couple I mentioned in Chapter 1, Mr. and Mrs. Post, who never made more than $30,000 per year, yet their portfolio was worth more than $800,000? How could this couple have so much money? Well, that is exactly what I asked, and they said, "We saved it and invested it in no-load funds." I said, "Please tell me your story. There's got to be more to this, right?" They sat back and shared some simple truths that every investor should follow. I call them the seven habits of very wealthy people, and I detail them in this chapter.

The seven habits for building wealth include saving every month, staying out of debt, shopping before you buy, buying used when you can, taking care of your stuff, investing in stocks, and taking time to plan your future.

1. Save Every Month

The Posts said that each month, no matter what they made in salary, they put money in savings and invested in no-load mutual funds. They said, "No matter what happens, pay yourself first and make it a habit." The combination of systematic savings and compound growth is incredible. Here are several ways you can start saving money now:

➤ **Maximize your RRSP contribution.** A Registered Retirement Savings Plan (RRSP) is an individual retirement account into which a maximum of 18 percent of your earned income to a maximum of $13,500 can be deposited each year. Your RRSP contribution can be deducted from your income, after allowing for pension-related adjustments. The true benefit of the RRSP is that all interest, dividends, and capital gains are tax-deferred; no part of your RRSP is taxed until money is withdrawn, at which time it is taxed as income. The second benefit is the flexibility of available investment alternatives. You can invest in GICs, stocks, bonds, and mutual funds. Since there are more than 1,300 different mutual funds, your alternatives are almost endless. The third benefit is convenience. An RRSP is very simple to start. All you have to do is fill out an application and make a deposit. A self-directed RRSP allows you to invest not only in mutual funds, but directly in individual stocks and other investments.

➤ **Write yourself a cheque.** Before you start paying your bills each week or each payday, write yourself a cheque and deposit it into a separate account. The whole idea is to pay yourself before anyone else. Your goal should be to save your target savings goal. Then use the remainder to budget your spending. Act like the target savings goal amount doesn't even exist, and budget accordingly.

➤ **Let a mutual fund direct-debit your account.** Most mutual funds and other investment accounts offer a direct-debit feature that automatically withdraws a predetermined amount from your chequing account each month. This is one of the easiest ways to save money. Each month at bill-paying time, just record the withdrawal in your cheque register. Don't be afraid of this feature. Try it for a year and cancel if you don't like it.

➤ **Save your pennies, nickels, dimes, quarters, loonies, and twoonies.** I save my change every day in a bowl. When the bowl is full, I deposit it in my investment account.

➤ **Save your raises.** Another trick is to ignore any raises in income when budgeting for expenses. When you get a raise, save the entire raise. Instead of increasing your spending habits, increase your saving habits. Let the raise boost your saving percentage.

2. Avoid Debt

Many rich individuals pay cash for everything and avoid debt (except for their home mortgage). Instead of borrowing money to purchase an item, they wait until they save enough money to buy the item with cash.

Here are four ideas that will help you eliminate debt faster and reduce the total cost of debt interest:

➤ **Refinance your mortgage.** Shop around when mortgage rates drop to see if you can get a better fixed rate. If you plan to stay in your home for more than two years, and you can improve your mortgage rate by as much as 1 percent, you should consider refinancing. This may reduce your mortgage payments and reduce the amount of money you spend each year on interest payments. Try to avoid fees. These are often negotiable. Offer to refinance if the mortgage company will reduce its fees.

➤ **Avoid paying credit card interest.** Don't make purchases on your credit card unless you're sure you can pay off your balance before interest charges kick in. And never use credit cards for cash advances, since interest charges begin immediately.

➤ **Apply for a home-equity loan.** If you have a great deal of credit card debt and own your own home, you might consider applying to your bank or mortgage company for a home-equity loan. Then use the money to pay off your credit card debt.

Treasure Tip

Use only one no-fee credit card with low rates, in case you're unable to pay off your balance in time.

➤ **Pay more each month on your mortgage.** If you can afford to add to your mortgage payment each month, you will reduce the overall interest costs on your mortgage and speed up the time it takes to retire your mortgage. If you can double your payments, your home will be paid off much faster.

3. Shop Before You Buy

The Posts also said that they shopped extensively before they bought anything. This is a very simple concept, but few people take the time. It is my belief that women by nature are shoppers and men are not. My personal habit is to go into the store, buy exactly what I need, and get out. Take a moment and think about your own habits. Do you take the time to shop around, or are you an impulsive buyer?

➤ **Shop at warehouse clubs.** I learned many years ago that I could save a lot of money by shopping at discount warehouse clubs. It was difficult to store the large quantities when I lived in my tiny, 500-square-foot apartment, but it is much easier now in my house.

➤ **Buy seasonal items out of season.** If you want to buy a boat, start shopping towards the end of the summer. Owners will accept a lower price, knowing the expense of keeping it in storage another winter. Most people buy their boats in the early spring. Avoid the buying pressure, and get it cheap later in the summer. The same thing is true of lawn mowers, convertibles, and landscaping materials. If snow is a problem in the winter, buy a snowblower in the late spring. If you time your purchases right and negotiate properly, you might pay only a fraction of the normal in-season price.

Words of the Wealthy

The word **haggle** came from the Old English term *heawan*, which meant to beat or cut. Haggling is the process of negotiating the lowest price possible in a purchase transaction. Canada is one of the few countries where haggling is not a normal part of everyday shopping.

➤ **Learn to haggle.** Canada is the only country I know of where people accept paying the full price on merchandise without negotiation. Always ask, "Is there any way I can get a better price on this?" It works. A few months ago, I offered to purchase $8,000 worth of antiques from a large antique warehouse. I asked if they would give me a discount for the amount of money I wanted to spend. They gave me more than 10 percent off, which added up to more than $800. What a great reward for asking such an easy question! The next time you buy a big-ticket item, try to negotiate.

➤ **Delay purchases of items you don't need.** Before you rush out to the store or pick up the telephone to buy that widget you just have to have, write it down and think about it for a week. Then ask yourself if you still want it as much. How many things do you have in your closet, storage room, or drawers that you only used a few times? I've practised this over the past five years, and even built a file of things I've wanted to buy. Would you believe that I've bought about 10 percent of them? This habit also cuts down on the amount of stuff you'll be selling in your next garage sale.

4. Buy Used When You Can

The Posts often bought used merchandise, especially if they could find good quality at lower prices. They spent a lot of time shopping for used items in the local want ads. They said they saved a lot of money over the years focusing on used instead of new cars. They bought quality used cars from previous owners and eliminated the commission paid to the salesperson, along with the heavy depreciation incurred in the first year. Don't be a fanatic about buying everything new. Consider a used car before you purchase a new one. Consider antique furniture instead of new. Check the want ads before you buy.

Treasure Tip

If possible, sell your own car instead of trading it in. You have a better chance of getting a higher price than a dealer will offer.

Used cars seem more attractive than ever before. New car prices have risen sharply in the 1990s, fueled by insatiable demand from buyers willing to lease or finance their purchases. We have also seen a huge supply of "program cars" or previously leased cars hit the market. This large supply of two- and three-year-old cars has resulted in more competitive prices.

If you have to buy a new car, call eight of the surrounding dealers within four hours' driving distance and ask them for their best price on the automobile of your choice. Be specific with your model and desired options.

For about $56 a year, the Automobile Protection Association, a non-profit organization, (416-204-1444) will provide you with a breakdown of dealers' actual costs (quotes) on two new cars as well as recommended dealers, leasing firms, and brokers who agree to offer prospective customers a straightforward, no-hassle price.

When you buy a used automobile, focus on quality and resale value. Hondas, for example, hold their value for longer than other cars, and command higher resale prices. And seek to buy a used car privately through the classified ads, rather than a dealer. Most dealer mark-ups are outrageous, and it's easier to haggle with people wanting to sell their cars privately.

That Reminds Me...

If at all possible, don't lease a car. The commission and financing charges are all disguised in the payment, which makes it very difficult to make an intelligent decision. Most of the time, the lease is much more expensive in the long run. If you purchase a used vehicle, take care of it with regular maintenance, and sell it later. Your total out-of-pocket expense should be much less than with a lease agreement.

Wealth Warning

Before you buy a used car, take it to an independent car repair service for a checkup. If you unknowingly buy a poor quality, unreliable car, you may end up with big problems later. There's nothing worse than sinking your hard-earned money into something that's not reliabl unless it's having to sell it later.

If you want to know approximately what an automobile is worth, call your bank and ask for Blue Book values. There are three prices to pay attention to. First is the loan value, which is the amount of money a bank is willing to lend to a customer to buy the car. Second is the trade-in value or wholesale price, which is what a car dealer might be willing to pay for the car on a trade-in. Third is the retail price, which you might pay if you were buying it from a used car dealer. Your goal as a buyer is to buy the car at or below the loan value. Your goal as a seller is to sell it at or above retail. Either way, if you don't get the price you want, you have to be willing to walk away.

If you do have to get a loan to buy a car, be sure to ask several banks for the best rate. If you do this before you look for a car, you'll be better prepared to negotiate.

Consider antique furniture. A few years ago, a very dear friend taught me an invaluable lesson. I was looking for furniture for my office and he said, "Larry, don't waste your money on new furniture. Buy functional antiques." He explained, "You can depreciate them on your balance sheet as they appreciate in value." This man is a genius. My office is full of these antiques. Not only are they beautiful, but they have also appreciated since I bought them.

Buy quality. If you do buy used, you must focus on quality and resale value. Always research the big-ticket items in the classified ads before you buy, and look at how they fall in price relative to their original retail price. How do they fall in price each year? Are there any consumer reports out on the product? Go to the library and look in the periodical index or do an Internet search for the particular item you want to buy. See if there are any studies done. *Consumer Reports* is a magazine that can save you a lot of money. It does studies on various products regarding quality, maintenance, and resale value. Why not subscribe?

5. Take Care of What You Own

Another little pearl of wisdom the Posts shared with me involved simple maintenance. They said they took care of what they owned. They said that it is amazing how long things will last if you take good care of them.

Keep up automobile maintenance. This couple had both of their automobiles serviced every 6,000 kilometres, which included an oil and filter change. They also waxed their cars every six months. These simple steps helped keep their cars running better and helped maintain the resale value. For example, my 1987 Mazda recently rolled over 200,000 kilometres, and is going strong. I make sure to change the oil every three months. A new muffler and some other parts every few years is a lot cheaper than a new car, and insurance rates on old cars are much lower.

Home maintenance is also important. Have your heating and air-conditioning system checked once a year to prolong the life of your equipment. Pay for a good pest control service now, so you don't have to pay later for termite damage. Prevent exterior damage of your home by regularly cleaning out your gutters and replacing the old ones.

6. Maintain a Basic Understanding of the Stock and Bond Markets

The next habit this couple taught me was to develop a basic understanding of the stock and bond markets. They studied the basics, knew the benefit of owning stocks, and invested in stocks through no-load funds. They learned a great deal from the mistakes they made, and understood that investing money in the stock market involves making occasional mistakes. In spite of all that, they kept learning more each day and stayed the course.

If you feel uncomfortable with your investment knowledge, be proactive and do something about it. There are books and classes available that can

Words of the Wealthy

When you buy shares of **stock** directly or through a mutual fund, you become part owner of a company. These shares can build your wealth by paying you dividends and by rising in price.

That Reminds Me...

When you purchase a bond or bond mutual fund, you are essentially buying IOUs of companies or the government. The total interest paid each year is your reward for loaning the money. Additional reward comes when interest rates fall and the price of the bond increases. The reverse is also true. If rates go up, the price of the bond will fall. A bond is simply a source of future cash flow that can be bought and sold at different prices until maturity. However, at maturity the bondholder is paid only the face amount or maturity value of the bond along with the appropriate interest.

teach you everything you need to know. Do yourself a favour and learn all you can—now.

The best way to learn is to start investing. You'll want to learn more because your money is at stake. If you don't already, strongly consider subscribing to either *The Globe and Mail* or the *National Post,* or both. Their business sections are very good and are loaded with personal finance commentary. The next best way to learn is to join an organization dedicated to educating investors. You might also read some books on investing. Here are some of my favourites:

➤ *A Random Walk Down Wall Street,* by Burton Malkiel

➤ *Beating the Street,* by Peter Lynch, retired manager of Fidelity's U.S. Magellan fund

➤ *One Up on Wall Street,* by Peter Lynch

➤ *Value Investing,* by Ben Graham, father of value investing

➤ *Bogle on Funds,* by John Bogle, past chairman of Vanguard Funds

➤ *The Complete Idiot's Guide to Personal Finance for Canadians,* by Robert Heady, Christy Heady, and Bruce McDougall

7. Take Time to Plan, Research, and Systematically Measure Your Results

Treasure Tip

Time is money and therefore requires just as much management as does your money. If you don't have a day planner, get one. If you do have one, shop around and make sure yours is the best for your needs. I've used a day planner since I was 13 years old! They just make my life so much easier.

Finally, Mr. and Mrs. Post also did their homework. They took time to research their options before they made an investment, and they understood that quick decisions get you hurt in the market. Rumours get started and before you know it, a "hot tip" turns out to be a cold nightmare. They recognized and avoided the traps.

Don't forget to measure the results of your portfolio. This is one of the most common mistakes made by individual investors. They invest for years, never actually knowing their true performance on a monthly or yearly basis. They might estimate it, but they rarely do it accurately and they almost never compare it to the proper benchmark indices. We'll talk more about this in Part 2.

Characteristics of Wealthy People

If you want to improve your odds of achieving your desired level of wealth, you have to think like a wealthy person. Over the last 10 years in the investment business, I have spoken to thousands of wealthy individuals like Mr. and Mrs. Post. I've learned a great deal from these people. Mr. and Mrs. Post taught me the seven habits just listed, but they and other wealthy individuals also taught me unspoken lessons through the characteristics they portrayed. All these people were happy and enthusiastic about life, and I have a lot of admiration for them. In fact, I had so much admiration, I began to make notes about them. It was fascinating because they all seem to have several mental characteristics in common. The rest of this section presents the four most common. If you incorporate them into your life, you will have little difficulty getting to Wealth Level 2.

Wealth Warning

Remember that no matter what you do in life, you will always reap what you sow. Therefore, in your journey towards wealth, make sure your work helps others or improves the world in some way. If not, your efforts will eventually backfire and reverse the wealth–building process.

A Passion for What You Do

The world is so competitive now that markets around the world have opened up their doors to outside consumers. To compete in any business today, you have to work harder and be smarter than your competition. In the long run, the winners in any industry will be companies and individuals who were passionate enough about their work to spend the time and effort it takes to produce outstanding products and services. Without this passion, a company or individual will be less likely to make the effort or spend all night to meet a deadline. During the first four years of building my company, I spent at least one full night a month in my office working. Sometimes I would work 32 hours straight! I have even fallen asleep right in the middle of a conversation with a client!

It's not that I'm an advocate of working this many hours. It's very unhealthy. My point is that I was excited enough about my company to want to! The question I'm asking here is this: in your current position, are you willing to work all night on a project if you have to? If the answer is no, then you need to seriously consider making a job change or starting your own business doing what you enjoy.

The happiest wealthy people I know have a passion for what they do, which seems to naturally create a certain level of tenacity and perseverance in achieving their goals. They have a vision and they have a sincere enthusiasm about life that comes from deep inside. They don't necessarily have a passion for building wealth. Wealth, for them, is a result of their passion and effort for the work they do.

A student asked me recently, "If you could change anything in the business world, what would it be?" I told her that if everyone loved what they were doing in their life today, or if everyone at least had a plan to achieve this, the world would be a better place. There would be less frustration, anger, and unhappiness. People would feel more gratification.

When you love what you do, your chances of great achievement improve dramatically. If you are unsure about where your passion lies, here are three questions that will give you some ideas to consider. Go to a quiet place where you will not be interrupted. There are no right or wrong answers, so relax and enjoy yourself. Write down exactly what comes to mind. *Do not judge any answer!* Let your mind go and list anything that comes to mind, no matter how impossible it might seem. Write each question at the top of a separate page.

1. Your doctor calls and tells you that in exactly six months, you will die a peaceful death due to a weird virus. What would you do during this six-month period? Who would you spend time with? What activities would you spend time doing? What would be important to you? (List at least 20 answers.)

2. An unknown relative dies and leaves you a portfolio of cash totalling $2 million. What would you do? Who would you spend time with? What activities would you spend time doing? What would be important to you? Would you quit work? How would you spend your money? (List at least 20 answers.)

3. What three great endeavours would you dare to attempt if you were guaranteed you could not fail?

The answers to these questions simply give you insight into your most important values. If you really took the time to list 20 or more answers, you might have found some things you enjoy doing that you haven't participated in for a long time. One of your answers could be something you're passionate about that you can use as a business idea. It might be another position within a company or your own company.

If you can't figure it out now, put the three pages away and try this exercise again in a week. Be sure to change your surroundings next time. Sit in a comfortable spot with no interruptions. Try it a third time if you have to.

Decision-Making Ability

The wealthiest people I know are good decision makers. They don't procrastinate or live in denial. They take the time to identify all the issues, research the alternatives, and select the best answer. They also look carefully at all the possible consequences of each decision. They list the pros and cons, take time to think about all the options, and finally ask themselves, "What is the worst thing that can happen?" If they can accept the worst possible outcome, they press forward. If not, they hold back. They understand *zero-based thinking*, which I will cover later in more detail. These are the keys to making educated decisions.

Discipline

The clients I have who built their wealth from the ground up have a certain discipline that helps them adhere to the simple habits necessary to build wealth. Climbing the social ladder is unimportant to them. They focus instead on what they are passionate about.

Discipline is simply a subconscious habit that is established by repetition. It's difficult to start a habit, but I'm told that after 21 days, it becomes part of your life. Here's an idea. For 21 days, take 15 minutes in the afternoon to plan tomorrow. This will give your brain time to think about what you have to do, which will help you get closer to your vision.

Patience

Wealthy people are patient and maintain a long-term outlook. They plan for the future, do what it takes to build wealth, and over time they know they will succeed. When they're faced with failure, they get right back on track again and go for it. They understand that wealth-building is a journey, not a destination. It's a practice of patient habits that naturally produces riches.

The Least You Need to Know

➤ The best thing you can do to build your wealth is to save systematically every month and avoid debt.

➤ Delay purchases you don't need by writing them down, filing the list away, and not thinking about it for a week or month.

➤ Used cars and antique furniture can save you a fortune in commission and depreciation expense.

➤ To be really wealthy in life, you must have enough passion for what you do to lose yourself in your work.

➤ Building wealth requires certain habits that are easy to implement and maintain.

Chapter 6

Building Wealth as an Employee

In This Chapter

➤ Getting the job you've always wanted

➤ Finding out what you really enjoy doing

➤ Developing a job proposal

➤ Maximizing income while working for others

➤ Buying your company's stock

If you have a high level of excitement about what you do, you will be the best at it and people will want to hire you. Every employer in your field will want to have you around, and they might be willing to pay you a lot of money to get you on their team. Enthusiasm is contagious and employers look for it. They know that's the one thing they can't teach. Some people are naturally enthusiastic, and that's great.

However, if you put a naturally enthusiastic person in a job they hate, you kill the enthusiasm. Therefore, to maintain your enthusiasm and get paid what you're worth, you must enjoy your work. It may take some time to figure it out, but to maximize your salary, you have to be good at what you do. As I said in the last chapter, to be good—I mean *really* good—at what you do, you have to be passionate about it. To be passionate, you have to love what you're doing.

Wealth Warning

Wealth is never worth sacrificing your happiness, family, or integrity for.

How to Get Your Dream Job

Many people live their lives in frustration and unhappiness, working at jobs they despise and for people they don't respect. They stay in this self-imposed prison, locked in by their own fear of change, their inflexible standard of living, or procrastination. Often it takes something dramatic or life-threatening to break them out. What they don't realize is that this eats away at their self-confidence and self-worth. Don't let this happen to you.

Three Questions Revisited

If you don't know what you like to do, or you lack the vision or ability to see yourself advancing from your current position, don't get discouraged. That's a common problem that you can solve, and here's how to solve it. Go back again to the three questions in Chapter 5 in the section titled A Passion for What You Do. Follow the instructions and list your answers. If you have already done this, try it again. Your answers will give you insight into what you are the most passionate about. Find something you can focus on that will make you money.

If you think you can't make money doing what you love, you might be right. If nothing else, you could write a book about it. As I said, if you are passionate enough about your work, you will be the best at it and people will want to be a part of your world. If you are passionate about painting, then focus your time and energy on being the best painter you can be. A high school student asked me recently if I thought he should get a "real" job or continue pursuing his first love, which was painting in oils. I said both, but I also said that he should focus most of his attention on painting. People love art and are often willing to pay big money for it. Several friends of mine are now professional artists. They took the hobby they were the most passionate about and made it into a business. One of them travels the world and sells his paintings to people in many different countries. One of his paintings recently sold in an auction for more than $2,500. His wife manages his business affairs and schedules his appearances. What a great idea. No matter what your passion is, find a way to make money doing it.

Do You Enjoy What You Do Now?

Take some time to answer the above question. Here are a few more that might help you decide:

➤ Do you find yourself stressed-out on Sunday night before work on Monday?

➤ Do you have a vision of what you want in life?

➤ Is your current job part of that vision?

➤ Do you see yourself working at your present job for a long time?

➤ Does your employer treat you with respect?

➤ Is your job a stepping-stone for what you really want to do?

➤ Do you have a plan for the next step?

Your answers should tell you whether or not you are in the right job now. If you're not, why waste your time, your life, or the money you could be making? Develop a plan and move on.

The Perfect Day at Work

Next, find an hour of peace and quiet when you can think clearly. Take a piece of paper and write a vision of yourself at work, doing what you love to do. Title it, "The Perfect Day At Work." Make sure you have no interruptions and let your imagination run free. Don't worry about grammar, spelling, or order. Just write whatever comes to your mind. Get as specific as you can. Where are you? Describe your surroundings, the people you work with, your boss, and the company. Fill at least one page, if not several.

Treasure Tip

One of the most common characteristics of happy wealthy people is their attitude every Sunday night before work. Most of them enjoy their work so much that they don't know the difference between a weekday or weekend night.

Once you complete this exercise, take some more time to brainstorm how you can make this dream a reality. Don't accept defeat immediately by saying, "This is only a dream. I can't really do this." This is a self-imposed limiting thought. If you can think it and believe in it, it's possible. But if you don't believe in your vision, you'll never get there. Brainstorm for a minute on how you can make this dream a reality.

Once you finish brainstorming, design a plan to get there. If the dream is really worthwhile, it will take some time to accomplish. But if it's what you really want, you won't mind the effort it takes to get there.

Looking at Your Options

Now that you have a better idea of what's important to you, think about all your options. They are unlimited. I can think of four basic directions you can go:

1. Stay with your current employer and design a job proposal to move into the position you want or into a new position that might not yet exist.

2. Look into other companies or employers within your industry who might appreciate your work and give you more opportunity. Find the best firm in the industry and submit a job proposal.

3. Study other fields of interest. Find the best companies or employers in that industry and submit a job proposal.

4. Start your own company. We'll discuss this in Part 3.

Each option involves some homework on your part. For now, focus on role models and job proposals.

Find a Role Model

Spend some time identifying the people who do what you want to do. Then find the very best in the business. Ask everyone you know in that field, "Who's the best at this?" Find at least three people who are successful at what you want to do. If you can, find out in advance what makes them different or special. Call these people or write them a letter. First, compliment them by saying, "I've been told that you are one of the best (whatever) in the country." Compliment them further by mentioning what you think makes them so special and unique. They will be impressed with what you know. Second, tell them that you are very enthusiastic about learning more about their industry and business. Third, ask them if you can talk with them for a few minutes about their success. Just say, "I'd like to hear your story. Would you have a minute to meet with me now or next week (over the phone or in person) for a few minutes?" If you compliment these people (without overdoing it) and ask them about their story, most of them will meet with you.

When you do meet with them, ask them specific questions and let them talk. Here are some questions to choose from. Don't forget to take notes.

➤ What do you love about your work?

➤ What do you dislike about your work?

➤ What are your biggest concerns each day?

➤ What do you focus most of your time on?

➤ Describe a typical day.

➤ If you had to do it all over again, what path would you take?

➤ Where would you start?

➤ Would you share with me your five- or 10-year vision?

Now take some time and review their answers. Did you find what you expected? Are you still as excited as you

Treasure Tip

Some of the best advice I ever received on achievement was to find the people who were the best at what I wanted to accomplish and learn from them. This single idea always helps me reach my goals faster, with less effort.

were? After the appointment, be sure to write them a thank-you note. You might even mention in the letter the one thing that excited you the most. They will appreciate your attention to detail and welcome another contact from you—which could prove to be valuable later.

The Job Proposal

This is an idea I came up with years ago to help my brother get the job he wanted. It's a simple idea that can get you the job you want. The first step in building the job proposal is to know what you really want to do. The job for which you are making the proposal must be your dream job, or a stepping-stone toward your dream job.

Wealth Warning

The job proposal is a very unique and powerful tool. If you use this just to get a job, with no attention to your values or interests, you may get a job you eventually dislike. Before using this technique, make sure you know what you enjoy doing.

Second, your vision must match the vision of the company or the duties of the position you want. To ensure this, interview the company or supervisor for that position. Study everything you can and make sure this is where you want to be.

Third, describe the position you want on paper and be as specific as you can. What are you willing to do? What are you willing to be responsible for? What are you willing to accept in salary and benefits?

Fourth, design the employment (job) proposal. I have included a copy of the proposal I helped my brother design. He is an electrical engineer who wanted to work for a small software company. He interviewed for the job first and was told they were going to hire someone else. He was discouraged, but still wanted the job. We sat down and came up with a job proposal that he submitted later that week. A week later, he got the job.

There are no rules here and your proposal will be completely different from his, but I thought that an example might help you to design yours (see page 73).

The proposal should be done on a word processor and printed on bond paper. It doesn't have to be fancy. It just has to look good and use correct grammar and spelling. Be sure to present this proposal in person and go over it if you can. If you cannot get a face-to-face meeting, then send it registered mail. Then call within two days of receipt. Don't ask what your contact thinks of your proposal. Instead say, "I'd like to stop by next week on Wednesday. Would 10 in the morning be good, or would two in the afternoon be better for you?"

If there's no interest, go to the company's competitor and offer the same proposal. Don't waste your efforts on someone who doesn't appreciate your enthusiasm and talent.

How to Maximize Income while Working for Others

The one thing I learned while working for others was that salary is always negotiable. The second thing I learned was that if I was good at what I did, there was always another company out there willing to pay me what I was worth. At least I had to convince my current employer of this fact. If I was successful, I would be paid what I was worth. If I was unsuccessful, I moved on to an employer who recognized my talent and the value I could add to the company. Therefore, you should always make it a habit to do some research into the salary range of your current job. What are other people in your field getting paid? How do these salaries compare to yours? Be sure to take into account the living expenses of the cities these people live in. For example, everything else being equal, someone in Vancouver will naturally be paid a higher salary than someone in Edgewater, B.C.

If you think you are worth more than what you are currently paid, but you think that getting a raise is impossible, I have got an idea for you. Don't ask for a raise. Raises are the traditional means to higher pay, but they are limiting and often obscure in nature. Most companies don't even have a written policy on how raises are given. Many employers don't realize that this can lead to a lot of disenchantment among the employees.

The better alternative is what I call performance-based bonuses, which are bonuses usually based upon a percentage of a company's net income. The benchmark that measures the bonus must be a net result of income and expenses. If they are based solely on gross income, employees pay little attention to expenses. But, if they are based on net income after expenses, something magical happens. Employees begin to consider the cost of everything. Your employer may not understand this concept.

I know this from experience. Until recently, my employees earned a bonus on gross income. The day I changed the benchmark to net income, the entire atmosphere changed. My employees began to act like shareholders and started paying much more attention to the costs of everything. We'll get into more detail about performance-based bonus programs in Part 3, but my point is that if your company does not have a performance-based bonus program, ask for it. Convince your boss that if you and the other employees were paid a bonus based upon net profits of the company, you would all pay more attention to reducing expenses and increasing gross income. This means that the company would make more money, which would, in turn, more than pay for the bonuses. If your company does not start one, put together a proposal. Include in that proposal all the benefits, which include:

➤ More productivity, because employees will be more motivated to produce.

➤ Employees paying more attention to the cost of everything.

➤ Employees being more efficient.

Employment Proposal for XYZ Company

I. Why I want to work for XYZ Company.

A. I want to work for a small, growing company.

B. More opportunity for growth and experience.

C. Opportunity to work in a team-oriented atmosphere.

D. I admire the management's philosophy and vision.

II. What am I able to offer XYZ Company?

A. Sales assistance in the marketing department as you acquire new clients.

B. Project assistance.

C. Hardware design, development, and installation.

D. Programming assistance in producing the best software available.

E. Troubleshooting and maintaining the highest-quality service in the industry.

III. What I expect to be paid initially.

A. Hourly pay of $X per hour.

B. $X per hour after 40 hours in a one-week period.

IV. Available working hours.

A. Regular working hours (8:00 A.M. to 5:00 P.M.).

B. After hours.

C. Weekends.

D. Moment's notice.

V. Future compensation expected.

A. To be negotiated in two months.

B. Subject to the value you think I can add to your business. (You could be more specific here if you want.)

C. Bonuses based upon a percentage of net profits.

D. Full benefits including health insurance and retirement plan.

VI. Trial period.

A. Two months.

B. If things do not work out, I will walk away with no questions asked.

VII. Vision for the future: My goal is to be the chief engineer for XYZ Company and, if possible, stockholder/partner in the firm. I would like to develop new product services that complement existing ones and participate in strategic planning and development for XYZ.

Conclusion: The best thing that can happen is that you get a good engineer with education and experience who adds more value to your company than you pay him. The worst thing that can happen is that you get a good electrical engineer at an annualized salary of $XX,000 ($X per hour) for two months.

➤ The company's increased capacity for work.

➤ Employees being willing to do more.

➤ Decreased expenses.

➤ Increased income.

Note, however, that this might be difficult to do if you work for a large company with policies already in place.

How to Maximize Savings while Working for Others

Can you get to Level 3 or 4 without starting your own company? Absolutely! I've met hundreds of people who've done it. If you want to build serious wealth, whether you work for yourself or someone else, the key is to live well within your means so you can save money systematically each month. At each pay period, a certain percentage of your income must go to your investment account, retirement plan, and savings account. It's even better if this takes place automatically at the time you get your paycheque.

If you are not doing this now, or haven't made the decision to do this, then stop right now and make the decision. Read this out loud: "I am a saver and a good steward of my money and financial future. I save a significant percentage of my income each month, which I invest for my future." If you don't make this a habit now, you may never reach Wealth Level 3 or 4. You might believe you have an excuse now to wait, but you may *always* have an excuse.

Treasure Tip

Most of my clients have a net worth that exceeds $1 million. How did they do it? Did they sell a business? Did they inherit money? No! The characteristic shared by these clients is that they all systematically contributed to an RRSP.

Maximize Contributions to Your Retirement Savings Plan—The Last Tax Shelter

An RRSP is a great way to save money systematically by depositing a percentage of your salary before tax. Your money can then be invested in stocks and mutual funds within the account. The taxes you would normally pay on the income are deferred until you withdraw the money after you retire. Plus, the capital gains taxes you would normally pay on the growth are deferred until you start making withdrawals. The combined effect of compound growth and tax deferral can be very powerful in building your portfolio.

Think of an RRSP as a briefcase. The briefcase keeps its contents protected from elements outside. An RRSP protects your money from government taxation. On money held in an RRSP, you pay no taxes. And when you first put the money into an RRSP, you can deduct it from your total annual income when you're calculating your income tax for the year. That means you pay less tax. And your money grows tax-free.

Once the money's in an RRSP, you shouldn't just forget about it. It's like any other investment. It can grow quickly; it can grow slowly; sometimes it doesn't grow at all; and sometimes it even loses value. The big difference between money invested in an RRSP and money invested in a conventional investment is that your RRSP grows tax-free.

Treasure Tip

Visit your human relations department or employer and try to maximize your retirement savings plan contributions. You not only get a tax deduction for the deposit, you also get the benefit of tax-deferred growth.

Outside an RRSP, your money may earn $100, and you'd pay, say, $25 in tax, leaving you with $75. Inside an RRSP, your money may make $100, and you'd pay no tax. So you still have $100 left to reinvest.

Get into Another Qualified Defined-Contribution Plan

There are other types of retirement plans in which your employer can contribute to a tax-deferred account on your behalf. These plans are known as defined-contribution and defined-benefit plans. These can be somewhat complicated but they are a great company benefit. If your company doesn't offer these, you might want to suggest them.

Maximize Savings in Your Investment Account

Even though you might have maximized your RRSP contributions, you should continue to maintain your own investment account deposits. Look back at Chapter 5, where I discussed several different ways to save money so you can invest it. You should always continue saving in as many ways as you can.

Now you need a place to put that money you save. Where should it be invested? If you work for someone else and you want to get to Wealth Level 3 or 4, you have to invest in stocks (also known as

Wealth Warning

The real risk in maximizing RRSP deposits is higher tax rates at the time of withdrawal. If you believe in your heart that tax rates will be higher tomorrow, then investing after-tax dollars outside the plan may be the better alternative.

Treasure Tip

If you want to build wealth, you must consider investing in something that can produce a double-digit return. The most common invest-ment with this potential is stock in a fast-growing company. There is risk, but your exposure can be reduced by spreading your investment among many different companies.

equities). This includes the money in your retirement plans and investment accounts. It may also include privately held stock of your own company or your employer's company. The stock market is one of the most powerful tools you can use to truly see your portfolio grow and to beat inflation. Don't overlook ownership of your employer's stock as an investment alternative. My research has convinced me that in the last century, more fortunes have been built with stocks, both private and publicly traded, than with real estate or any other asset.

In the next chapter, I will cover more on the benefits of owning equities of publicly traded companies. For now, take a look at the company you currently work for. Would you ever want to be a shareholder?

Buy Stock in the Company for Which You Work

First, before you even consider doing this, look back at the answers to the questions in the earlier section titled Do You Enjoy What You Do Now? If you answered favourably and you plan on staying with this company for a long time, then buying their stock might not be a bad idea. You also need to consider your employer's earnings growth potential. Is your company making any money? If the company's earnings aren't growing, you may want to avoid their stock.

Second, you have to consider the size of the company and the availability of the stock itself. If the company is small and owned by a few people (that is, if it's owned privately rather than traded on a stock exchange), then it may be difficult if not impossible to become a shareholder. You might have to convince the owners to let you buy shares or take shares instead of salary or bonus. Your employer might say "no," but it won't hurt to ask. Remember, if your company is small and experiencing normal cash flow problems, your employer might welcome the idea. He may prefer to pay part of your salary or bonus in stock.

If you work for a large company that has stock publicly traded on an exchange, this becomes much easier. Whether your company is small or large, or has closely held or publicly traded stock, it might be available through an employee stock ownership plan or ESOP. ESOPs are becoming very popular now as employers begin to see the benefits of employees being shareholders. The plan issues shares to its employees each month or year based upon their salary or profits of the company. ESOPs can also be part of a retirement plan, which means the gains and dividends can be tax-deferred until retirement. It's a great idea if you want to own your company's stock. If not, don't participate. One of the most successful ESOP plans ever was Wal-Mart's employee stock-purchasing plan. This plan made hundreds of their employees—who might otherwise have retired with a little pension and a small Social Security cheque—millionaires. However, if you do decide to buy shares of the company you work for, be sure it's just one of several different investments. Diversification—not putting all of your eggs in one basket—is crucial.

The Least You Need to Know

➤ To be happy and get paid what you are worth, you have to have passion and enthusiasm for what you do.

➤ Consider all your employment options, which include staying where you are, looking at other similar companies, looking at other industries, or starting your own business.

➤ Decide what you want to do, find role models, and build a job proposal that can help you get there.

➤ Maximize your income at work, save as much money as you can in tax-deferred qualified plans, and buy stocks.

Part 2

Achieving Wealth Level 3 by Taming the Portfolio Beast

If you know how to get to Wealth Levels 1 and 2, then Wealth Level 3 is easy to accomplish. All you really need to know is how to properly manage an investment portfolio. Your portfolio can be like a wild animal. Occasionally it will seem like it's turning against you, especially when the market takes a dive. However, if you know how to tame this beast, you'll sleep better and build wealth faster.

First, you need to be able to recognize the investment tools that should be avoided. Second, you need to understand the investment tools that will help you achieve your objectives. Third, you should learn how to hire professional help. Fourth, when you're ready to take your first step into the investment world, you need to know what to look for. Fifth, in order to be your own successful portfolio manager, you must understand six key fundamentals. Sixth, you need to know how the investment cycle works. Seventh, there are 10 investment tactics you should know. Eighth, you must know how to keep your investment-related expenses and mistakes to a minimum. Ninth, there are certain laws of investing that might come in handy. Tenth, it might also be helpful to know the most common mistakes made by investors. I discuss all of these in this part.

Chapter 7

Portfolio Tools You Need to Avoid

> **In This Chapter**
>
> ➤ Why most investors continue to use bad tools
>
> ➤ What happens if you use the wrong tools
>
> ➤ Three killers of wealth
>
> ➤ The worst investment tools
>
> ➤ What your broker doesn't want you to know

Have you ever noticed that in every nice neighbourhood, there's always one house that just doesn't fit? Maybe the builder used poor-quality materials, wrong tools, or just did a poor job altogether. Whatever the case, you know the end result is a money pit, and every home owner's nightmare is to own one of these. I look at portfolios the same way. I meet these wonderful people who have built their portfolios from scratch. Many of the portfolios have been built correctly and only need an adjustment or two. But a good number of them are just waiting to cave in. I call these "investment pits." The investor usually doesn't have a clue as to the risks and costs she's incurring.

Before you can build anything, you need to know what proper tools to use. Whether it's a house, building, or investment portfolio, if you use the wrong tools and materials, eventually you're going to have problems. Unfortunately, you may not know you've made a mistake until it's too late. The tools I'll be discussing in this chapter are all financial tools, most of which are investment vehicles used to

Words of the Wealthy

A **secondary market** is any market where previously issued securities are traded. The Toronto Stock Exchange (TSE) is the best known example in Canada. Here investors can buy and sell stocks from each other through the designated traders on the floor of the exchange.

Wealth Warning

The biggest investment nightmares I've observed in the last 10 years seem to be the result of complicated tax shelters, limited partnerships, bad stock tips, life insurance products, or futures contracts. As long as there are unsuspecting investors and commission-based salespeople, the nightmares will continue. The best defence is knowledge.

maximize a portfolio's total return. I've met thousands of investors over the last 11 years, and a great many of them were using the wrong tools to accomplish their goals. These tools were either too expensive, mediocre in quality, unsuitable, or all of the above. Why is this the case? I explain the answer in this chapter and show you how not to make the same mistake.

Reasons Why People Use the Wrong Tools

One of the first keys to building wealth is knowing the correct investment tools, which means you also need to know the tools to avoid. It might be appropriate to start with what you should avoid. Improper tools are the most common killers of wealth. If that's true, why don't people do something about it? Well, as I said before, most of them have no idea there's a problem. Here are some of the reasons people get themselves into the wrong investment tool.

They Don't Do Their Homework

First, most investors simply do not do enough homework before they invest their money. I've met hundreds of investors who spend more time planning a vacation each year than they do planning or researching their own investment portfolio. This is scary. Maybe they know the basics, but they make quick investment decisions using limited knowledge.

They Take Advice from Commission-Based Salespeople

The second most common reason investors use the wrong investment tools is that they buy their investments from commission-based salespeople. Not all commission-based brokers are bad, but there is a conflict of interest here. If you are an experienced investor, and understand the details of the market and how brokers charge for their services, then you probably know how to work with a broker. You use their research, you both come up with ideas, and then you make a decision. You also know how these folks are paid and you know commissions are negotiable. However, if you do not fully understand the details of the market, why would you buy from someone who gets paid a commission every time you buy or sell an investment? Since their paycheques depend upon you making transactions, their natural motivation is to promote transactions—and not performance. If they are paid a commission on each trade, can you really count on the investment to be in your best interest most of the time? You have to ask yourself this question: what motivates the commission-based broker?

Toward the end of each month, brokers all across the country have to make their commission quota. What do you think is going through their minds during the last week of every month? I've been there. I was a broker for almost five years. If you deal with a commission-based broker, take a look at all your trades for the last year. Are most of them made during the last half of the month? Before you make another investment decision with a commission-based broker, read the next chapter on how to select an investment advisor. One thing I can almost guarantee is that a commission-based salesperson will ignore non-commission-based alternatives that might benefit you. Commission-based salespeople include financial advisors selling deferred sales charge mutual funds, which carry a potential sales charge that declines over time. These advisors typically receive a commission of about 5 percent of the funds they sell.

That Reminds Me...

The biggest problem I see with commission-based brokers is the hidden fees they charge. These are fees you might never find or know about. Before you buy any investment from a commission-based broker, have him describe in detail every expense involved in the investment. Then read the prospectus. If the broker left anything out, stay away from the investment. If the broker says there is no commission or the commission is built in, ask exactly how much it is. Demand an answer. If you can't understand all the fees and commissions, leave it alone.

They Don't Check for Bias and Conflicts of Interest

Many people use the wrong investment tool because they don't check for bias before they make a decision. They mistake marketing information for good advice. I believe that approximately 95 percent of what you read and hear about investing in your lifetime is marketing related. Most of the investment information available today is biased and does not portray the whole story. Your job as an investor is to uncover the

Words of the Wealthy

All mutual funds have a **prospectus**, which is the fund's disclosure document. This multipage document explains in great detail all the aspects of the mutual fund, such as fees, commission charges, fund manager restrictions, and the fund's objective. Newly issued stocks and bonds also have prospectuses.

Wealth Warning

I hosted a radio show titled *Arkansas Moneytalk* for three years and was never paid a penny by any fund or investment product I suggested on the show. But not all investment shows are the same. Beware of the TV and radio talk shows on investing, with hosts who get paid to promote mutual funds, insurance products, or any investment. Most listeners don't understand the conflict of interest inherent in these programs.

truth to help your portfolio. If you can't find substantial unbiased evidence to support your investment choice, I suggest you keep looking, be patient, or move on to something else.

Why is bias so important? If the person is paid by a company to promote its investment products, she may have a one-track mind and focus only on the product. The biased result is that she tends to ignore the alternatives and drive investors into decisions based on limited thinking. Unfortunately, most investment decisions are made this way and knowledge of the mistake may go unrecognized for years. Often, the undoing of the mistake involves a penalty or exit commission, which in itself tends to further compound the mistake. Investors don't like paying penalties. They would rather wait and keep the mistake alive until there's no penalty. It seems ironic, but I've seen this happen hundreds of times. If it's not a penalty, it's the absence of a secondary market that keeps the mistake alive. A secondary market enables you to sell the investment at a later date. If there is no secondary market and you have no buyers, you end up with a worthless investment—which is an even worse mistake. Therefore, recognizing the bias before taking advice can reduce your chances of making a mistake.

The Results of Using the Wrong Investment Tools

The end result of these bad tools is an investor with an unsuitable, expensive, or mediocre investment. The first is the most common.

Unsuitability of the Investment

Investors sit in front of me every day with portfolios filled with unsuitable investments. Usually it is one stock that represents a huge chunk of their net worth. For example, some people have half the farm bet on BCE Inc. or Microsoft Corp. or Dell Computer Corp. I can't call these people investors. I call them speculators or gamblers. If something went wrong with that one company, their net worth would take a big hit. If they really understood the risks, they would sell at least most of it immediately. Even after I explain the risks, do you know how they justify hanging on? They say, "Well, I'll wait until the price comes back up to my original purchase price." Or they'll say, "The capital gains tax is too large." This is crazy.

My next question is always, "If you had the value of this investment today in cash, would you buy this investment?" Their answer is almost always, "No." I then tell them they ought to consider selling the investment because their subconscious is telling them something. This is referred to later in the book as "zero-based thinking." The reality of the risk, unfortunately, sets in too late. People may say they can handle risk, but they don't know the truth until the market takes a big fall.

Unknown Expenses

The second result is a portfolio filled with unknown expenses that eat away at the profits, if any are even made. This is what I call slow portfolio death. Many individual portfolios in Canada are experiencing slow death. This percentage is beginning to decrease because investors are finally beginning to learn more about all the charges investment companies levy on their clients and shareholders. Publications like *The National Post* and *The Globe and Mail* do teach investors most of the traps out there. Unfortunately, most novice investors don't read these publications.

Mediocrity

The third result of using the wrong investment tool is mediocrity. Again, most investors don't know their portfolio performance is mediocre. Often, they don't even know how their own portfolio is actually performing. They get a monthly statement showing the dollar amount of change from last month, but that's it. Brokerage firms normally do not illustrate portfolio performance for their clients. I've always wondered why. It would be so easy to do. If my company can do it, why can't theirs? Instead of waiting for your brokerage firm to measure your percentage performance, learn how to do it yourself, or get someone to do it for you. Your accountant might help.

The Tools to Stay Away From

Some investment tools are good, and some are bad. If you know what tools to avoid, you can save yourself from expensive, unsuitable investments and significantly reduce the chances of mediocrity in your portfolio.

Proprietary Investment Products

Proprietary investment products are "packaged" securities that are sold by brokerage firms, usually in the form of unit trusts, limited partnerships, and mutual funds. They are underwritten or managed by the brokerage firm that offers them, and they are your portfolio's primary enemy. They will slowly squeeze your portfolio to death through unnecessary fees or bad investment performance. There are many different possible conflicts of interest involved with these securities. For example, the manager might feed all his trades to one firm, resulting in two possible conflicts of interest. First, the manager might not be getting you the best commission rate available on the securities he's buying for you. Second, the brokerage firm could be filling the orders for the manager and adding points to the spread that make the purchased stocks more expensive. This is especially true with over-the-counter stocks. Run away from these blood-sucking investments.

High-Cost Mutual Funds

The Canadian mutual fund scene is full of traps that can strangle your long-term investment performance. While many new, attractive funds have been launched in recent years (which we'll discuss later), most Canadian mutual funds ought to be avoided. This is largely because management expense ratios are very high. The management expense ratio, or MER, is the annual percentage of your investment that you will pay to the company managing your fund.

Words of the Wealthy

A **full-service brokerage firm** is one that offers its clients securities as well as advice. The firm is compensated by commissions paid at the time transactions are made. A **discount brokerage firm** offers the same selection of securities, but because it does not offer advice, its commissions are usually far lower. Seek to do your investing with a discount broker, since it's more economical. Each of Canada's major banks has a discount broker, and there are a few others.

The average MER for mutual funds that invest primarily in Canadian stocks is around 2.2 percent. It doesn't sound like much, but it is. Statistics show that the average Canadian stock fund tends to fall behind the Toronto Stock Exchange 300 composite index by more than 2 percent per year over long periods of time. This isn't a coincidence. The 2.2 percent average MER is being subtracted from the funds' annual returns, but not from the TSE 300.

For example, for the five-year period to the end of November 1999, the average Canadian stock mutual fund return was 12.2 percent, while the TSE 300 return was 15.1 percent. If you invest $10,000 and get an annual return of 12.2 percent in an RRSP over 25 years, you will end up with $177,755. If you invest $10,000 and get an annual return of 15.1 percent over 25 years, you will end up with $336,421. What a difference a few percentage points per year can make!

That's why it's so important that you invest your money cost-effectively, with the lowest-possible MERs you can find in mutual funds. Alternatively, you can build your own portfolio of stocks using a discount broker. We'll examine both issues in depth later.

When it comes to mutual fund investing, there's absolutely no reason to pay a load of any kind. That includes deferred sales charge (DSC) funds. Load and DSC funds are sold by such firms as Trimark, Investors Group, Mackenzie, Fidelity Canada, and AGF. Their funds are sold by commission-based financial advisors or financial planners, who usually receive a commission of around 5 percent of the funds they sell to their clients, plus an annual trailer fee of about 0.5 percent of their clients' assets. Who pays for the commissions? The investor, of course. As a result, load and DSC funds have high MERs, which drastically restrict your long-term returns.

Avoid all load and DSC funds, and look toward the growing number of low-MER, no-load funds, mainly index funds, for mutual fund investing.

Limited Partnerships

These are the real killers of wealth. They're not as popular as they were in the 70s, but they are still around. I personally have met hundreds of investors who have lost their entire fortunes in limited partnerships. The chain of events usually unfolds like this. The investor buys a limited partnership from a broker or advisor. The first problem that's encountered is a commission charge of unknown proportion. Unfortunately, the commission is not indicated on the confirmation slip you get in the mail and it may not be clearly stated in the disclosure document, either. You can't see it, but believe me, it's ugly.

Wealth Warning

I remember the last limited partnership I was pushed to sell. It took me nearly five hours reading the prospectus to find all the fees and expenses involved. I estimated them to be a total of 19 percent. The deal was eventually pulled and never sold. I wonder why?

The second problem is the pricing of the limited partnership on the brokerage statement each month or quarter. This price is usually held at the original purchase price—which is total garbage. After you purchase the partnership, you never know what your units are actually worth because there is no secondary market available. You might not ever know the true value of your units. If you did, it would make you sick.

The third problem occurs when you decide to sell the limited partnership. That's when you find there is no place to sell it, and no one to sell to. The only way you can sell is to accept the price a "scrap yard" will offer you. A *scrap yard* is a company that researches limited partnerships around the country. It makes its living by offering limited partners 20¢–50¢ on the dollar for their units. Scrap yards are scavengers. They will buy the units and attempt to sell them at a higher price later, or dismantle the whole partnership and sell off the partnership's individual securities, land, and so on. There are certainly exceptions to this rule. Not all limited partnerships are bad. The most common exception would be a private venture that just happens to be beneficial to all parties. If you are considering a limited partnership and are well aware of all aspects of the venture, then by all means explore this as an investment. However, if you are approached by someone offering you a limited partnership in a venture you do not understand, chances are you're better off running away.

Initial Public Offerings of Closed-End Funds

A closed-end fund is a unique type of investment company or mutual fund that issues a set number of shares, after which no additional shares can be sold. The fund theoretically "closes" the door and manages the money. If you purchase closed-end shares when they are initially offered to the public, your money goes directly into the fund to be managed. If you want to sell your shares later, you must do this in a secondary market. Most closed-end funds can be sold on the TSE.

Closed-end funds by their nature and function can be very attractive—with one big exception: when they are offered to the public. Just like a stock, closed-end funds are underwritten by a brokerage firm. That firm is paid by marking up the shares of the fund above their net asset value. This markup is normally about 8.5 percent and is not felt until a few weeks after the underwriting is completed. Why a few weeks? Well, the firm underwriting the issue holds back some shares for its own account, and attempts to keep the price of the issue at least as high as the initial public offering price. Since the firm only buys a

Words of the Wealthy

The **net asset value** of a fund is the actual true value of each share of a mutual fund. This is calculated by dividing the total value of the fund by the number of shares outstanding.

That Reminds Me...

An initial public offering or stock underwriting is the process by which a brokerage firm or investment banker promises a company a certain amount of money for the securities they issue. The brokerage firm hires people to sell the securities and takes the risk of not being able to raise all the money promised. The brokerage firm is paid by marking up the shares before selling them. This is important to understand because many brokers explain this by saying, "The shares are offered net commission," which implies no commission. You better believe that if a broker is selling it, you're paying a commission.

certain number of shares, it can only keep this up so long. After the initial public offering, the shares become available on the secondary market and their price usually falls back to approximately what the shares are actually worth—which is the net asset value. Therefore, there is usually little reason to buy a closed-end fund until it hits the secondary market.

Options

Options are marketable securities that give their owners the right, but not the obligation, to buy or sell a stated number of shares (usually 100) of a particular security, at a fixed price, within a predetermined period. There are many different books published on this subject that go into great detail. Fortunately for both of us, this is not one of them! The one thing you need to understand is that such options are complicated, involve a lot of risk, and are not worth any attention. What kind of risk am I talking about? You can lose 100 percent of your investment very quickly. I can tell you that I don't know anyone who has made any significant money in the long run using options. One of my first investment experiences involved a $1,500 option on gold. I lost every penny of it, but I learned two great lessons: avoid options, and don't always listen to investment advice from friends. No matter what your friends tell you, the risk in options is not worth the reward. The only possible exception is a strategy known as "selling covered calls." If you want to learn more, there are many other books available that can teach you about this technique.

Futures

A futures contract is a legal agreement in which a buyer promises to pay a seller some fixed price for a specified quantity of a particular good at some future date. The goods can be commodities or financial instruments such as treasury bills, or market indexes. These contracts are negotiable financial instruments that are bought and sold like stocks in secondary markets called commodity exchanges. Futures contracts are usually referred to as "futures" or "contracts." Just like options, the risk in futures is not worth the reward. You can lose more than 100 percent of your investment. Avoid futures like the plague.

Penny Stocks

Penny stocks are stocks that are initially offered to the public at a price of $1 or less and are traded primarily in the over-the-counter markets of the CDNX or the Nasdaq bulletin board. Penny stocks are the bastards of the investment industry. The brokerage houses that specialize in penny stocks are notorious for using fraudulent sales pitches. It is estimated that penny stock fraud costs North American investors more than $2 billion each year. The U.S. Securities and Exchange Commission came up with three primary warning signs of penny stock fraud.

➤ Unsolicited phone calls from brokers offering penny stocks

➤ High-pressure sales tactics

➤ Inability to sell the penny stock and receive cash

All considered, stay away from penny stocks.

Rumours and Hot Tips

It seems as if every investor in the world has fallen victim to a rumour or hot tip. I certainly have. I get one almost every day. Rumours and hot tips are normally intended to show others at parties and meetings the brilliance of the person sharing them. The person might mean well by sharing the information, hoping that others can profit, too. However, what people don't realize is that these rumours and hot tips usually have the opposite result. First, they can show the ignorance of the person sharing them. Second, if the information is garbage, the person hearing it may act on it and lose money. Avoid these in your wealth-building program.

Words of the Wealthy

Major stock exchanges in North America include the Toronto Stock Exchange, the New York Stock Exchange, the Nasdaq Stock Market, and the American Stock Exchange (AMEX). There's no need to buy shares of companies listed on other exchanges.

Insurance Products

Insurance products are not bad for what they are intended to be, but they are horrible if used for investment purposes alone. A variable life insurance policy can be a whole life or universal life insurance policy with a cash value and death benefit that varies in value according to the performance of a portfolio of mutual funds from which the policyholder can select. Typically these policies offer a stock fund, a bond fund, and a money-market fund.

They are described as mutual funds covered by a tax umbrella that allows them to grow tax-deferred. The variable life insurance policy even allows the withdrawals to be completely tax free as long as the withdrawal is considered a loan against the policy. However, there are three primary problems with these as investment products.

First, they are extremely expensive. You have to pay both the money management fees and the costs of the insurance. Second, the selection of mutual funds within these policies is usually very limited and mediocre. Third, these investments can become a ball-and-chain later in life. If you want your money back, you might have to pay an early withdrawal penalty to the insurance company. Plus, if you terminate the policy,

Words of the Wealthy

A **fixed annuity** is a contract with a life insurance company whereby you give them a sum of money, and based on your age, life expectancy, and current interest rates, the company calculates how much it will send you each month for as long as you live. You decide when you want to receive payments, and until then, the money grows tax-deferred.

Words of the Wealthy

A **variable annuity** works the same way as does a fixed annuity, except its value and pay-out amount varies according to the performance of a portfolio of mutual funds from which the contract holder can select. Typically these policies offer a stock fund, a bond fund, and a money-market fund.

you have to pay taxes on all your capital gains since the beginning. The variable life policy might offer tax-free loans, but you have to keep the policy intact for the rest of your life to keep them tax-deferred.

Variable life policies might be an excellent vehicle for estate planning, but not for investment purposes alone. We'll talk more about that later in Part 4.

Treasure Tip

Real wealth is built by owning equity in a company—if not your own, then someone else's.

The Least You Need to Know

➤ Before you make any investment decision, do some homework and make sure you fully understand the investment.

➤ Always be aware of the three biggest killers of wealth: biased investment advice, unknown risks, and high commissions and fund expenses.

➤ Avoid proprietary investment products, load, DSC and high-MER mutual funds, limited partnerships, initial public offerings of closed-end funds, options, futures, penny stocks, and rumours and hot tips.

Chapter 8

Portfolio Tools That Work

In This Chapter

➤ Questions you need to ask before you buy an investment

➤ Hidden costs and conflicts of interest that most often destroy a portfolio

➤ When and when not to use fixed-income tools

➤ Why stocks are so powerful in the wealth-building process

➤ Why mutual funds are no longer just for small investors

The tools presented in this chapter are the ones most often used by the wealthiest people I know. I have presented them in reverse order of importance and power.

You can certainly buy non-liquid securities, but as I said in Chapter 2, you had better understand what you're getting into. This chapter deals with liquid securities—ones you can quickly sell and convert to cash.

Five Questions to Ask Before You Buy Any Investment

Before you buy any investment, you need to fully understand what you are buying. There are many hidden traps. Here are five questions that will help you make better investment decisions:

1. **In one sentence, what exactly am I investing in?** If you or the person selling you the investment can't explain, in one sentence, what you are investing in, then the investment might be too complicated. If so, don't buy it.

2. **Does this investment fit into my plan?** Make sure the investment meets your own personal goals. If you want no risk of fluctuation, you'll need to focus on money-market funds, short-term GICs, treasury bills, and savings accounts. If you have a long-term horizon and can withstand higher levels of fluctuation, then stocks may be what you need. Just make sure the investment accomplishes your mission, and fits into your portfolio goals. Don't worry, you may not know the details of your portfolio goals now. The next several chapters will help you narrow them down.

3. **What are the risks involved in owning this security?** Risk is always a confusing subject and will be discussed in a later chapter. For now you just need to remember to ask this question before buying an investment.

4. **Is there a secondary market for this investment?** This is *very* important and yet so few investors ask this question. You must have a secondary market that will allow you to sell the security later. If the security is stock-listed on the TSE, then you know there is a real secondary market. If it is a packaged product like the ones mentioned in the previous chapter, then you need to stay away. Markets do change and you need to know whether you will be able to sell the investment later. If there is no established secondary market, the security becomes illiquid, and you need to avoid it.

    Another problem is monthly pricing data. Without actual known transactions involving the security, there is no way to get an accurate price each month. Therefore, the price on your monthly statement becomes an estimate.

5. **What will this investment cost me?** Investment costs are so easy to hide. If you buy a stock from a brokerage firm, you will be charged a commission on top of the purchase price. What can be hidden from you is an additional commission, which is part of the spread. The spread is the difference between the price the brokerage firm paid for the security, and the price at which they sold it to you. This is true for stocks and bonds.

    There are more ways commissions are hidden from the investor than I even know after almost 11 years in the business. You can always look in a prospectus when buying a mutual fund. But if there's nothing like that available, just ask this question: "If I sell this investment tomorrow and the price of the security remains unchanged from today, what will it cost me?" If your proceeds are significantly lower than your original purchase price, don't buy the security. It's probably a commission trap.

The tools listed in this chapter were selected based on certain attributes that correspond to the questions just listed. Almost all of them can be easily researched and understood. They all have certain types of risk that are somewhat measurable, and each has a secondary market that is easily accessible. These securities will cost you less relative to most other types of securities. However, each one of them is still used today to indirectly hide commissions and fees. If you are aware of this possible practice and learn more about how to prevent it, you shouldn't have many problems.

The Fixed-Income Tools

Fixed-income securities are basically IOUs issued by companies and the government that pay a certain amount of interest each year and pay the full principal amount at a certain known date, called the maturity date, in the future. By their very nature, fixed-income securities pay a fixed rate of interest that today, depending upon maturity and quality, is only a few points above the inflation rate. Since your goal of building wealth involves beating the rate of inflation by a significant amount, fixed-income securities are not very powerful tools. However, if your goal is to reduce risk and maintain your principal instead of maximizing its growth, then fixed-income securities may be just the thing for you. Consider keeping most of your portfolio in stocks, and some in bonds to reduce your overall risk.

Many investors think the price of a bond stays constant while it pays its interest. This is not the case. In fact, bond prices fluctuate more than people know. Most bondholders only get a chance once a month (on their brokerage statement) to see their bond's price as opposed to stocks and mutual funds that are priced daily in the paper. What makes a bond fluctuate? Interest rates. When interest rates go up, bond prices fall, and when

That Reminds Me...

Bonds represent the debt of a government or company, while stocks represent equity ownership. Therefore, if a company files for bankruptcy, a bondholder will be paid off first, then the stockholder. The equityholder's claim to the company's assets is said to be subordinated to the bondholder's claim. Government bonds are guaranteed, which means the provincial or federal government that issued the bond will do everything in its power to pay the interest and principal of its bonds. That could include raising taxes, or selling government-owned businesses.

interest rates fall, bond prices go up. Therefore, when is the best time to own a bond? When interest rates go down. I'll discuss this in more detail later in the book, but for now you just need to understand that to get an above-average return from bonds, interest rates must fall. Otherwise, they are not very powerful wealth-building tools.

Everyone has her own individual goals and risk tolerances. Both stocks and bonds carry risk, but Canadian and U.S. government bonds are generally less risky than stocks. If you buy a government bond, the price of the bond will fluctuate, but as long as you hold the bond until it matures, you will receive the bond's yield at the time you bought it. What is a bond yield? It's the annual percentage return you will receive from a bond at its current price, if held to maturity. For example, you might read in the newspaper that a government of Ontario bond maturing in December 2008 has a yield of 6.6 percent. That means if you buy the bond, you are guaranteed an annual return of 6.6 percent as long as you hold the bond until December 2008, assuming the government doesn't go bankrupt.

Stocks offer no such guarantee. Though stocks have traditionally outperformed bonds over long periods of time, there's no guarantee this will continue. In fact, there have been periods lasting as long as 15 years where stocks remained flat. That's why it's smart to own at least some bonds as you get older and into retirement. When you are older, it's also important to buy bonds with relatively short maturities. That is to say, for example, when you are 70 years old, you shouldn't be buying bonds that mature in 25 or even 10 years. You might need the money in a few years, just as interest rates are rising and bond prices sinking. As you get older, buy bonds with shorter maturities, and you will avoid locking in your bond investments for long periods of time.

Money-Market Funds

A money-market fund is actually a mutual fund of short-term, fixed-income securities that all have maturities of less than one year. Some investment accounts are automated now, which means that all deposits, dividends, interest, and proceeds from sales are automatically deposited into a money-market account. These funds are primarily used as parking places for cash.

If you have a substantial sum of money, say $1,000 or higher, that you're not sure what to do with, it's wise to put it in a money-market fund until you decide. Be careful of money-market funds with high MERs. Many money-market funds have MERs above 1 percent, which is unacceptable. Often you will find that savings accounts with high interest rates (such as ING Direct and President's Choice Financial), are a better deal than money-market funds. Look in the mutual fund listings in the newspaper to get an idea of the "current yield" of the various money-market funds. The current yield is the current annualized return you get from the fund, but it will fluctuate.

Don't, however, let your money rot in a money-market fund for years on end. For long-term savings, look for a low-MER, no-load mutual fund or a diversified group of stocks.

For shorter-term savings that you don't want to expose to too much risk (such as a down payment on a house), consider buying a treasury bill or a government bond that matures in one or two years.

Guaranteed Investment Certificates

Guaranteed investment certificates (GICs) are useful when you have short-term goals. If you have a sum of money that you know you'll need within three years, GICs might be a perfect idea. The advantages include the fact that they are insured up to $60,000 and the fact that they pay higher rates than money-market funds.

The main disadvantage with GICs is the penalty for early withdrawal. This can be eliminated if you purchase marketable GICs from a brokerage firm. Many banks and brokerage firms offer GICs. If you want to sell before maturity, the brokerage firm will offer you a price based on current interest rates. Just like a bond, if interest rates go up, the GIC's price will fall. If rates have fallen, then you might get a capital gain on your GIC when you sell. However, if you plan to hold the GIC until maturity, it really doesn't matter if the price fluctuates, because you are guaranteed to receive the face value at maturity.

The primary benchmark to use when comparing your GIC's yield is the yield on a money-market account. If a money-market account offers higher interest, you might want to reconsider the GIC.

Government Bonds and Treasury Bills

Let's discuss government bonds a little more in depth. The government of Canada and each of the provinces issue bonds, with maturities of two to 30 years. U.S. federal government bonds are referred to as Treasuries. There are also treasury bills, which are like Canadian or U.S. bonds, but mature in less than a year. Money-market funds are usually invested mostly in treasury bills.

Government bonds usually pay a fixed rate of interest twice a year. When the bond matures, the government pays back the principal, or face value, of the bond to the bond holder. Bond prices fluctuate with interest rates. When interest rates go up, bond prices fall. When interest rates fall, bonds become more valuable and their prices go up. A bond's yield moves in the opposite direction of its

Words of the Wealthy

Treasury bills are issued with 13-, 26-, and 52–week maturities. They are normally sold at a discount to the face value, which is $1,000 per bond. The difference between their face value and their discounted value is the interest you will receive at maturity. Until maturity, their price fluctuates daily according to short–term interest rates.

Words of the Wealthy

Bonds with longer maturities, say 10–25 years, fluctuate more than bonds with shorter maturities.

Words of the Wealthy

A junk bond or high-yield bond, is any corporate bond rated below a BBB rating by Dominion Bond Rating Service or Canadian Bond Rating Service. Junk bonds are also known as non-investment grade bonds or high-yield bonds. It's best to stay away from junk bonds.

price. If the price of a bond falls, its yield goes up and vice versa. It's a difficult concept to grasp, but think of it this way: if a bond price falls, then someone who now buys the bond will get the same fixed rate of interest payments at a lower cost, thus earning a higher yield. The yield, as you will recall, is the annual return you will earn from your bond purchase, if you hold it until it matures.

Traditional bonds pay interest in cash twice a year. For long-term investors, especially in an RRSP, this cash can be a nuisance to reinvest elsewhere. That's why strip bonds are better suited for your RRSP. A strip bond doesn't make regular interest payments; rather, the bond is sold to you at a big discount to its maturity value and slowly climbs to its maturity value as the maturity date approaches. This way, you're not saddled with frequent cash payments that you must worry about reinvesting.

Canadian provincial bonds usually have a somewhat higher yield than federal government bonds. This seems to be because there's a slightly higher perceived risk to owning a provincial bond. But since provincial bonds are guaranteed just as federal bonds are, it's good to go for the extra yield from provincial bonds.

When building a bond portfolio, be sure to spread out your maturities. This means buying bonds with various maturity dates. For example, if $60,000 of your portfolio is dedicated to bonds, you could buy $20,000 worth of bonds maturing in three years, $20,000 maturing in six years, and $20,000 maturing in nine years. This way, you'll be spreading out your interest-rate risk. As your bonds mature, you will reinvest them at the prevailing interest rates.

Discount brokers and full service brokers will sell you Canadian and U.S. government bonds, both regular and strip bonds, provincial and federal. When you call to buy one, have a rough idea about the maturity and type (strip or regular) of bond you want, and your brokerage will tell you what they have available in their inventory.

Corporate Bonds

Corporate bonds do offer higher yields than treasury bonds, but they involve a little more risk. They are also rated according to the issuing company's estimated ability to pay their interest and principal payments on a timely basis. High-quality corporate bonds are designed to give a portfolio stability. They are not designed to produce double-digit total returns.

Higher-yields among corporate bonds are found in the lower non-investment grade issues called *junk bonds*. A junk bond represents an IOU issued by a company whose ability to repay its interest and principal in a timely manner depends on the economy and on the company's ability to sell its products or services.

If you consider buying these bonds individually, you are asking for trouble. But if you purchase a fund, you will get a manager who knows the junk market better than you ever will, because this is all he or she works with on a daily basis. The fund owns many different junk bonds, thus reducing risk.

Words of the Wealthy

Risk/reward ratio is a term used to describe a security's return relative to its risk. If a security has the potential for a 10-percent return on the upside, you should only be willing to accept an equal or lesser degree of risk on the downside. For example, why risk a 20-percent loss for a possible 10-percent return?

Hybrid Fixed-Income Securities

You can also use convertible bonds and preferred stocks, which I call hybrid fixed-income securities. I call them hybrids because, like a bond, they do well when interest rates go down; like a stock, they go up when the underlying company's earnings grow substantially. Occasionally these types of investments become attractive, but not very often. When you need to stabilize the value of your portfolio, these types of securities can help. They can be defined as a cross between a bond and a stock. They pay higher income than traditional stocks, but don't fluctuate as much in price. Don't bother with them.

The Equity Tools: Stocks and Such

Where do you invest your money? You can invest your money in a conventional savings account or in GICs or bonds, but your net return after inflation and taxes will not likely be strong enough (at least at today's rates) to compound the portfolio growth at a sufficient pace. However, equities, or stocks, stand a much better chance. Whether they are publicly traded or privately held, they can compound much faster because their value or price is directly related to the earnings growth of the company. That's what makes them the wealth tool of choice. They are the key to building wealth because they represent equity ownership in a company and their value will grow relative to the growth in net earnings. If a company is expected to have continued earnings growth of 30 percent or more, then its stock price may have the same growth potential. There are

Words of the Wealthy

The **P/E ratio** is a stock's price per share, divided by its earnings per share. It is used to estimate the true value of a stock and is often used in comparison with other stocks. If Canadian Tire's market price closed at $25 per share today and its current quarterly earnings equaled 25¢ (or $1 on an annualized basis), its P/E ratio would be 25.

Words of the Wealthy

A **value investor** is someone who looks for good value in the market. A stock selling at an unusually low P/E ratio is a great example. Occasionally stocks drop in price well below what they should. Value investors search for opportunities like this and try to take advantage of the stock's price returning to more normal (higher) levels.

very few opportunities in the investment world that offer this much growth potential. This is the single biggest and most popular wealth builder in the world, but ironically, many people don't take the time to understand the concept or its power.

The market value of a stock is based on what people perceive to be the value. This perception of value is normally based upon the amount of net cash the company produces (or is perceived to produce) on a per-share level after expenses. This cash is referred to as earnings or earnings per share. The majority of these earnings are usually retained by the company and are used to finance further growth, with the remainder being distributed as dividends to shareholders. Small or fast-growing companies usually do not distribute any earnings as dividends because they need the money to continue their fast-paced growth. On the other hand, larger or slower-growing companies usually distribute a great deal of their earnings as dividends. In the past, smaller companies proved to be faster-growing and more rewarding to investors. But in the 1990s, many big companies such as Wal-Mart Stores, Microsoft, Home Depot, and Nortel Networks displayed astounding growth rates.

The relative comparison of a company's stock price to its earnings is commonly referred to as the *price/earnings ratio* (or P/E). Traditionally, the P/E ratio has been a useful tool to gauge whether a stock is cheap or expensive. But in recent years, the P/E ratio has provided little guidance for investors. For example, the P/E ratio for Nortel Networks was traditionally in the 25 to 30 range, but in 1999 the stock soared and its P/E ratio using expected 2000 earnings shot up to more than 75. Similarly, stocks of many large U.S. and Canadian companies greatly increased in the 1990s. The P/E for U.S. and Canadian stocks as a group shot up to more than 30, compared with traditional levels of well below 20. Using this and other measures, some long-time stock market analysts believe U.S. stocks have never been more expensive and are heading for a nasty fall.

The P/E ratio is useless when evaluating most Internet-related stocks. At the turn of the century, Internet mania had taken the valuations of such companies as AOL, Yahoo, Amazon.com, and eBay into the stratosphere. Many Internet companies don't have net income, which means it's impossible to calculate the P/E. The ones that are profitable typically have P/E ratios in the hundreds or higher, which means investors are taking enormous risks.

But not all companies are trading with huge P/E ratios. In fact, despite the overall expensiveness of the North American stock market, many well-known companies are selling rather cheaply. For example, the Canadian banks at the start of 2000 were selling at P/E ratios between nine and 15, good prices for cautious investors.

Domestic Stocks

Domestic stocks are stocks of companies that are headquartered here in Canada. They should make up a good bit of your investment portfolio, but not the whole thing. This is a common mistake made by investors in Canada. I'll talk more about this later.

Domestic stocks can be purchased individually through a broker or through a mutual fund. One advantage stocks offer is protection from the risk of inflation, which bonds don't seem to do as well. The only real disadvantage is the performance risk that stocks carry. If the underlying company goes bankrupt, the stock could become worthless. You are also tied to the overall Canadian market, which can correct unexpectedly. Therefore, domestic stock prices can be volatile.

Successful investors use certain stock indices as relative benchmarks for their own portfolios. Therefore, it is important to understand the most common indexes and what makes each unique. The TSE 300 index represents 300 different stocks. Another Canadian stock index is the S&P/TSE 60, which measures the performance of 60 of Canada's big-company stocks. There are many other narrowly gauged indexes, but it's difficult to list them all. These indices all act as broad-based windows into the stock market. If you were really interested in health-care-related stocks, there are several health-care-related indexes of stocks and mutual funds available. If you knew the health-care-related stock index took a dramatic dive over the past year, you might consider this to be an overreaction by the market and decide to buy a mutual fund specializing in this area.

If investing is your hobby and passion, it's okay to build a portfolio of individual domestic stocks. If it's not your hobby, and you're picking your own stocks, you may be setting yourself up for future losses. If you don't enjoy investing, you will not do a very good job. Consider buying mutual funds or hiring a fee-only investment advisor.

Foreign Stocks

Only in the last few years have investors started to understand the value of foreign stocks. If your portfolio is invested only in Canadian companies, you are actually taking more risk than is someone with a portfolio diversified all over the world. Allocating approximately 35 percent of your portfolio into a diversified mix of foreign stocks will actually reduce your risk and, at the same time, increase your performance potential. I firmly believe that all stock portfolios should have a certain percentage allocated into foreign stocks.

The most popular benchmark that represents a portfolio invested all over the world is the Morgan Stanley World Market Index, which can be found daily in the business pages.

The Mutual Fund Tools

A mutual fund, also known as an investment company, is a corporation, trust, or partnership in which investors combine their money to benefit primarily from professional management, diversification, and liquidity. Each fund has a manager or management team responsible for making the investment decisions for the fund and for purchasing securities with the money invested by the shareholders. The securities can include stocks, bonds, options, GICs, and real estate, depending on the fund's stated objective.

What makes each mutual fund different is the fund's objective, explained in the prospectus. The objective of the fund outlines the intentions of the manager, including the type of investments he will be using as well as the different philosophies or strategies he will employ. This is the most important item in the prospectus to understand. The second is the list of restrictions: guidelines set up to help keep the fund manager focused and on track.

Mutual Funds Are No Longer Just for Small Accounts

Conventional wisdom might have you believe that mutual funds are designed to help investors diversify small amounts of money. It's certainly true that mutual funds offer a great deal of diversification, but they offer many other benefits that most investors completely overlook. Here is a list of what a portfolio of mutual funds offers the shareholder:

➤ The synergy of combining several money managers' unique investment styles into your portfolio.

➤ Services such as automated chequing account debit purchasing that make it a lot easier to invest on a monthly basis.

➤ An inexpensive way to hire a group of investment managers, since the management fees are so inexpensive compared to the expenses of hiring a private individual money manager.

➤ A cost-efficient method of investing all over the world, considering the high cost of foreign security commissions charged to individuals.

➤ The ability to diversify among hundreds of securities all over the world that would be almost impossible for an individual investor with a small amount of money and a limited amount of time to research.

➤ Greater diversification in your portfolio, because building a portfolio of several different funds means benefiting from managers who may have different investment philosophies.

➤ A great deal of portfolio liquidity, because you can sell your mutual fund almost as quickly as you can a stock.

➤ Peace of mind that someone is watching the portfolio.

Mutual funds are not perfect. They do have their limitations and disadvantages. The advantages certainly outweigh the disadvantages, but here is a list of *possible* problems:

➤ High management fees.

➤ Limitations of mutual funds because they can only invest in marketable securities.

➤ Loss of control over when taxable gains are taken.

➤ Poor performance.

➤ Legal limitations of the fund manager that could affect performance.

Mutual funds aren't just for small accounts anymore. As investors learn more about what it takes to build wealth, they quickly realize the advantages mutual funds have to offer.

Which Mutual Funds Are Best?

Mutual funds are not all created equal. In fact, there are startling differences that greatly affect your long-term returns. As we've discussed before, the paramount consideration when choosing mutual funds is fees. You must familiarize yourself with mutual fund management expense ratios (MERs), which you will find in a fund's prospectus and in the monthly mutual fund reports that are included in the third week of each month in *The Globe and Mail* and the *National Post*.

On average, the higher a fund's MER, the lower your long-term returns will be. For years, there were very few low-cost mutual funds to choose from in Canada. But in recent years a bunch of new low-cost funds became available. Most of these are index funds.

What are index funds? Index funds are mutual funds that buy stocks in correlation to a stock index, and therefore seek to provide substantially the same returns as the index they're trying to match. For example, an S&P/TSE 60 index fund buys the same stocks, in the same proportion, as the stocks that make up the S&P/TSE 60 index. There are also index funds that match the following indexes:

➤ S&P 500 (U.S. big-company stocks)

➤ Dow Jones Industrial Average (30 U.S. big-company stocks)

➤ S&P 400 mid-cap index (U.S. mid-size company stocks),

➤ Nasdaq 100 (primarily U.S. technology and Internet stocks)

➤ Morgan Stanley Europe, Australia and Far East index (EAFE)

➤ Morgan Stanley Europe Index

➤ Morgan Stanley Japan Index

➤ Morgan Stanley Asia-Pacific Index

➤ Scotia Capital Government Bond Index

There are fully RRSP-eligible versions of most of these index funds, which means they won't use up your allowable foreign content in your RRSP.

While most Canadian mutual funds charge MERs ranging from about 1.5 percent to 3 percent, many index funds have MERs of about 0.5 percent or even lower. Over long periods of time, this makes a big difference.

Some market analysts scoff at index funds because they ensure your returns will be no better than the market averages. What these people fail to mention is that the vast majority of mutual funds provide returns well below the indexes they're trying to beat. That's because high MERs and high cash levels prevent most mutual funds from beating the indexes. All mutual funds hold some cash, because money is flowing into and out of the funds all the time. Cash provides low returns and holds back long-term returns. Because index funds are mandated to follow an index (which holds no cash), they hold very little cash.

The lowest-cost index funds are offered by Toronto-Dominion Bank (TD eFunds), Altamira (Precision Index), and Royal Bank (Royal Index Funds). Other banks and fund companies offer index funds as well.

An alternative to index mutual funds is index-tracking stocks. These are trusts that trade like stocks on the major stock exchanges. For example, iUnits trade on the Toronto Stock Exchange under the symbol XIU. IUnits track the S&P/TSE 60 index. If you buy shares of iUnits, you are investing in 60 of Canada's biggest companies, including Nortel Networks, BCE, Bombardier, Royal Bank, TD Bank, Canadian Pacific, Magna International, and so on. To buy index-tracking stocks, you must have a brokerage account (preferably at a discount broker) and pay a commission to buy and sell them.

Here is a list of index-tracking stocks that trade on the American Stock Exchange, with the stock symbol and a quick description. Check out www.amex.com for more details.

➤ Spiders S&P 500 (SPY): invests in the companies in the S&P 500 index (MER 0.18 percent)

➤ Spiders S&P 400 (MDY): invests in the companies in the S&P 400 mid-cap index (MER 0.3 percent)

➤ Nasdaq 100 (QQQ): invests in the companies in the Nasdaq 100 index (MER 0.18 percent)

➤ Diamonds (DIA): invests in the 30 companies of the Dow Jones Industrial Average (MER 0.18 percent)

➤ U.S. sector-specific index-tracking stocks (MERs of about 0.65percent):

➤ Basic Industries (XLB)

➤ Consumer Services (XLV)

➤ Consumer Staples (XLP)

➤ Cyclical/Transportation (XLY)

➤ Energy (XLE)

➤ Financial (XLF)

➤ Industrial (XLI)

➤ Technology (XLK)

➤ Utilities (XLU)

There are also index-tracking stocks for 17 countries around the world. These are called WEBS (World Equity Benchmark Shares). They trade on the AMEX and have MERs of about 1 percent, which is far below most international mutual funds. Some of the more popular WEBS include: Japan (EWJ), Singapore (EWS), Malaysia (EWM), United Kingdom (EWU), Mexico (EWW), Hong Kong (EWH), and Germany (EWG). Investing in four or five WEBS from around the world gives you as much diversification as an international equity mutual fund, at a much lower annual cost.

The advantages of index-tracking stocks over index funds are that the MERs can be even lower, and they're suitable for inside and outside an RRSP. Many index funds that don't use up your RRSP foreign content aren't suitable for outside your RRSP, since the gains they produce are considered income and not capital gains. That's because they use futures contracts based on Canadian treasury bills (a complicated investing technique) to get around the foreign content restrictions for RRSPs. Index-tracking stocks produce capital gains (or losses), which are taxed at a lower rate than income. Only three-quarters of capital gains are taxed, while all of your income is taxed.

The advantages of index mutual funds over index-tracking stocks are that dividends are reinvested in more fund units automatically, whereas index-tracking stocks pay cash dividends that can be a nuisance. Also, no-load index mutual funds don't involve a commission, but most have minimum investment requirements.

105

Strongly consider using a variety of low-fee index funds and/or index stocks for the bulk of your stock investment portfolio. A simple, yet effective portfolio would be to buy one Canadian index fund, one or two U.S. index funds (such as the S&P 500 and the S&P 400), and one or two broadly diversified international index funds (such as one based on the EAFE index). Or instead of an international fund, buy a handful of different WEBS. You can round out your portfolio with low-fee, non-index (actively managed) funds, including small-cap funds, which invest in smaller companies in Canada and around the world that aren't included in the major indexes.

Actively Managed Funds

Despite the growing popularity of index funds, most Canadians who buy mutual funds are still invested in actively managed funds. Who can blame them? After all, we all would like above-average returns on our money, and index funds certainly won't provide index-topping returns.

People are attracted to star funds with eye-popping historical returns. Funds with one- or two-year returns of 50 percent, 75 percent, or higher tend to attract a flood of new investors, all seeking the same returns for their portfolios. There's only one problem with chasing hot funds – you usually get in too late. Nothing lasts forever. By the time a fund has posted some hot historical numbers, its glory days are usually coming to an end – much to the disappointment of thousands of new investors in the fund.

As we've discussed, most actively managed mutual funds fall behind the indexes because of high MERs and cash levels that provide low returns. This, however, doesn't mean there are no reasons to buy actively managed mutual funds. Low-MER mutual funds make sense when you are looking to invest in stocks not included in the major indexes, such as small-cap stocks, or stocks from countries not represented by the major indexes.

Of course, if you're shooting for above-average returns, and you're willing to accept that your funds might underperform the indexes, then you might decide to go with some no-load, low-MER actively managed funds. By low MER, we're talking at least below 1.5 percent, but below 1 percent would be much better. The downside to this strategy is that the list of low-fee, actively managed mutual funds in Canada is quite short.

If you do go with actively managed funds, go with broadly diversified funds that invest in a range of industries, rather than specialized funds. If you just invest in a few specialized funds, such as health-care stocks or financial stocks, your overall portfolio will be poorly diversified and exposed to too much risk. If you invest in a whole bunch of specialized funds, you will be defeating the purpose. Your overall portfolio will end up looking a lot like one with a few broadly diversified funds, and will most likely cost you a lot more in MERs.

Also, avoid balanced funds. These funds invest in a mixture of stocks and bonds. The problem with them is they usually charge high MERs, in the 2 percent range and higher. Buy lower-cost stock funds and your own bonds instead, directly from a discount broker.

Closed-End Funds

One of the most overlooked investment vehicles is the closed-end fund. You know from the previous chapter not to buy these during an initial public offering because they are too expensive. However, once these funds make it to the secondary market, they can trade at a discount to their actual net asset value. Because they trade like a stock, their market price has little to do with the actual net asset value. I've seen some funds trade for as little as 65 cents on the dollar. This may be hard to believe, but it's true.

Just like open-end funds, closed-end funds can focus on many different sectors. Most of the closed-end equity funds focus on one individual country or geographic region. Therefore, closed-end funds can be a perfect way to invest in a specific country or region that you might be excited about.

Closed-end funds offer two unique advantages. There is certainly the advantage of having the opportunity to buy a mutual fund at a discount to its net asset value. However, the most important advantage is rarely discussed. What makes a closed-end fund so attractive is the fact that the manager doesn't have to worry about shareholders withdrawing money on a daily basis. Open-end fund managers have to worry about this every day. Closed-end fund managers don't have to worry about this, which means they can focus single-mindedly on managing the portfolio.

There are very few closed-end fund indexes available for comparison. Therefore, most of the time you will have to compare performance to other similar closed-end funds. Often you might find other open-end funds that are also similar. Closed-end funds generally require more homework than traditional open-end funds, and are therefore better suited to sophisticated investors.

A Little Secret About Bond Funds

Bond funds, just like stock funds, do give the shareholder diversification into many different individual bond issues, which is a great benefit. However, if you are going to build a portfolio and you need to allocate money to bonds, you should first consider buying individual bonds. Unless you're dealing with junk bonds or small amounts of money, it's more cost efficient to build your own portfolio of individual bonds. Why? What's wrong with a bond fund? Individual bonds are primarily purchased for their interest payments, which are usually fixed at a given rate. Given current interest rates, these bonds don't pay a lot of money, and if they're purchased within a mutual fund, you're going to receive even less money in interest payments. Bond funds, just like all other mutual funds, have management fees. I've seen 1.35-percent management fees on a bond fund that only paid about 6-percent interest. The net interest payment to the shareholder was only 4.65 percent! That means that 22.5 percent of the interest payment went to management fees—which is crazy. And, people actually buy these things every day! Just be aware of the details before you buy a bond fund.

The Best Tools of Wealth

I have found that most wealthy people use the same wealth-building tools. The following is a list of the most lucrative ones.

The Best Tool: Your Own Business

Equity in a fast-growing company, preferably your own, is the best tool to use when attempting to achieve Wealth Levels 3, 4, and 5. Why? Because your own business may be the only way to get potential returns in excess of 10 percent. The value of the stock is tied to earnings growth of the underlying company. If earnings are growing at 50 percent, then the stock is likely to be growing at 50 percent. This is truly the only way to achieve consistent returns that exceed the stock market. You might be able to accomplish above-average returns in the stock market, but you don't have the same control over that return unless it's your own company. We'll discuss starting your own business in Part 3.

A No-Load Mutual Fund Portfolio

There are two types of investors: hands-on investors who monitor their portfolio's every move, and hands-off investors, who barely glance at their monthly financial statements. Most people are hands-off investors or at least don't devote substantial amounts of time to tending to their investments. These people are better off with low-MER, no-load mutual funds and index funds. They are a snap to purchase, and once you do, you need not think about them very often.

Others, however, like to put more time into their investing, and are inclined to buy their own stocks and bonds. These people are hoping their research and hard work will result in above-average returns. Individual stock investors, however, must pay close attention to diversification. If their portfolios aren't properly diversified, they risk suffering substantial losses if a few of their stocks sink. A portfolio of individual stocks without funds should include, at the very least, 20 different stocks in order to provide adequate diversification. Owning 50 stocks would be even better. Because discount brokerage commissions are quite low, in the range of $25 a trade, it's possible to build a diversified portfolio of stocks that actually costs less than even a low-fee mutual fund over the long term. You aren't restricted to buying so-called "board lots" of 100 shares when you buy stocks. You can buy 10 shares, 25 shares, 50 shares, whatever you want to suit your needs. But an individual stock investor must stay on top of her investments and make adjustments to keep her portfolio current and diversified.

The Perfect Portfolio

The optimal wealth-building portfolio has these characteristics:

➤ The portfolio is built primarily of stocks and maybe some bonds in an automated account—the aggressive investor may not own any bonds, while the conservative investor may have 60 percent in bonds.

➤ The stocks are globally diversified among Canada, foreign developed countries, and foreign emerging-market countries—the ideal percentage of foreign securities for a moderate-risk investor is approximately 30 percent.

➤ The portfolio should be broad-based, invested in a variety of companies, industries, and countries.

➤ The portfolio can be quickly, easily, and cost-efficiently adjusted to take advantage of better opportunities.

➤ The overall annual cost of your portfolio should be as low as possible, under 1 percent.

Tools To Help You Invest

There are many terrific publications and Web sites to provide guidance as you invest, whether you're an indexer, active fund buyer, or stock picker.

First, strongly consider subscribing to *The Globe and Mail* and/or the *National Post*. Both papers have excellent business sections, full of useful commentary and statistics regarding personal finance. The cost of subscribing is a pittance compared with the knowledge you'll gain and the ability you'll have to stay current on a range of financial issues.

Another publication you might look at is *Canadian MoneySaver*, which is full of commentary about current investment topics. Check www.canadianmoneysaver.ca or call 613-352-7448. A subscription is $21.35 (11 issues a year). *Canadian Business* also covers investing topics well. *The Globe and Mail* operates two handy Web sites: www.globeinvestor.com for stock investors and www.globefund.com for fund investors.

Each of the discount brokers have Web sites that outline the services and fees and carry some information about investing. Check out www.tdwaterhouse.ca, www.investorline.com, www.actiondirect.com, www.canada.etrade.com, and www.invesnet.com.

For U.S. investment topics, you can't beat *The Wall Street Journal*, which also operates a terrific subscription-based Web site: www.wsj.com. Other good Web sites include: www.morningstar.com, www.fool.com, www.smartmoney.com, and www.vanguard.com.

The Least You Need to Know

➤ Always look for hidden commissions and fees that can eat away at your portfolio.

➤ Identify the possible conflicts of interest before you take any investment advice.

➤ If your goal is to maximize the growth of your portfolio, use stocks.

➤ The best portfolio for beginners is one that is diversified internationally through low-fee, no-load mutual funds and index funds.

Chapter 9

Five Things You Must Know Before You Hire Professional Help

In This Chapter

➤ Where to look for an advisor

➤ What to look for in an advisor

➤ What you should avoid

➤ Questions you need to ask the advisor

➤ Questions you need to ask the advisor's clients

When you have achieved the advanced stages of Wealth Level 2, where your return exceeds your target savings goal (TSG), you must pay close attention to the management of your portfolio.

If you feel you have a good understanding of the main investment areas, such as diversification and keeping fees low, then don't feel you have to hire an investment advisor. In Canada, in fact, most financial advisors or financial planners will sell you only high-cost mutual funds that generate commissions for the advisor. If investing, however, is not a hobby or passion of yours, you might need to consider getting some help from a professional in the investment industry. Every investor has different needs, and every professional offers somewhat different services. This chapter will help you match your needs with the best professional available: a financial planner, full-service broker, or other professional.

Whatever professional you need, one thing they all can do for you is eliminate procrastination in your financial plan. They can keep you accountable and even make decisions for you. The key question is whether the advisor can do better than you can. If you think an advisor can beat your performance at least by the amount of fees and commissions charged, then you should consider hiring that advisor. If you think you can do a better job, then try it yourself.

Will All the Great Advisors Please Stand Up?

The best place to start looking for an investment advisor is among your friends. Find friends whose investment knowledge you respect, and ask whom they recommend. You can also talk to your accountant or tax preparer, if you use either; these folks see brokerage statements every year and know first hand which advisors make money for clients. Watch your local newspaper for investment seminars and workshops in your area. Otherwise, you may have to resort to the *Yellow Pages*.

The most difficult question an investor will ever have to answer is, "What kind of professional should I trust?" This decision is usually the first one to make and often the least researched. Many people in my workshops ask me to explain the difference between fee-only investment advisors, investment advisors, money managers, brokers, and certified financial planners. Therefore, I thought it might be useful to discuss the various titles that accompany these professionals in the investment industry. The primary differences to be aware of include services offered, source of compensation, influences, and regulation.

That Reminds Me...

If you are just starting out with your portfolio and you have less than $20,000 to invest, you are in what I call the "grey zone." If you look for help, you'll find very few quality investment brokers or advisors willing to spend any significant time with you. Why? Because the commission or fee income from $20,000 isn't usually enough to get most brokers or advisors excited. If you're in the grey zone, you need to be sure not to let an unscrupulous advisor steer you into a "commission trap" to make up for your lower portfolio size. The commission trap is any investment that charges above-average commissions. If you don't understand the possible hidden commissions and fees, you'll be easy prey. The next chapter will help you through the grey zone.

Full-Service Investment Brokers

The first and most widely known investment professional is the *full-service investment broker* (broker). Other titles that describe a broker include "registered representative," "financial consultant," "investment banker," and even "vice president" (usually awarded when certain levels of commission are achieved). Investment brokers are security salespeople who help investors buy and sell securities for a commission. Brokers seldom have fiduciary responsibility for clients' accounts, so the clients must be contacted prior to, and must agree to, any investment transaction. Some brokers may also offer financial planning, estate planning, and retirement planning services.

Brokers are regulated by the provincial securities commissions and the Investment Dealers Association. The primary advantage of using a full-service broker is the extensive research about investment decisions they can provide. However, many discount brokerage firms now offer the same research information. The full-service brokerage firm might have a team of security analysts—but they make plenty of mistakes, too. When selecting stocks and other securities, pay attention to facts, not to the opinions of security analysts. With a little experience, your instincts may produce better results.

The primary disadvantage of working with a full-service broker is the way they are compensated—via commission for each investment purchase or sale you make. Commissions usually range from 1.5-percent charges on stock trades to 8.5-percent charges on mutual funds and other packaged products. Many investors feel commission-based investment advice is a conflict of interest. When you have any investment planning done by a broker, make sure you know the full extent of the commissions involved in every recommendation. Unless you feel you're clueless about investing, avoid stock brokers.

Words of the Wealthy

A **fiduciary** is an advisor who has been authorized to buy and sell securities on behalf of the client, without the client's express permission. This authorization is given in the form of a limited power of attorney signed by the client. An advisor has *fiduciary responsibility* when he is responsible for buying and selling securities for the client. Avoid this type of arrangement; you lose control of the decision-making.

Words of the Wealthy

The primary influence over the broker is the investment firm's branch manager, who is also compensated based on the amount of commissions and proprietary investment products sold. Proprietary investments are those that the broker's company underwrites and exclusively distributes or sells.

Words of the Wealthy

A **fee-only advisor** is a money manager or financial planner who receives a fee for service that is usually based on a percentage of assets under management or time. Fee-only advisors do not receive commissions for any investment they recommend.

Financial Planners and Advisors

Almost anyone can describe himself as a financial planner or advisor, so you should do some digging before you choose one. Check his educational background, for example, and ask for references. Ask for verification of training by the Institute of Canadian Bankers, the Canadian Securities Institute or the Institute for Financial Planning. Members of the Canadian Association of Financial Planners need two years of working experience and must have liability insurance to qualify for a CAFP designation.

CAFP (www.cafp.org) provides a free consumers' guide to financial planning, including a detailed list of member planners. (To reach CAFP's Toronto head office, call 416-593-6592.)

To simplify, I will use the term "advisor" to refer to professionals I've mentioned in this chapter.

The Four Cs: Compatibility Questions You Should Ask Your Advisor

If you decide to hire an advisor to help you in your journey toward the next Wealth Level, you need to know what to look for and the right questions to ask. What you should envision is a relationship between you and your advisor that is based on trust and compatibility. You need to focus on finding someone who will keep your best interest in mind and be rewarded for doing so. Your goal is not only to find the best

Treasure Tip

If you're starting from scratch, you should interview at least three advisors before making a decision.

advisor for you, but to gain a certain degree of respect from that advisor. Often, the amount of attention and service you get from the advisor is directly related to the amount of respect he has for you.

How do you gain that respect? First, by asking the right questions. There are four Cs of advisor-client compatibility: credentials, compensation, characteristics, and customer service. Your questions should at least cover these four areas. The rest of this section explains each area, including the key questions that you need to ask before you hire an advisor.

Credentials

Just what exactly qualifies your advisor as a professional? Some advisors just hang a shingle outside their doors and go to work. The following questions will help you to separate the wheat from the chaff.

1. **Whom are you registered with?** The advisor should be registered with one of the following:

   ➤ The Canadian Association of Financial Planners (416-593-6592)

   ➤ The Investment Dealers Association of Canada (416-364-6133)

2. **Where did you graduate from university?** This might not be important to you, but it will sure answer the real question, which is, "Did you go to university and did you graduate?" If you doubt the answer you get, call the university and check. You shouldn't base your entire decision on whether or not the advisor finished university (I know several brilliant people who never went to university), but university is a test of tenacity. If the advisor you're interviewing didn't finish university, make sure she can show you at least five good years of investment experience.

3. **How long have you been in the investment business?** Don't be a guinea pig. If this is the advisor's first few years in the business, you might want to wait. Most advisors make their biggest mistakes during the first year in the business. If you do hire a neophyte advisor, start with a small amount of money. The best advisor is someone who has experienced at least one big market correction (a period where many securities "crashed," or went down in value) such as that in 1987.

4. **Who was your previous employer?** You might even ask for a resume. If your advisor has jumped around from firm to firm, you might want to reconsider. If you were hiring an employee, would you hire someone who has jumped between jobs each year over the last several years? There can be exceptions to this rule, so ask why the advisor jumped around. He might have done it by design, to learn more about the business before starting an investment firm.

5. **What certifications do you have?** The most important certification a money manager can possess is a CFA or Chartered Financial Analyst. This is a comprehensive three-year course developed and maintained by the Institute of Chartered Financial Analysts. It is not the most important thing to look for when hiring an advisor, but it is impressive. Comparing the CFA designation to the CAFP designation is like comparing university to high school. The CFA is much more difficult and comprehensive than is the CAFP.

   The only possible problem with the CFA is that it can make your advisor too academic. Academic investors can sometimes be too rigid in their investment strategies, meaning they focus on certain kinds of conventional portfolio strategies, but disregard others that also may be beneficial. Therefore, the most intelligent are not always the best money managers. As I will explain in Chapter 11, it takes much more than intelligence to be a successful portfolio manager.

Treasure Tip

If you divide the amount of money under management by the number of clients, you'll find the advisor's average account size.

6. **How many clients do you have?** The advisor can have too few or too many clients. Too few may imply that he has little experience. Too many may mean that he can't serve all of them effectively. There is no magic number, and you'll just have to judge for yourself. The more clients the advisor has, the more experience she has. If you are hiring a money manager, you also may want to ask how much money she has under management. If the manager has more than $30 million under management, she's built a significant business.

7. **Questions to ask yourself. Are you impressed with this person?** Does he have his credentials? Does he have enough experience to make you comfortable?

Compensation

If you spend time regularly attending to your portfolio, then use a discount broker and do it yourself. However, if investing is not a hobby of yours, you should focus on fee-only advisors who can't try to rack up commissions by steering novices into commission-heavy investments. Be wary of any advisor that tells you there's no charge to use his services. There's always a charge—it's just a question of how it's paid, and how much. Advisors who sell deferred-sales-charge funds, for example, earn commissions through the MERs you pay to own the fund.

You've got to fully understand the costs involved before you hire anyone to help you manage your money. As noted earlier, an advisor's method of compensation will dictate the conflicts of interest you may encounter. So, regardless of whether the advisor is commission-based or fee-based, ask these questions:

1. **How are you compensated?** If the answer is "fee-only" then ask the percentage rate. In my view, 1 percent should be the upper limit, and it should be capped at a certain dollar amount. These fees are usually negotiable, so don't be afraid to ask for discounts. Then compare these rates with the other fee-based advisors you interview. If the advisor is paid commission, it may be difficult to compare apples to apples because of all the different investment products they can sell. One way to do this is to compare the commission of 100 shares of stock at a hypothetical price of $25. Most brokerage firms also have minimum commission amounts. Be sure to

compare these, too. The most important thing to remember is that if you hire a commission-paid broker or salesperson, there is always a commission paid somewhere, somehow. Unfortunately, it's your job to ask about it. It's also your job to double-check the accuracy of the answer you get. Numerous hidden costs can slowly eat away at your portfolio.

One common hidden cost is the underwriting fee that is added to a new issue or investment product. If a newly issued stock, fund, or other investment product is offered to you by a broker with no commission charge, ask what the total underwriting fee adds up to. Often you'll find these underwriting fees to be in excess of 6 percent. What amount is too much? You'll have to be the judge. I avoid these fees altogether.

If a commission-based broker recommends a mutual fund to you, be sure to ask how you'll pay his commission. If he says the fund pays his commission, you should reply, "No, I'm paying your commission; just tell me how much it is and how I'm paying it." Listen to how he explains it. Ask him to explain the management fees. You might want to ask him to show you the explanation in the prospectus. The broker is paid to sell the fund, and keep you in it. Many of these funds, especially the proprietary funds, pay the broker "trailers" that are extra commission payments paid as incentive to keep clients in the funds. Ask your advisor about these details. Your knowledge will certainly get their attention.

2. **Will you explain to me all the costs involved in each investment?** There are additional fees of which you need to be aware that do not go to the broker or advisor. The most common are the management fees charged by mutual fund managers. The average domestic stock mutual fund management fee is approximately 2.2 percent. Foreign funds charge a slightly higher fee, while bond funds charge lower fees. Another fee to look for is a custodian fee, which is normally charged by the brokerage firm for holding your account. If your advisor is paid a fee and uses a brokerage firm for trades, you also need to be aware of the commission and transaction fees charged by the brokerage firm.

3. **What if I want to change my mind and fire you?** Very few people think to ask this question. It may seem a bit harsh, but you need to ask it. If you are a positive person, firing the advisor may be the last thing on your mind, but you need to know the logistics and costs involved. You also need to know the cost of liquidating your account. Anything you buy should cost little or nothing to sell, and should have a secondary market where it can easily *be* sold.

Most of the hidden costs are listed somewhere in the agreement you signed to open an account or to go with an advisor, or in the prospectus of the specific investment you bought. There are a few that aren't listed, but it would take another chapter to explain all of them. Just remember that nothing is free and that if it sounds too good to be true, it probably is.

4. **Questions to ask yourself.** After you have analysed all the costs, do they seem reasonable? If you have hired a discretionary money manager, the total cost should not exceed 1.5 percent of your principal per year. Compare other money managers to see if they are more competitive. If your advisor's rates seem too high, ask for a discount. If you have hired a broker, compare the commission rates with those of other firms. If the rates seem too high, ask for a discount.

Characteristics

Each advisor has a unique personality that ultimately affects the contents and, therefore, the results of the portfolio. You need to understand this personality before you hire the advisor.

1. **What is your investment philosophy?** The advisor's investment philosophy is very important to your future. It dictates how your portfolio will be managed and, therefore, how your wealth will be built and maintained. Most investment professionals either don't have a philosophy or have difficulty explaining their investment philosophy in a few sentences. That frightens me. You want someone who can tell you his philosophy easily, briefly, and with conviction. When you ask this question, look not only for these qualities, but also for understanding. Do you understand the philosophy? Are you comfortable with it? If you can't understand it, how will you know if you agree with what she thinks? For example, my investment philosophy reads: "Investment excellence is the synergy produced when you achieve high performance with global trend diversification, cost efficiency, convenience, and the proper level of risk. This process often requires the investor to break down the walls of conventional wisdom."

2. **Do you focus on the domestic market, foreign markets, or both?** The answer should be both. Many advisors focus only on the domestic market, which is a shame. To establish the proper level of diversification, you must have both domestic and foreign securities in your portfolio. If the answer is both, ask if the advisor uses mutual funds or individual stocks for the foreign portion of the portfolio. If the answer is individual stocks, find someone else. Not many advisors can pick individual stocks and bonds around the world successfully. If the advisor can show you a track record of success using both domestic and foreign stocks, consider working with him. For example, I think every investment portfolio should have both domestic and foreign stocks, as well as bonds. Instead of using individual stocks, I use low-cost mutual funds or index funds to accomplish this for my clients.

3. **Tell me a little about yourself.** Get to know your advisor as a person. You have to understand the person before you'll know whether she will be compatible with you and your needs. Ask her about her hobbies and interests. Ask her what motivates her. Ask where she grew up.

4. **What is your specialty? What are you the best at?** You need to know what your advisor is good at. You need to know what he enjoys most about the investment business. What he enjoys most is what he will more than likely be the best at, and provide the best results in. My specialty, for example, is global portfolio management using no-load mutual funds.

5. **How do you view risk, and how does your philosophy fit with my risk tolerance?** Let the advisor explain how your risk tolerance is calculated and how your portfolio will be designed accordingly. Don't be afraid to ask questions here. The stock market can be volatile, so make sure you understand the risks involved.

6. **Questions to ask yourself.** You have to consider compatibility. Will you be comfortable with this person? What kind of attitude does he have? Is he patient with you or just trying to sell you something? Do you trust this person? Is he trying to confuse you with investment jargon? Will you worry about your money after you hire this advisor? Is this person a good listener? Did the advisor ask about your goals and objectives? You need to make certain that your advisor will help you achieve your goals. If you don't have any, then he should at least help you establish your expectations for risk and return.

Customer Service

If you pay close attention to the level of service offered by the advisors you interview, you'll more than likely find a large discrepancy. Most advisors offer a status quo level of service. However, as advisory firms and full-service brokerage firms become more competitive, you will begin to see additional services, such as monthly newsletters, quarterly market reports on audio tape, and detailed transaction explanations as to why each trade was made.

1. **What services does your firm offer?** If you need a fee-only financial planner, ask what services are offered. The answer is different with each planner. The same is true with brokers and advisors in the money management business. The level of client services offered varies with each firm. Some firms are very competitive; others don't seem to care. The following list of services will give you an idea of what advisors can offer you (if they want to), and the services you should ask about:

   ➤ Quarterly, if not monthly, brokerage statements (ask to see an example).

   ➤ Quarterly performance statements (ask to see an example).

   ➤ Performance compared to a domestic index and a world index.

➤ Advisor availabilty by phone.

➤ A sufficient number of client service people who can answer administrative questions.

➤ Yearly one-on-one client reviews.

➤ Yearly tax information statements to help you prepare your taxes.

2. **Where will my assets be held?** If you are considering an independent money manager, there should be an independent third-party custodian holding your assets for you. This custodian should be a brokerage firm that sends you statements every month. The money manager should have a limited power of attorney agreement with the brokerage firm that allows him to buy and sell securities for you, deduct his fee quarterly, and get a copy of your monthly statement and daily account information. Having this independent firm separates your money manager from your account and reduces the possibility of fraud.

3. **How accessible will she be?** It can be very frustrating not to have access to information or answers when you need them. Who do you call when your advisor

That Reminds Me...

Years ago, in a small retirement community, one of my clients hired a man who called himself an advisor. She opened an account with the advisor and began receiving statements showing above-average results. She began hearing other clients of his complain about not getting their monthly cheques. Since she didn't need income from her account, she didn't have any problems—at least that's what she thought.

The next thing she knew, the advisor had skipped town with her money. Every client this guy had was not only scared to death, but furious and even embarrassed. How could this guy get away with this?

It was easy! He was depositing the money in his own account and fraudulently producing his own statements. There was no independent third party producing a second statement. Approximately $10 million in client assets was lost.

Therefore, when you open an account with an independent advisor, make your cheque out to the brokerage firm where your account is being held, not to your advisor. When your account is opened, call the brokerage firm and check your account number and balance. You should also receive a confirmation by mail of the account being opened. Be sure to compare the statements you receive from the advisor with those from the brokerage firm.

is on vacation? Make sure the advisor has hired other advisors who can help you. This is called "depth." A firm has depth if it has employed more than one advisor.

4. **What has been your year-to-year performance vs. the TSE 300?** All advisors should be able to furnish you with a track record. This track record should be presented along with other relative indexes against which you can compare. It should reflect the combined performance of all the advisor's accounts and should mention that it was prepared using AIMR standards. The most common broad market indexes are:

   ➤ The TSE 300
   ➤ The Lipper Balanced Fund Index
   ➤ The Morgan Stanley World Market Index

The best index to beat would be the last one, because it represents an index of stocks diversified around the world. If the advisor lagged all of these indexes, indicating lower than expected performance, you might want to ask why. Remember, don't base your entire decision on the advisor's past performance. Just because the advisor did well last year (or for the past 10 years), doesn't mean you can expect the same performance this year. Be sure to consider the philosophy of the manager before you eliminate him just because his track record is bad. His philosophy might be right on target next year.

If you are hiring a commission-based broker, you will not get a track record. Brokerage firms do not offer track records on their individual brokers' performances, nor on the clients' individual accounts. You'll get individual performance data on your account if you are in a wrap account, but otherwise you're on your own.

5. **What was your worst year? Best?** Wouldn't you like to know the advisor's worst year? Ask him what happened and listen to his answer. You want an advisor who takes responsibility for his results. If he defends his performance too much, he might not be willing to admit a mistake later. All advisors make mistakes. You want an advisor who's honest about it. If he's willing to admit it, he's also more likely to correct it more quickly.

6. **Do you use AIMR standards in reporting performance?** The best industry standards for reporting investment performance is the Association for Investment Management and Research (AIMR) Standard. These standards are intended to foster a fair representation and full disclosure of performance results. The second goal of these standards is to promote greater uniformity and comparability among performance presentations. The guidelines are strict and comprehensive. If your advisor does not claim to use these standards, you should ask him why he's not willing to comply with industry standards.

That Reminds Me...

The organization that administers the Chartered Financial Analyst (CFA) course and exam is the Institute of Chartered Financial Analysts (ICFP), which is a subsidiary of the Association for Investment Management and Research (AIMR). If your advisor is a CFA, his performance numbers must comply with AIMR standards. Otherwise he will lose his designation. The first objective of the AIMR standards is to establish a common, accepted set of ethical principles that ensure fair representation and full disclosure in investment managers' presentations of their results to clients and prospective clients. Their second objective is to achieve greater uniformity and comparability among such presentations. Without these standards, an advisor can manipulate his performance data to seem more attractive than it actually is.

7. **Do you offer financial planning, money management, or both?** If you hire a financial planner, she needs to know every aspect of planning, which includes spending control, retirement and estate planning, saving, asset protection, life insurance, and taxes. If you hire a money manager, she needs to know every aspect of investment management, which includes investment strategy, global investment trends, domestic industry trends, interest rates, and all the best investment products available.

You may find that you need both a money manager and a financial planner. If you hire one person to do both, make sure you check her references. It's very difficult to be good at both. There are certainly exceptions to this rule. I personally know several advisors that do both well, but they are the exceptions, not the rule.

8. **Can you show me your clients' portfolio performance each quarter for the last few years?** This is similar to numbers 4 and 5, but in more detail. These statistics might not be available, but if you can observe quarterly performance, you can get an idea of the volatility this manager has produced. Pay attention to the best- and worst-performing quarters. If you can't handle the kind of fluctuation you see in these numbers, don't hire this person.

9. **How many clients did you lose last year? Why?** Every advisor loses clients each year for many different reasons. Before you hire an advisor, ask how many clients he lost and why. If he says none, you should be suspicious. There are many different reasons why advisors lose clients. It's a natural occurrence that cannot be

prevented. I personally lost 12 clients out of 350 in 1995. Most of the reasons had nothing to do with me or my service. They either moved away, got scared of the market, or wanted to manage the money themselves. If the advisor says he hasn't lost a client, he might have lost several for reasons he doesn't want you to know.

10. **Questions to ask yourself. Do you feel that this firm will take care of your needs?** Does it have a bias toward customer service? Is it open to your questions? Does it try to educate clients? Find out specifically what makes this firm different. Does it have any unique services? Does it have sufficient staff to cover its clientele? How many advisors are registered? Does it have enough knowledgeable staff to cover its clients' needs or is it understaffed?

Treasure Tip

You may find that most money managers will help you with the basics of financial planning. However, if you need more detail, find a fee-only financial planner who can help you. Make sure she spends time educating you so you can eventually do most of the planning yourself.

Client References

It is standard procedure in almost any service business to ask for client references. The only thing different about the investment business is that advisors have to ask a client's permission prior to using that client as a reference. Once the client agrees, the advisor can offer her name and phone number to other prospective clients who inquire. Some advisors don't offer references and when asked, they reply, "My clients are confidential." Don't accept this answer. It ought to be a warning signal. If the advisor has a legitimate business and does a good job, his clients should be willing to be references. I did a survey of my clients in 1994, and asked them if they would allow me to use their names and phone numbers as a reference. Out of all the responses we received, only one declined. He said he was just too busy to take any calls.

Words of the Wealthy

Don't accept the opinion of a client referral who is related to your advisor. Ask for one of the advisor's first clients. That individual can tell you the most about the advisor.

Get at least three references that have been with the advisor longer than one year. You might ask for the client that has been with the advisor the longest. You need to talk to clients who have been with the advisor during bad market years such as 1994 or even 1987. The advisor will naturally give you a list of his happiest clients, but you should still make the call. When you do talk to the references, assure them that their answers are confidential and that you have no intention of sharing them with anyone, including the advisor. Here are some questions you might ask:

1. **How long have you known (the advisor)?** I have clients that have known me since I was five years old. They know much more about me than does a client that hired me just last year.

2. **What do you like best about (the advisor)?** What do you like least about (the advisor)? These are my favourite questions. They are seldom asked, but they are probably the most powerful. The answers may tell you something about the advisor that you'd never otherwise know. You might find a personality trait that makes you feel more comfortable about working with the advisor. You might also find a monster in the closet! Whatever the case, the answers to these questions are usually by far the most interesting.

3. **Knowing what you know now, would you hire (the advisor) again today?** This is called zero-based thinking. The question is whether or not the client would hire the advisor if he had to do it all over again. The answer often gives you more insight into how the client really feels about the advisor. If the answer is yes, you might even add, "Do you mind telling me why?"

4. **Has (the advisor) made you money?** You might want to be more specific and ask if the advisor has beaten the TSE 300 or other indexes that are important to you. You might also ask if the advisor achieved the return goal he set for his clients.

5. **Did (the advisor) do what he said he was going to do?** Did he make any promises he didn't keep? This is the ultimate question that sums it all up for you.

Background Check

Finally, before hiring any type of advisor, broker, or planner, you might even want to call the Canadian Association of Financial Planners, the Investment Dealers Association, or your province's Securities Commission to see if there have been any complaints filed on the advisor. If you want to get an idea of the kind of professional to avoid, just ask about the most common complaints. Most consumer complaints involve financial planners, brokers, and advisors who earn their income solely by commissions, especially those who represent only one company, such as one mutual fund family.

The biggest scam in the investment business is the salesperson who calls himself a financial planner to disguise his true colours. If you hire a financial planner who charges you a fee for a financial plan and then gives you a plan with loaded (commissioned) mutual funds, you should run away as fast as you can. If the plan suggests proprietary funds (funds run by the firm the advisor works for), you should run even faster. This is one of the biggest conflicts of interest in the business.

The Least You Need to Know

➤ If investing is not your hobby or passion, you might consider hiring a fee-only advisor and avoid commission-based brokers.

➤ The best advisor to hire is a fee-only advisor who may be a money manager, financial planner, or both.

➤ Before you hire any professional, make sure he is compatible with your personality, risk tolerance, and financial goals.

➤ Make sure the advisor is registered with either the Investment Dealers Association or the Canadian Association of Financial Planners.

➤ Be sure to ask for references, and call at least three of them.

➤ Seek to eventually become your own financial advisor. You'll save a tonne of money in fees.

Chapter 10

Getting Your Feet Wet with the First Decision

In This Chapter

➤ What to look for in your first investment

➤ How to avoid the commission trap

➤ Measuring your risk tolerance

➤ Setting up your return expectations

➤ Specific mutual fund ideas

In Wealth Level 1, when you make your first investment decision, you might feel somewhat overwhelmed. This chapter will help you narrow your focus considerably and get you started on the right track. The first mistake most investors make when they begin investing is procrastinating. Most investors fear their first investment decision so much that they procrastinate, sometimes for years. They think they have to buy a stock or something complicated that requires days of study and research. If you follow the five questions in the first pages of Chapter 8, you'll instantly narrow down your choices considerably. Therefore, the first investment decision should actually be the easiest, and this chapter will give you a nudge in the right direction.

Most first-time investors are also so afraid of making a mistake that they actually freeze. Don't let this happen to you. Remember from Chapter 3 that the most important element initially is the amount of money you save, not total return. Your first investment decision is important, but the amount of money you save is much more important. Mistakes early in your journey can often be completely covered by one or two savings deposits down the line.

Don't Be a Sucker

Yes, the first investment for most people can be the most expensive. Why? Because the first-time investor usually knows the least, which means he falls prey to commission traps by brokers, insurance agents, and other salespeople. The typical first-time investor buys an insurance policy as an investment or a fully loaded mutual fund.

Some loaded mutual fund investments are sold as contracts that require monthly deposits, usually in the form of automatic chequing account debits. The debit concept is great. Automatically, without any effort on the part of the investor, money is withdrawn from his chequing account and invested for him. However, if he is buying a loaded fund, the commission usually bites heavily into the deposit before any money actually gets invested.

That Reminds Me...

I have a client who was sold a mutual fund with a 50-percent commission charge on the first year's monthly deposits. He was sold one of the most expensive investment products known to man. Fortunately for him, his tenacity and market performance prevailed and his account grew substantially as he continued his deposits. However, he said, "If I would have known there were such things as no-load mutual funds, my account might have performed a little better."

If you are a novice investor, it's difficult to prevent a smooth salesperson from selling you an investment product with heavy commissions. Salespeople are trained to sell and they are wonderful at it. Your best defence is knowledge. Chapters 7 and 8 should have helped explain the basics of the good and bad alternatives.

For your first investment, pass on anything that seems to have a high commission attached. Also, trust your gut and pass if the salesperson is using heavy-handed tactics or is trying to rush your decision.

What Should Your First Investment Look Like?

If you understand the necessary characteristics of a properly diversified portfolio, you'll find that the list of investments is quite short. Because the list is so small, you may not need an advisor to help you. If you are uncomfortable with making a decision after reading this chapter, then you may want to get some help from a fee-only investment advisor, using the questions in Chapter 9 to help select one with whom you're comfortable.

Near the end of Chapter 8, I gave you a list of optimal wealth-building portfolio characteristics. Here's a reminder of the most important elements:

➤ The portfolio is built primarily of stocks.

➤ The stocks are diversified among many different countries and industries, to help maximize return while reducing risk.

➤ The portfolio can be cost-efficiently adjusted.

One stock can't meet all these characteristics. However, if you think the above characteristics are boring and you have your heart set on buying a stock or on another investment idea, go ahead and try it. Make your mistakes now while they don't hurt so much. Go with your gut, and with a little luck you might do well.

The easiest way to design a portfolio of less than $100,000 using the portfolio characteristics listed above is with low MER, no-load mutual funds, including index funds and index-tracking stocks. Therefore, before you make your next investment decision, let's explore mutual funds again.

Treasure Tip

If you had to pick one investment idea that covered all the necessary characteristics of an optimal wealth-building portfolio, it would be a low MER, no-load mutual fund.

You Have to Meet the Minimums

All mutual funds have a minimum investment amount you must meet to initially buy shares in the fund. Therefore, you have to pay attention to minimums when you design your portfolio. If you have only $1,000 and want to get started with a mutual fund, your choices might be somewhat limited. Some funds have a $5,000 minimum, but a typical minimum investment is $1,000. If you have less than $1,000 to invest, you can either wait until you've saved that much, or find a fund with low minimums. Some funds will accept less than $1,000 if you agree to purchase at least that amount over the course of a year using monthly deposits.

Narrowing the List

Your first step should be to buy a single fund that is globally diversified. You need a fund that invests not only in Canada but in other developed and emerging-market countries. Very few funds do this well, so your list of alternatives is quite small.

If you're looking for a globally diversified fund (that invests in Canada and foreign countries), you may encounter some confusion. These funds go by different names depending on which mutual fund rating service or publication you choose. The most common title is International Funds, which includes mutual funds that invest in Canada and foreign countries. You might also find the title Global Funds, which should be the same. Regardless of what they say, make certain you know how these funds are allocated. Be sure not to mistake a foreign fund for an international fund. Foreign funds invest exclusively in foreign countries.

You should remember, too, that the federal government limits the amount you can invest in foreign securities in your RRSP portfolio. However, as we've seen, several index funds invest internationally and don't use up any of your allowed foreign content. These funds are usually called International RSP funds, and today the lowest-cost ones are offered by TD Bank eFunds (www.tdfunds.com), Royal Bank (www.royalbank.com), and Altamira (www.altamira.com). There are other non-index international funds that don't use up your allowable foreign content, but their MERs are very high, well above 2 percent in most cases.

Risk and Return

The stock market lost almost 80 percent of its value in the crash of 1929. The market did come back, but it took a few years to do so. The possibility of a crash like this is highly unlikely today. However, the risk is there. The more likely scenario is a 10- or 20-percent drop in stock prices. Many investors refer to this as a stock market "correction." The question you need to ask yourself is whether you could handle the potential damage to your portfolio. If you can accept this risk, then you are what I consider to be an aggressive investor who should focus 100 percent on stocks or stock funds diversified throughout companies all over the world.

"To Thine Own Self Be True"

Most investors overestimate the level of risk they can actually handle. Their true risk tolerance is unmasked only when an actual correction is experienced. When this happens in Wealth Levels 3, 4, and 5, it may be too late to make any adjustments. Therefore, either lean a little more to the conservative side or accept the risk of a correction. Keep in mind that you are investing for the long run.

What Kind of Return Do You Expect?

An aggressive investor should target investments with annual returns in excess of 15 percent; moderate investors should shoot for 12 to 15 percent; and conservative investors, 8 to 12 percent. Don't try to hit home runs, no matter how much risk you think you can tolerate. Investing is like baseball. It's won with base hits, not home runs. The more home runs you attempt, the more you'll strike out. However, if you're bored with base hits, go for the fence now, early in your career. When you do make a mistake, learn from it. Spend some time learning why you failed. Ask yourself:

➤ What could I have done to prevent this loss?

➤ If I had to do it all again, what would I do differently?

➤ What will I do next time to improve my results?

Take some time to learn from the loss, but don't let it discourage you. Too many people take their mistakes personally. They say to themselves, "I guess that's just the kind of investor I am." I hear them say to me all the time, "If you want something to go down, just let me buy it." This is a horrible attitude to have, and, ironically, it is a self-fulfilling prophecy. If you think this way, you better believe you'll lose money. But if you take the time to learn from your losses, you'll be all the wiser.

Treasure Tip

On your way to Wealth Level 2, if your yearly savings deposit exceeds 10 or 20 percent of your total portfolio, don't concern yourself with any possible stock market correction—at least not until after the first stage of Wealth Level 2.

Investment Ideas for the Confused and Bewildered

If you're starting to work on your portfolio, there are some key investment tools to consider: stocks, real estate, and mutual funds.

Individual Stocks

If your heart is set on individual stocks, that's great. Be sure to learn all you can about buying stocks. There are a number of books on stock picking that you might want to read. The two best authors I've found are Peter Lynch and Ben Graham. Check

Treasure Tip

Waschka's law of market corrections says selling is the worst thing you can possibly do during a correction. A correction is simply an absence of buyers amidst a flood of investors wanting to sell. If you join them, you'll completely miss the market rebound when there's an absence of sellers and a flood of buyers. Stay off the bandwagon.

your local library or bookstore. You might have heard of Warren Buffett, the multibillionaire investor. His learned comments about investing in the stock market can be found at www.berkshirehathaway.com.

Real Estate

If you decide you want to try real estate, that's also fine. Be sure to learn all you can before buying your first rental property. Property management can be a nightmare. Waking up to a tenant's call at 3 a.m. because the toilet broke is not my idea of fun. If you want to speculate on undeveloped land, just remember this is one of the riskiest investments available. Therefore, you had better make real estate your business before you make a purchase. For example, if you are a licensed real estate appraiser, then by all means focus your attention on real estate as an investment. You'll see deals before anyone else does.

Real estate is just like any other industry or business. I don't believe real estate is a better industry than any other. It has its good years and its bad, just like other industries. In the late 70s, for example, we had double-digit property appreciation almost nationwide. Banks would loan money on almost any property. Those days are long gone and we don't have that environment available anymore. It's just another industry now—one that happens to be filled with con men on TV offering "no money down" books, cassettes, and videos that lead to very little actual success. However, many fortunes have been made in the real estate market, and if you expect to make your fortune this way—go for it. Just remember one thing: no matter what industry you use to build your wealth, you had better have a passion to be the best at it. Otherwise, you won't have the desire to learn all you can about it.

Mutual Funds

I prefer to use mutual funds. They require less attention and offer a level of diversification beyond any other investment opportunity in the world. I've tried individual stocks, bonds, options, futures, real estate, and even dividend reinvestment plans (DRIPs). From the standpoint of balancing risk with returns, nothing builds wealth better than mutual funds.

Don't Spend Too Much Time Monitoring Your Investment

If you are focusing on achieving Wealth Level 2, now is not the time to look at your investments every day. There are two much more important things to focus on now: your savings amount and your investment knowledge.

The Tortoise and the Hare

Most beginning investors worry too much about picking the fastest growing investment. They focus too much on the market and not enough on minimizing expenses or meeting their target savings goal. The result is portfolio mediocrity as their unbalanced portfolio never grows significantly in size. Such investors end up with a volatile portfolio that *might* be growing at a 15-percent rate—but it doesn't really matter. Because they didn't meet their target savings goal, their account never grew very big. It's the classic tortoise-and-the-hare story. While the hare runs around frantically trying to buy the best performing stocks each month, the tortoise wins the race because he saved as much as he could each year. His returns might not be all that incredible, but his account value sure is. Try to be the tortoise, not the hare.

Invest Automatically

Most mutual funds offer an automatic debit service from your chequing account. This is a no-brainer, yet so few people take advantage of it. More than half the people I suggest this to are afraid of it. I've narrowed down the list of fears most people have of the automatic debit service:

➤ Fear of the mutual fund company taking advantage of them

➤ Fear of an invasion of privacy

➤ Fear of losing control

➤ Fear of forgetting to record the deposit in the cheque register

First, the mutual fund can't take advantage of you. Why would they jeopardize their legal status and reputation just to get a few more dollars out of your account? Second, the mutual fund can only debit a certain amount, not check your balance! Third, this service is a way to gain control over spending, not to lose control. Fourth, write a big note where you pay your bills to record the debit each month. The debit service is too easy and powerful not to take advantage of it.

Treasure Tip

Waschka's law of savings says save automatically by letting a mutual fund debit your chequing account each month.

Where to Put the First Investment

Your first investment could be purchased within an RRSP, which would allow it to grow tax-deferred. You can deduct the deposit from your taxable income; what's more important, though, is the tax-deferred growth and the almost unlimited investment alternatives to choose from. Therefore, consider your first investment going into an

133

Words of the Wealthy

A **value-oriented** manager searches for undervalued stocks priced below what the manager actually thinks they're worth. The goal of the value manager is to sell at a profit when the market realizes the stock's true value.

Words of the Wealthy

A **growth-oriented** manager searches for stocks with high earnings growth. Investors are willing to pay relatively higher prices for these stocks on the chance that they may go even higher later.

RRSP. Any of the types of investments listed here in this chapter can be purchased within an RRSP (with the exception of foreign securities, which are subject to limitations.

You could also start your own investment account for yourself (and your spouse). The first decision you'll have to make is whether or not to buy directly from a mutual fund or through a discount brokerage firm. For now, as long as you are buying only one or two funds, going with the discount brokerage firm doesn't give you much of an advantage. Later, when you own three or more funds, the discount brokerage firm will let you consolidate your portfolio into one account. This is a real time-saver. Investing directly with several different funds can be time-consuming. To buy a fund, you have to call for an application, wait for the application to arrive, fill it out, send it in, wait for them to receive it. Then they purchase the fund for you. This could take 10 days. Yet, this entire procedure can take place the same day if you have an account with a brokerage firm that offers no-load funds. Instead of getting many different statements in the mail, the brokerage firm will consolidate all your mutual funds on one statement. Instead of getting several different tax forms at the end of the year, you get one.

Remember, discount brokerage firms are somewhat limited in their list of available funds. Therefore, your favourite fund might not be on their list. You can call the firm and ask if they plan to add that fund, or you can just go directly to the fund itself. A self-directed RRSP at a discount broker will allow you to buy a range of mutual funds from various companies, and buy stocks and bonds for a reasonable commission.

Graduating to More Than One Fund

The best advice I can give any novice investor who's looking to do more is to learn all you can. Graduating from one fund to two or three requires a little more knowledge and confidence, which are easily attained through books and investment classes. If you want to learn more about mutual funds, read one of Gordon Pape's mutual fund guides. If you just can't stand this stuff, get a fee-only advisor to help you get started.

Graduating to Two Funds

Assuming you chose one mutual fund in your investment portfolio, sooner or later you're going to have enough money to diversify into two, three, or more funds. There's no magic amount at which to begin this split; it's all a matter of preference and whether or not you can meet the minimums on the funds you have selected. You want to be sure to build a mix of domestic and foreign invested funds. If you tend to be a little conservative, focus on stock funds that buy relatively large companies using a value-oriented philosophy. You might also keep your foreign fund allocation at or below the 30-percent level, which leaves 70 percent of your money domestically invested.

If you are an aggressive investor, you might want to focus on stock funds that buy stocks of relatively small companies using a growth-oriented philosophy. Your foreign allocation could be as high as 50 percent.

When you select each fund, look for a fund manager who thinks the way you do. The only way to find this out is by reading the manager's objective and philosophy in the prospectus. You might get lucky and find an article or television interview, but chances are you're going to have to do some searching. Don't worry; the next six chapters should make the search a little easier.

Graduating to Three Funds

You might consider three funds when your portfolio grows beyond $15,000. If you are a moderate-risk investor, your three-fund portfolio should look something like this:

> 35%—Small-cap domestic stock fund
>
> 30%—Big-cap domestic stock fund or index fund
>
> 35%—Foreign stock fund or index fund

Basically, you would be adding a small-cap fund to your portfolio at this point. If you are conservative, you can still use a value manager with a 30-percent or less foreign allocation. Aggressive investors can use a growth-oriented manager and up to 50-percent foreign allocation (but not within your RRSP).

You don't really need any more than six mutual funds in a portfolio. Graduating beyond the three-fund portfolio takes more time and effort. The next six chapters will help you to be more effective and efficient in that effort.

The Least You Need to Know

➤ Your first investment should meet basic portfolio characteristics, which include a focus on stocks (a stock mutual fund) that are globally diversified and cost-efficiently managed.

➤ Don't let a smooth-talking salesperson take advantage of you by selling you an expensive investment product.

➤ Learn as much as you can from your mistakes by asking yourself what you will do next time to improve your results.

➤ If you are a conservative investor, focus on value-oriented mutual funds. If you are aggressive, focus on growth-oriented mutual funds.

➤ On your way to Wealth Level 1, don't monitor your investment every day—focus on learning more about the market and maximizing your savings amount.

Chapter 11

The Investment Management Cycle

In This Chapter

➤ Real-life asset allocation strategy

➤ The most important portfolio management strategy

➤ When you should sell

Wouldn't it be great if you could make a few smart moves periodically in your investment portfolio that gave you returns way above everybody else's and the market averages? Of course it would, but unfortunately, very few people, including the highly paid investment professionals, have demonstrated an ability to do this. Just about everybody is hoping for above-average returns, but of course it's impossible for everyone to be above average.

That's why, when making changes to your investment portfolio, never lose sight of the factors that really matter over the long term. These are: proper diversification and keeping fees low.

Of course, we all like to fiddle with our investment portfolios, believing that we can get into a particular market or industry at the right time, get out of the market at the right time, or find the best company or fund to invest in by doing tonnes of research. It's fun to make decisions in the quest for higher returns. Just ensure that your decision-making doesn't alter your game plan too much, and doesn't cost you significant amounts of added commissions or fees.

There's plenty of proof that extensive research and decision-making don't translate into higher returns. The best evidence is the fact that the vast majority of mutual funds in Canada and the U.S. weren't able to keep up with the market averages during the 1990s, a period when stocks performed uncommonly well. Despite having all the best research tools and information at their fingertips, the "professional" investors fell well behind the market averages. The vast majority of U.S. stock fund managers failed to provide returns as high as the S&P 500 average annual return of about 18 percent during the decade. The average U.S. stock fund return was only about 15 percent per year. And a large majority of Canadian stock fund managers couldn't keep up with the TSE 300's average annual return of 10.6 percent in the 1990s. The funds' average return was just 9 percent. Keep in mind that several poorly performing funds were merged into better performing funds during that time, which unfairly skews the funds' results higher. In the last five years of the 1990s, the funds were more than three percentage points behind the TSE 300's average annual return of 17 percent. Except for a few lucky investors who picked the handful of funds that outperformed the indexes, it was the low-fee index fund investors who were best off.

All this doesn't mean it's impossible to make timely moves with your investment portfolio. It just means that you must be aware that it's very difficult to top the market averages. Highly educated and highly paid investment professionals all around the world are constantly trying, but very few succeed.

So read this chapter to understand some of the concepts that investors use to make decisions, but don't get carried away with constant tinkering to your well diversified, low-fee investment portfolio.

This chapter is designed to give you some ideas about building wealth through your investment portfolio. When your portfolio exceeds approximately $10,000, which is large enough to easily diversify among more than three mutual funds, you're ready to take advantage of another level of opportunity called multi-fund portfolio management. You now have the ability to add layers of diversification to your portfolio, hire a team of investment specialists, and build a synergistically profitable portfolio.

But how do you select the investments to build this portfolio? Most investors use past performance. All the fine print says not to do this, but investors do it anyway. Markets do change, meaning that your investment strategies should reflect these changes. That's what this chapter is all about: incorporating a portfolio management cycle that keeps up with the changing markets.

This chapter primarily refers to mutual funds, because that's where I spend most of my time helping my clients. However, you can use the same principles in this chapter for stock investing. It's a lot more difficult to do, but it can be done if you have the time and passion necessary.

The Portfolio Management Cycle Asset Allocation

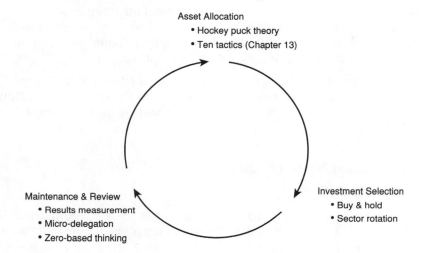

Asset Allocation
- Hockey puck theory
- Ten tactics (Chapter 13)

Investment Selection
- Buy & hold
- Sector rotation

Maintenance & Review
- Results measurement
- Micro-delegation
- Zero-based thinking

Asset Allocation

The first step in the portfolio management cycle is asset allocation, which is simply dividing your assets among several different types of investments or asset classes for the purpose of diversification and profit. An asset class can be stocks, bonds, money markets, gold, or even real estate. Asset allocation is based on the idea that a portfolio diversified among many different asset classes will incur less risk than a portfolio invested in only one class.

Throw Away Your Asset Allocation Software

There are also several very expensive software programs available that will calculate your "optimal" asset allocation based on your risk tolerances. Unfortunately, the outcome is based on years of past performances of each asset class. This means that the allocation you get assumes that the future will be similar to the past—which is simply not true. Therefore, don't waste money on these programs.

Don't Base It on Your Age

How do you know how much to place in each asset class? Most brokers and investment advisors use some type of rule to decide how an investor's assets should be allocated. The rule is usually pretty dogmatic. For example, many of them believe that an investor's bond allocation should be based on age. If you are 25, then 25 percent of your portfolio should be in bonds and 75 percent should be in stocks. If you are 80, then 80 percent of your portfolio should be in bonds and 20 percent in stocks. Remember this: the market doesn't care how old you are; it will take your head off whether you are 25 years old or 80. If you had 80 percent of your money in bonds in 1994, your portfolio got hammered, but if they were in short-term bonds, which they should be if you are 80, then you did just fine, because your bonds matured soon after.

Instead, your allocation in any type of investment should be based on your risk tolerance and how you feel about that investment, as well as on the risk you are willing to assume to meet the goals you want to achieve. You can also take into account the hockey puck theory, described next.

Base Your Asset Allocation Upon the Hockey Puck Theory

It's said that Wayne Gretzky, the most popular hockey player in the world and definitely one of the best, was asked by a reporter one day, "Wayne, I don't get it. Why are you so much better than your teammates and opponents? You are not a faster skater. You are not a quicker puck handler. You're not even any meaner. What makes you so much better?"

Wayne stopped a minute and said, "Well, most of my teammates and players skate to where the hockey puck is. I skate to where I think the hockey puck is going to be." This has nothing to do with investing, but it has everything to do with excellence in portfolio management. If you think about it for a minute, most investors don't even invest where the market is. They invest where the market has been, right? So, your goal should be to invest where the market is going, and not where it has been. You must be willing to invest your money based on what you think is going to happen. To do that, you have to understand trends. A trend is a three-, five-, or 10-year series of events that affect a niche of the world economically, politically, and socially. The most dramatic trends go on to affect the entire world.

The whole idea behind investing for profit is to position your money to take advantage of the best investment opportunities available. These opportunities are best found by focusing your attention on trends, especially the ones indicated by small revolutionary changes in the world that have the potential to

➤ Spawn new products and maybe new industries

➤ Improve the health and lifestyles of people all over the world

➤ Help emerging countries catch up with the modern world

➤ Help corporations be more productive and profitable

Therefore, instead of allocating assets the conventional way—using different asset classes—position your assets to take advantage of trends. By diversifying your money

That Reminds Me...

The current trend on everyone's lips is certainly the Internet. By the end of 1999, the stocks of many Internet companies, such as Yahoo, CMGI, Amazon.com, eBay, and America Online, had risen to astronomical levels, even as many of these companies had no profits and only modest sales. Investors were feverishly bidding up Internet stocks on the hope that the Internet will continue to transform the way people shop, do business, and communicate. Here is a fearless prediction: a handful of Internet stocks will be solid long-term performers, but it's too late to catch the big gains from the majority of Internet stocks. Many are priced so high that even years of fast-paced growth won't be enough to make their share prices anywhere near reasonable levels. Some investors argue that the old rules about net income and P/E ratios don't matter anymore. This is craziness. If a business doesn't make money, eventually it goes under.

When considering investing in Internet stocks, remember the California gold rush. Few prospectors got rich from gold, but the service industries, such as the manufacturers of Levis that catered to the needs of the prospectors, made millions. When it comes to the new frontier of the Internet, the service providers (AOL, Rogers Cable, courier companies, etc.) are a better bet than trying to pick the one-in-a-million, content-oriented companies (Amazon.com) that will be wildly successful.

among several different unrelated trends, you dramatically increase your potential for returns and reduce your risk of loss.

If you are going to forecast trends, you have to be able to develop scenarios based on events that are currently unfolding. This requires some knowledge, imagination, and a heavy reliance on the latest flow of economic data. You need all this to provide you with some hint of a realistic prediction of the future. Your prediction doesn't really have to be exactly on target; you just have to be close. It's a little like landing an airplane in the midst of a hurricane using only your instruments. It may be difficult, but it certainly beats flying completely blind.

So the first thing you do is find the most dramatic trends in the world. You can start simply by asking your spouse or parents what new things they are spending money on. You can also find trends in the news media. Instead of just listening to the news, spend time thinking about how you could profit from the events being covered. Look for statistics whenever you can (like the number of people using cellular phones or beepers, for example). Select the three to six best trends you can find and design your portfolio to take advantage of these trends. If you select unrelated trends, your portfolio will have a certain amount of diversification. You have to expect to be wrong to some degree. At least one of these trends might not develop the way you anticipated. If you diversify among several trends, your mistake won't hurt so much. You can divide evenly among the trends or weight some trends more than others. What does a trend look like and how do you find one? Chapter 13 will help you easily identify these trends.

Second, find ways to exploit trends. You can do this with individual stocks and bonds or mutual funds. The most convenient method would involve mutual funds. While the mutual fund manager focuses on the micro view of the corporate world, you have more time to focus on the macro view of the world. If you allocate your assets among these funds according to the amount of confidence you have in the trends you've selected, your portfolio will be more customized to your personality and beliefs. That's the way it should be. You should invest in what you believe in.

Why not take a minute to write down the five most influential trends in your life. Observe what you have purchased in the last several months. Look at the magazines you read, especially any trade magazines you might use in your business. What's new? What changes do you foresee? Here's a list to get you started:

➤ Advances in health care for the aging baby boomers who'll need it

➤ Advances in communications via cellular phones and pagers

➤ Growth of emerging-market countries and their communications industries

➤ The desire of aging baby boomers to travel more for pleasure as they approach the age of 50

This method of asset allocation is what I call real-life asset allocation. Most investment professionals and professors will argue that it doesn't work because it's not based on specific procedures, has no equations or formulas, and doesn't have any set guidelines. However, neither does the market!

Because of the market's tendency to continuously change, you can't expect quantifiable logic to work. If the market were quantifiable and easy to profit from, everyone would be rich! But that's not the case. Therefore, if you want to flow with the market and make any money, you have to escape from conventional wisdom and remain flexible in your strategies. Your success will be directly related to your ability to stay flexible and adapt to the changes.

Investment Selection

The second part of the portfolio management cycle is investment selection. Most people just pick stocks or mutual funds without any thought to allocation. They grab a magazine from the shelf at the grocery store checkout stand, pick a great-performing fund off the Top Picks list, call the company, and—just like that—they're invested. As soon as their fund is off the Top Ten List, they swap into another fund. This is the scary truth about investors today. They spend more time cleaning their car than they do planning their investment portfolios.

There are basically three types of fund selection strategies. These strategies work, but you cannot be dogmatic with them. You have to be flexible and adaptable to change. The market is not dogmatic, and neither should you be when investing in it. You are also going to be wrong a certain percentage of the time. When you make a mistake, first you have to be willing to admit it without taking it personally. Then, you must be proactive and correct it.

Each selection strategy is used in conjunction with your asset allocation decision. If you have decided to devote 20-percent of your portfolio to technology stocks, then you need to select one or two technology funds to fill that 20-percent allocation. These three selection techniques will help you do that: buy and hold, market timing, and sector rotation.

Buy and Hold

This is the single most common strategy used by mutual fund investors. It simply is what it says: buy a security and hold it through good times and bad. You should use the buy-and-hold strategy to build the core of your portfolio, which should, in turn, deliver stability to your overall portfolio. Core funds are rarely traded and are usually held two to four years.

When using this strategy to purchase mutual funds, a low MER is the most important factor. And you want to ensure your fund is broadly invested, not just in a few sectors. To see what stocks the fund manager has chosen, request the financial statements of the fund from the fund company. Going with funds that have a good long-term track record isn't a bad idea, either, but it by no means ensures you will get good future results.

For your core buy-and-hold funds, you must resist the temptation to sell them, even if they go on a big tear and you feel as if you should lock in the gains, or if they fall hard and you think they'll never bounce back. Buying and holding ensures you capture all of a fund's long-term returns.

Market Timing

Market timing is simply the strategy of being in the market when it is going up, and out when it's going down. This is quite a seductive strategy, but it's almost impossible to accomplish consistently over time. Market timing is also known as technical analysis, which includes primarily the study of information in the form of charts. Technical

Words of the Wealthy

Fundamental analysis is the study of the basic facts that determine a security's value. A fundamental analysis of a mutual fund includes the study of the securities within the fund, the manager, the philosophy, the expenses, and the average P/E ratio.

Words of the Wealthy

Using charts to read the price history and other statistical patterns of stocks or mutual funds is known as **technical analysis**. Many investors and most professionals use these charts to make investment decisions. A technical analyst is also known as a "chartist."

analysts attempt to predict the movement of a particular market or security based on past behaviour in similar market circumstances.

Be careful not to take this strategy to the extreme. One of my clients called me just recently and asked me to sell every mutual fund he owned and buy a money-market fund. This is the extreme. I use money-market funds to a certain degree for market timing purposes, but timing the market properly is very difficult.

Sector Rotation

Many investors use this strategy for selecting investments without even realizing what it's called or how it actually works. It's a strategy based on several theories. The first theory is that there are many markets or sectors of the market that can act independently of each other. These sectors can be industries, countries, or any specific type of security. The second theory is that there will always be opportunity in the market. (As my friend Dave Muller says, "There's always a bull market somewhere." He writes a little known monthly investment newsletter titled *Foreign Markets Advisory*. In his newsletter, Dave uses a graphic illustration that compares the performances of each country's stock market to the others. When I want to compare the stock market trends of different countries, this newsletter is invaluable. If the theory is correct that there's always a bull market somewhere, this newsletter helps me find it.) The third theory assumes that an investor is able to invest in the sectors that are performing well, and get out quickly before the trend changes direction for the worse. The fourth theory says that by maintaining a portfolio focused on the best performing sectors, over time the investors will be able to beat the market.

The illustration (page 145) shows how the theory of sector rotation works in a perfect world. After identifying a major trend and investing in the corresponding sector, the investor rides the growth of one sector (or trend) and rotates to another sector (or trend) before growth begins to slow. You can ride the growth of a sector by using mutual funds that focus on that particular sector, or you can use individual stocks. This process is repeated over time to produce above average returns. This strategy requires a lot of work, and it's very difficult to employ successfully.

Sector Rotation

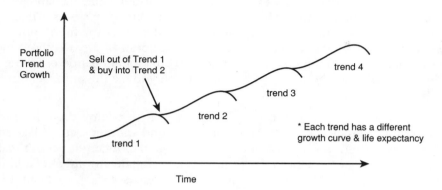

Portfolio Trend Growth

Sell out of Trend 1 & buy into Trend 2

trend 1

trend 2

trend 3

trend 4

* Each trend has a different growth curve & life expectancy

Time

You can compare this strategy of sector rotation to surfing in the ocean. First you find just the right wave, then you position yourself to take advantage of it. Before the wave crashes you against the beach or rocks, you turn back and find another wave. This strategy may seem seductive, but it is very difficult. It is a game of numbers, which means that you will fail part of the time. But with patience, research, and diversification, your winnings can cover your losses. It is not a question of "Will you lose?" It is a question of "When will you lose?" and "To what extent?" If you can win more than you lose, your portfolio will prosper. The only way to win is to buy an investment (from someone else) that you think is worth more than the money you paid. Then you must hold that investment until someone is willing to pay you more than you feel the investment is worth. Both transactions involve other people being wrong. What you are in fact saying each time you buy and sell is that the other person is wrong. That's pretty bold, wouldn't you agree? But this is only half of the boldness required. To increase your chances of profit, you have to increase your chances that the other person is wrong. The more wrong they are, the cheaper you can buy—and that means more profit for you. There are several ways to increase those chances:

1. Buy the sector that has fallen or corrected the most. What does everyone hate?

2. Buy the sector that everyone fears. What sector is somewhat new to the market?

3. Buy the sector that has the most negative media coverage. What does the media hate?

Treasure Tip

Some funds are managed by a committee instead of one manager. I prefer to have a single manager because one is usually more decisive and efficient than a committee. However, there are certainly exceptions to this rule.

145

The objective is to find the most hated or feared sectors, wait until they have hit bottom, and then buy. It's hard to know exactly when the bottom is hit. A chart can help. Check out www.bigcharts.com to chart stocks and index-tracking stocks. Check out www.globefund.com for fund information and charts. Make sure the fund's price chart verifies this bottom. What does a bottom look like? It doesn't really matter. What's important is whether or not the fund is trending upward after a long period of falling. Don't try to invest at the exact bottom. Buy the fund when you see the price trending upward.

Hold the fund until it hits a top. That's usually when everyone is talking about it or when it hits the front pages of Maclean's. Then sell it and find another sector. Make sure the fund's price chart verifies this top. What does a top look like? Again, it doesn't really matter. What's important is whether or not the fund is trending downward after a long period of rising. Don't try to sell at the exact top. Sell when you see the price begin to trend downward. As funds top out and are sold, it's important to have other funds available to buy. The perfect scenario would be to have another sector available to rotate into immediately. Therefore, you should always be on the lookout for other sectors that are beginning to trend upward.

The Flower Portfolio

All three fund selection strategies are best illustrated by the flower portfolio diagram in this section. The buy and hold strategy is used to build the core of your portfolio. Core funds are rarely traded and therefore make the base of the flower. The market timing and sector rotation strategies are used to build the next layer of sector-type funds, represented by the petals. As market trends change, so does the portfolio. If the market is underpriced or in a bull phase, the flower may have many petals. If the market is overpriced or in a bear phase, you may only see one or two petals. The core funds tend to be somewhat of a safe haven when the markets are overpriced. While the core remains intact, the petals occasionally fall off and are sometimes replaced with different petals. Therefore, the flower does change its design as the seasons of the market change.

The Flower Portfolio

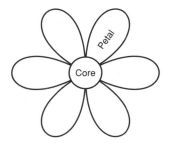

The only problem is that the seasons don't always repeat themselves each year. Core funds are normally held two to four years.

The second layer of funds (sector related) in the portfolio should be purchased based on the hockey puck theory. They are selected based on their potential ability to take advantage of a particular trend. These funds are normally held six to 18 months.

Maintenance and Review

The third phase of the portfolio management cycle—maintenance and review—is most often neglected by investors. For example, most investors have no idea how well their portfolio is performing. They try to do everything and rarely ever make transactions when they should.

Measurement of Results

At least once a quarter, you need to measure and review your portfolio's percentage performance. This can be a very difficult calculation if you are making regular deposits (or withdrawals). The easiest way to calculate your portfolio's performance for a particular period is to subtract your beginning balance from your ending balance and divide the result by your beginning balance. This will give you a simple rate of return for that period. If you've made deposits each month into your account, instead of using the beginning balance in your calculation, use an average balance. To calculate your average balance, just add up the beginning balances for each month and divide the total by the number of months. There are many more accurate, yet complicated ways to calculate your total return. These shortcuts will do for now.

That Reminds Me...

Sector funds invest in a particular sector of the stock market, such as financial services, technology, or consumer products. If you choose to invest in a sector fund, your broad-based portfolio will become "overweighted" in that sector. Essentially, you're making a bet that the sector you have chosen will outperform the overall market while you're invested in the sector. If you do choose a sector fund, keep it to a small portion of your overall portfolio, since a narrow investment increases your overall risk.

Treasure Tip

Some investment dealers publish mutual fund rankings and assessments. But these are often sponsored by mutual fund companies, who have an obvious stake in the issue. You can get more objective information from the Investment Funds Institute of Canada (www.mutfunds.com) and publications such as *The Globe and Mail* (www.globefund.com).

Words of the Wealthy

Micro-delegation is simply the delegation of the micro view responsibilities to other professionals. This strategy enables you to focus on the big picture. It also allows you to delegate the details to other people who are often better at them than you are.

Once you've done this, be sure to compare your performance to the TSE 300 market index, as well as the Morgan Stanley World Market Index. Record these indexes as often as you measure your portfolio results.

Your individual funds should also be compared to similar funds. You don't have to constantly switch back and forth between the best performing funds, but if your funds consistently underperform compared to other similar funds, then you may want to make a change. Also, if other similar funds in a sector you're heavy in begin to slow down and head south, it might mean that the trend is changing. Your fund may still be going strong, but all the other similar funds could be going down. If you know this, you can get out before your fund follows.

The Most Important Investment Strategy: Micro-Delegation

The macro view is the study of major trends around the world, while the micro view is the study of the specific stocks that take advantage of these trends. Most of the major trends can be exploited using mutual funds. If you want to focus on technology, for example, there are many funds that do so. If you do additional research, you'll find that some focus on hardware and some on software. Depending on your particular interests, you can usually find a fund that matches your specific goals. If you can't find a mutual fund that takes advantage of the trend you choose, then select several stocks that will.

Even if your passion is investing, the amount of time you have to research the world markets and the fine details that go along with them is very limited. Recognizing this limitation changed my entire outlook on investing. It brought me to the most powerful investment strategy I've ever used. I call it *micro-delegation*. If I'm going to really focus on worldwide trends, how can I expect to have the time to thoroughly study individual stocks and bonds? I couldn't answer this question, so I began to delegate the micro view responsibility to mutual fund managers. The simple purchase of a mutual fund automatically means that you have delegated the micro view responsibility to the fund manager. Since I made the decision in January 1992 to exclusively use mutual funds, the benefits have been incredible. The most important benefit went to my clients, who now have a higher potential for returns at much lower risk levels.

As outlined in the next chapter, your efforts in keeping up with the world markets and different economies will be rewarded. The 10 portfolio management tactics in Chapter 13 will help you interpret and exploit the information and market changes you'll encounter, which in turn will help you maintain sound asset allocations.

Zero-Based Thinking

As I've mentioned earlier in the book, all sell decisions should start with this question: if your portfolio were all in cash today, would you buy what you own? If the answer is no, then make the changes necessary to get to where you want to be. If the answer is yes, do nothing. Your decision should be based on your continued research of world markets and trends.

The Least You Need to Know

➤ Use the Wayne Gretzky asset allocation theory to allocate your assets among several different world trends.

➤ Build your portfolio by using several different mutual funds that position themselves to profit from the trends you feel the strongest about. Hold a core group of funds for the long term.

➤ Maintain your portfolio by focusing on the macro view of the world, while rotating portions of your portfolio to take advantage of the changing market conditions.

➤ Always ask yourself, "If my portfolio were all in cash today, would I buy what I own?" If the answer is no, make the necessary changes.

Chapter 12

Six Things You Must Have to Be a Successful Portfolio Manager

> ### In This Chapter
>
> ➤ A quick look at economic theory
>
> ➤ The best sources of investment information
>
> ➤ Charting mutual funds
>
> ➤ Unreasonable thinking

This is another chapter that will discuss the theories and lingo that professional investors use when deciding on investments. Unfortunately, you can study economic theory every day for your entire life and still not be able to predict economic developments in the future. Few predicted the sudden and sharp decline of Asia's economies in 1997, and the relentless pace of the U.S. economy throughout the 1990s amazed economists year after year.

So as you read this chapter, use the information to understand some aspects of how economies work, and how they affect markets. But don't begin to think that you will suddenly become able to predict market movements based on economic trends. Legions of professional economists make a living attempting to do this, and very few of them have accurate long-term track records.

You've Got to Know the Markets and World Economy

To really do well in the stock market, you must understand the basics of economic theory. There are many books available on this subject. For example, Steven Landsburg, an associate professor of economics at the University of Rochester, wrote an interesting book titled *The Armchair Economist* (The Free Press, a division of Macmillan, Inc.). It's easy to understand if you just take a little time to study it. A basic understanding of economics will help you to make many decisions in life, including when to buy a house, when to borrow money to start a business, and when to buy a stock or bond. It will also help to clarify the three most important aspects of economics: inflation, interest rates, and corporate earnings growth.

Inflation and Interest Rates

You need an understanding of inflation and its effect on interest rates. A basic economics book will teach you the details, if you want to get into them.

The key thing you need to understand is that the expectation of higher inflation will spur higher interest rates, and vice versa. Why? If investors anticipate inflation, they know that higher interest rates will follow, which will cause bond prices to fall. Therefore, they sell their bonds. Bond prices work on the age-old principle of supply and demand. No matter what inflation does, if a large number of investors sell their bonds at the same time, interest rates go up and bond prices fall. This is especially true for long-term treasury bonds. However, once interest rates on treasury bonds or corporate bonds approach an 8- to 10-percent yield, investors tend to sell stocks and buy bonds. Why? Think of it logically. Why would you want to own risky stocks that might (historically) have paid only 10 percent, when you can get a guaranteed 8 to 10 percent with a bond? How do you anticipate inflation and interest rate movements? Just watch the producer price index each month along with the consumer price index. (These are usually announced in major newspapers and on the national news.) The former will tell you how the latter will move in the future. We'll talk more about this in Chapter 13.

Earnings Growth: The Key to Making Money in Stocks

You also need to understand how corporate earnings can affect the stock market. Stock markets move primarily in response to the anticipated earnings growth of different companies. If the economy does well and corporations here are able to produce a higher amount of profit (earnings) than they produced last year, the stock market should do well.

The same applies to other countries around the world and their stock markets. If investors anticipate a country will grow economically, or if they see companies in that country beginning to improve their earnings, they will buy stocks there. You can make a lot of money investing in these countries if you get there before everybody else does. How do you anticipate the earnings growth of a country? Watch the economic growth, which is measured by the gross domestic product (GDP) growth rate. My favourite magazine is *The Economist. The Economist* will show you current and anticipated GDP growth rates each week. Look for the best scenario: a country that is turning around from slow or negative growth to faster, positive growth. Don't try to buy foreign stocks individually. They should only be purchased through mutual funds. If you want to focus on a particular country, look at WEBS and the closed-end funds that invest there exclusively.

Information: The Key to Wealth

You must have access to worldwide economic and market data. You can do this with a few publications or tap into the Internet. Once a week should be fine. When the market is volatile, you'll naturally want to check more often.

Treasure Tip

In your efforts to do research, don't spend too much money on subscriptions and online services. Visit your local library and see what publications are available there.

The most up-to-date investment Web sites are:

Globe Investor	www.globeinvestor.com
Globefund	www.globefund.com
Investorama	www.investorama.com
Thomson Information	www.marketedge.com
Morningstar	www.morningstar.com
Dowjones	www.dowjones.com
Wall Street Journal	www.wsj.com
U.S. Information	www.wallstreetcity.com
Quicken	www.quicken.ca

A Chart is Worth 1,000 Words

A picture is worth a thousand words and so is a chart. You can't pick a fund just by looking at its performance numbers. So what if it's up 20 percent for the year. Its price might be trending downward—and it could still be up 20 percent for the year. The only

Words of the Wealthy

Relative strength is a graphic illustration of the percentage (or fractional) difference between the price of a security and an index (or any other security). If the security and index rise and fall equally at the same time, the graph would be a straight line.

way to know this is to see a chart of its price over the past year or so. The pros use charts before buying. Why can't you? It's easy. You can find charts at several Web sites including www.globefund.com, www.bigcharts.com and www.investorline.com.

Basically, you want to look at three things in a chart: the general direction of price movement, how it relates to a market index, and volatility. First, you want to look at the general direction of the price movement. Is the stock or fund going up or down? Obviously, you want a security that is going up. Maybe it has trended downward for quite some time, but is now turning back up. This might indicate a turn-around opportunity. Second, you want to compare the stock or fund's price movement to a market index such as the TSE 300. Is the fund more volatile? Does it move with the market, or does it move somewhat independently? If you think the market is too high, you might want to find investments that move independently of the market. Third, how volatile is the security? Does the price move inconsistently up and down, or steadily across the page? If you are a conservative investor, you'll want to avoid the volatility and focus on stocks or funds that move steadily upwards. If you want to learn more about charting, read William O'Neil's book, *How To Make Money In Stocks* (McGraw-Hill, Inc.).

The Time Commitment

It takes time to make money in the market. The time you choose to spend will depend upon your passion for, and interest in, investing. Therefore, if you find yourself not taking the time, get some help. You don't have to watch the market every day, but you do have to watch it at least every month. As your portfolio grows, you'll need more time for research and decision-making. The majority of your time should be spent reading publications—and thinking. You need to follow inflation, interest rates, the stock markets, and other trends that I'll explain in more detail in the next chapter. The publications I mentioned earlier will help you to do this. The charting software I mentioned will help you keep an eye on your funds as well as others in which you may be interested.

A Little Discipline Goes a Long Way

You must have a certain amount of discipline to be a successful portfolio manager. You need the discipline to research, to know when to sell, to know when to buy, and to know when to hold.

Take the Time to Research

The changes in the market aren't always big enough to catch your attention. You have to see them take place gradually. If you don't watch the world markets and trends consistently (at least on a weekly basis), you may not see the gradual changes. If you are working on achieving Wealth Level 1 or 2, don't worry too much about the economy—focus on your savings target. However, once you reach Wealth Level 2 and you decide to manage your own money, it might help to pay attention to the world economy and stock markets. If you enjoy doing this and make this a hobby, it's easier than you think. All you have to do is read a few publications each month. *The Economist* will help you keep up with worldwide stock markets and trends. You don't have to read the entire magazine; just read what interests you. The *National Post* and *The Globe and Mail* will help you keep up with Canadian markets.

Sell When It's Time to Sell

This is the most difficult thing to do. It's easy to know when to buy, but it's really difficult to know when to sell. Here's an easy exercise we've discussed previously. Look at your portfolio once a month and ask yourself, if your entire portfolio were in cash today, would you buy what you own today? If your answer is no, make the changes necessary. Maybe you need money for another project or maybe you have a better investment idea. Whatever the case, make the changes. If your answer is yes, don't make any moves. This is what we have called zero-based thinking. I came up with this idea at lunch one day with Brian Tracy, who produced the tape series *The Psychology of Achievement*. It has helped me to develop my own "sell" discipline.

Another helpful sell discipline I use is the last half of Sir John Templeton's second law of investing. He said, "Sell at the point of most optimism." Most people call this contrary thinking. Whatever you want to call it, just do it. The investment game is won by those willing to sell when everyone else is buying like crazy.

Buy When It's Time to Buy

The best time to buy is when everyone else is selling. The first half of Sir John Templeton's second law of investing reads, "Buy at the point of most pessimism." If you have the discipline to follow this advice, you can make a lot of money in the stock market. Unfortunately, only a few investors have the guts or discipline to do it. Those who think and invest this way are called contrarians. What excites them the most is bad news because they know that investors will

Words of the Wealthy

Contrarian investors are those who invest contrary to everyone else. They buy when the market is correcting and sell when the market reaches new highs.

overreact and that, as a result, certain stock prices will fall lower than they should. That's when they buy.

Stick with Your Decision

Make your decision and stick with it until the reasons you bought the investment change. You don't have to trade a lot to achieve an above average return. This is especially true with mutual funds.

Imagination Is More Important than You Think

Albert Einstein said, "Imagination is more important than knowledge." Why do so many academically advanced investors do so poorly in the market? Do they know too much? Maybe they develop their brains but not their guts. Why do so many high school students beat investment pros in stock market contests? Your ability to process knowledge and data with an open mind is the first key to successful investment decisions. But an investor can know too much. If your knowledge limits your ability to objectively see all the possibilities, you know too much.

You Have to Be a Little Unreasonable to Be Any Good

George Bernard Shaw once said, "All progress depends on the unreasonable man." He deduced that the reasonable person adapts himself to the world. The unreasonable person tries to adapt the world to himself, and therefore changes the world for everyone. It is my belief that to be a successful investor, you must also be a little unreasonable.

First, the changes that are taking place in the world today are quite unlike the changes we've experienced in the past. They are unreasonable. They include social, economic, and political trends that most people don't even understand until they affect the local community. These changes often involve highly advanced technology that didn't even exist last year. Second, these unreasonable changes will transform the way we work, live, and think. Never before has it been so important to pay attention to what the future can bring. Third, if these changes are unreasonable, then our thinking must be unreasonable to deal with them. We're going to have to turn our normal patterns of thinking upside down—even if such thinking seems outrageous.

Companies today can design a product and put it on the shelf faster than ever, and they're getting faster every day. This means that the software or appliance you are using today will most likely be obsolete in 12 months. Someone, somewhere will come up with a better idea. That means that the company or even industry that produced the "old" product is at risk. If it doesn't stay in touch with its customer and the changes in the product, it's dead. More than ever, complete industries are now subject to forced "reengineering" at a moment's notice. Reengineering, to some, might be a new

That Reminds Me...

What if a company chooses to ignore these new changes or continues to think the old way? After years of extensive research and analysis, scientists have found that if you put a live frog in a pan of cold water and very slowly apply heat, the frog will not budge. Even after the water gets to a boiling point, the frog will not budge! It just sits there and dies. Why doesn't the frog react? Because each change in temperature is so slight that the frog continues to adjust to the water. It fails to realize that the net result of these changes should be an abrupt, energetic change in its behaviour—a new approach to new conditions. How many reasonable investors do you know that have been boiled alive as small changes in the market occurred over time, while no action was taken?

advanced product line to compete with the new model that was just introduced. Reengineering might also mean layoffs and plant closings because no one saw the trend or paid any attention to the customer. This scenario applies to all products, and no one is safe from it. The possibilities are endless. The best defence for most companies would be to distinguish themselves with outrageous customer service and extensive in-house research done by very open-minded people. Look what happened to Eaton's, the age-old Canadian department store. While the Gap and Wal-Mart invaded Canada with glitzy marketing and emphasis on customer service, Eaton's died a slow death because it didn't change with the times.

To achieve investment excellence, unreasonable thinking must be used. Successful investors today can no longer ignore the small market changes. They must be able to interpret the seemingly insignificant in order to "beat the street."

George Bernard Shaw also said, "The only person who behaves sensibly is my tailor. He takes new measurements every time he sees me. All the rest go on with their old measurements." Take new measurements often, and don't be afraid to be a little unreasonable.

You Have to Be Able to Think Creatively

Sometimes thinking differently means applying completely different logic. I like to use the phrase *creative thinking*. For example, imagine you wanted to travel exactly two kilometres while averaging 60 kilometres per hour. (You may want to write this down.)

If you averaged 30 kph during the first kilometre, how fast would you have to travel during the second kilometre to average 60 kph? Let's take out acceleration and deceleration to make it easier.

I've asked this question in my workshops for more than four years. Almost everyone answers "90 kph." They add 30 and 90 to get 120, which, when divided by two, equals 60 kph. However, this is incorrect. In this case, it is impossible to average 60 kph no matter how fast you travel. During the first kilometre, if averaged at 30 kph, two minutes are used, which is the exact required time needed to average 60 kph over the entire two kilometres. The problem here is that most people try to apply addition/division to a time/distance problem. Therefore, the answer can never be solved. Investors do the same thing every day. They try to apply three-, five- and 10-year past performance histories to a changing investment world. To beat the stock market averages in this world, you often have to ignore past performance and instead use creative thinking.

To be a successful investor, you have to look at current data (i.e., 3-, 6-, and 9-month economic data) and then project into the future any possible trends this data might show. Investment selection techniques must now be based upon these trend projections. To be any good at this, you must have a great imagination and be willing to make decisions that often fly directly in the face of conventional wisdom.

Desire and Passion Will Make You Very Wealthy

Show me an investor with passion, and I'll show you someone who's more than likely beating the market.

Those who do well in the market have a passion for it. They love the research and study that investing requires. They are natural sponges of information. They soak it all in and make decisions from the gut. They're confident and take responsibility for their mistakes. They know that mistakes are necessary for learning and improving their work. Here is a list of the most common desires I've found among wealthy people:

➤ A desire to learn

➤ A desire to be a proactive investor

➤ A desire to learn from mistakes

➤ A desire to beat the market

➤ A desire to manage risk

You can't force yourself to have these desires. Your interests may lie in a completely different field. If this is the case, don't worry about it. Just find someone who does have these desires and hire her to help you manage your portfolio.

The Least You Need to Know

➤ Understand the basics of economic theory.

➤ Focus on the best business publications and take advantage of the information available to you on the Internet.

➤ Use charting services to observe and compare fund performances with one another.

➤ Develop the discipline it takes to sell at the point of most optimism and buy at the point of most pessimism.

➤ Use your imagination. Knowledge is important, but your imagination will make you more money.

Chapter 13

My 10 Favourite Portfolio Management Tactics

In This Chapter

➤ Using interest rates to predict bond prices

➤ Taking advantage of panic attacks

➤ How the economic cycle can make you money

➤ The baby boom generation and stock market boom

➤ Natural and forced market inefficiency

If you ever want to achieve Wealth Level 3 using your investment portfolio, you need to be better than the average investor. This chapter will show you 10 tactics that will help you make investment decisions. These tactics are primarily mental mindsets, and while they'll help you think strategically about investment decisions, they can't guarantee above average results. They are like binoculars through which you can view the investment world.

Don't get carried away with making predictions about the economy, interest rates, or trends. Always keep a core group of broadly diversified funds or stocks in your portfolio that you never plan to sell (until retirement). Use a small portion of your portfolio for switching into different funds and following trends, if you want to take a shot at above-average returns.

Today, knowledge is power. For all practical purposes, it has become the most powerful tool in the world. Very few people realize this, however, and fewer understand it. It's been proven throughout history that whoever knows how to harness and use the most powerful tools has the potential to be wealthy beyond their dreams. Therefore, you must first focus on harnessing knowledge and information (which I covered in Chapter 11). Then you have to know how to use it. Specifically, you have to know how to think—and that's what this chapter is all about.

I have designed 10 portfolio management tactics that are essentially 10 different ways of looking at information. These are simply ways of thinking, or methods of looking at the world. They are also funnels of thought through which information is poured and processed into a more useful form. Their purpose is to help you discover and better understand the magnitude of specific trends in the world. These tactics will also help you to see each individual trend from many different perspectives. The more you understand these trends, the better chance you have of profiting from them in your ongoing efforts to build wealth.

With the growth of the Internet and other forms of media such as cable television, information is more easily accessible than ever before in the history of time. That's exciting. However, accessing the information isn't enough. You have to know how to process it. Your mind can be your greatest asset; it can also be your greatest liability. Here are 10 tactics to improve your investment mind.

Interest Rate Tactic

Bonds produce a fixed rate of cash flow (income) that investors are willing to buy for a certain amount of money. For example, if you bought a newly issued 30-year government bond at $1,000 and it yields 7 percent, you would get a $70 yearly fixed cash flow until the bond matures. If inflation dropped dramatically, interest rates would also fall. Therefore, let's say the government, a year later, is issuing the same 30-year treasury bond, but now it's paying a yield of only 5 percent, which is a $50 yearly fixed cash flow. If the same bond is only paying $50 now, what would *your* 7 percent bond be worth? It's paying two percentage points higher (or $20 more per year), so it's got to be worth more, right? Yes sir, your bond's worth more money. If you sold it, you would receive more than the principal you invested. How much more? By using certain yield-to-maturity formulas or a simple *bond yield book*, you can calculate how much more. You can find bond yield books at your local bookstore or library. Bonds do fluctuate in price over time; however, at maturity, that price fluctuation stops and the bond matures at its face value.

The most important thing to understand is how bond prices are affected by changes in interest rates. Let me explain using a seesaw. If you put interest rates on one side of the seesaw and bond prices on the other, you can see that when interest rates go up, prices of bonds currently trading in the market go down, and vice versa.

Notice how the seesaw is lopsided. This is to show the effect interest rates have on bonds with different maturities. A five-year bond (a bond that will mature in just five years) will fluctuate much less in price than a 30-year bond. The longer the maturity, the bigger the potential swing in price.

Interest Rate Seesaw

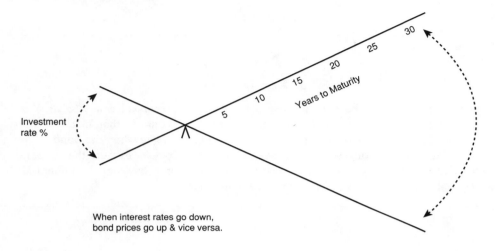

Investment
rate %

Years to Maturity

5   10   15   20   25   30

When interest rates go down,
bond prices go up & vice versa.

That Reminds Me...

One of the most important and influential forces in the stock and bond markets is the rate of interest paid on the 30-year Canada bonds—bonds issued by the federal government that mature in 30 years. When you hear someone mention the "bond market," he is specifically referring to the price movements of this particular bond. All other bonds seem to fluctuate in price according to the movements of the 30-year Canada bond, as do interest rates such as mortgage, GIC, and money-market rates.

Now that you understand this tactic, what do you think interest rates will do in the next 12 to 18 months? If you think they will fall, you might want to invest in the longest-term treasury bond or bond fund you can find. However, if you think rates will rise, you might want to avoid longer-term bonds altogether and invest in very short-term bonds (or even a money-market fund, which is considered to be the "shortest" short-term bond fund). If you are investing for the long term, don't worry about the maturity of the bond. Regardless of whether you select a 30-year bond or a one-year bond, these are liquid securities or tools that can be used to profit from short-term

That Reminds Me...

One of the best places to be when interest rates fall is in *zero-coupon treasury bonds*, also known as strips or zeros. These are bonds that are sold at a discount to their maturity; that is, you buy the bond at a particular price, then receive its full value when the bond matures. The zeros with longer-term maturities are the most volatile, because they offer no interest and only a principal payment at maturity. It is cheaper to buy these bonds individually, but you can also purchase them through a mutual fund.

moves in interest rates. For the purposes of this tactic, never buy these with the intention of holding them until maturity. Interest rates normally trend up (or down) over a period of at least a year. Therefore, I'm not suggesting that you make trades much more often than once a year.

Panic Cycle Tactic

The stock market has taught us over the years that its movements can rarely be explained or justified. The knee-jerk movements in the market (especially like the big one-day sell-off in 1987) have little to do with logical fundamental calculations. The most important discovery I have made during my 14 years of investing has been that market movements have more to do with emotion than with rational thinking.

I often refer to the market as "Mr. Market." When you go to Mr. Market's house, you never know what to expect. He's emotional, temperamental, and subject to wild mood swings. The headlines one week may be negative on interest rates. The next week it might be the trade deficit. Most major news coverage with a negative outlook causes Mr. Market to think a crash is coming. If you rely on Mr. Market for advice, as most people do, you'll follow in his footsteps and be persuaded to sell.

Then, out of the blue, good news will appear. It may be an earnings announcement or lower interest rates. It doesn't really matter, it's good news and that's what counts. Mr. Market jumps for joy and buys stocks like crazy. Most investors, just like clockwork, jump right in with him. Hey, the market's going up—can you blame them?

There's just one small problem with this story. Mr. Market and his followers never make much money. At best, if they are lucky, they might equal the averages. The biggest reason is that most stocks seem to be bought at their high. Plus, the excessive transactions necessary for this strategy cost a lot of money.

The irony here is that the true way to make money and build wealth is to do just the opposite of what Mr. Market does. Whatever he hates or whatever he is selling is more than likely what you need to be buying. This will help ensure that you are buying at the lower price. Remember, Mr. Market has loads of money. If you can buy what he might want later, you will be rewarded. The reverse is also true. Once everyone in his gang is buying, you need to be selling. This will help ensure that you are selling at the higher price.

I call this tactic (also known as the contrarian theory) of doing the opposite of what Mr. Market does the *panic cycle tactic*. It's the most powerful tactic in this chapter because it offers the most potential for profit. It also requires the largest amount of guts and faith.

First, being able to identify the point of most pessimism (panic) or optimism (euphoria) is almost impossible. However, you don't have to be exact, you only have to be close.

Second, when you really get close to the point of most pessimism, buying what everyone tells you not to buy isn't exactly easy. The last thing your friends or advisors are going to do at that time is suggest that you buy. The opposite is also true. When you get close to the point of most optimism, when everyone is buying like crazy and telling you to do the same, the last thing you're going to want to do is sell. (However, you might want to sell and take a profit, especially if you bought at a much lower price.)

The pendulum illustration in this section clarifies how the panic cycle works. You can apply this to individual stocks, bonds, industry sectors, countries, geographic regions,

Panic Cycle Pendulum

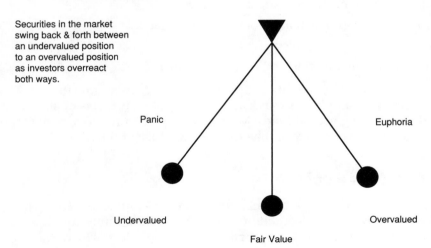

Securities in the market swing back & forth between an undervalued position to an overvalued position as investors overreact both ways.

Panic

Euphoria

Undervalued

Overvalued

Fair Value

and styles of investing. You can even apply it to real estate. The market pendulum swings between panic and euphoria. The middle equilibrium position of the pendulum represents fair value. Because investors tend to overreact, securities tend to be over- or underpriced.

Ask yourself this question: "What is everyone panicking over today? What does everyone hate to invest in now?" It's not always easy to find something everyone hates; it may take some time. But you'll find it eventually.

Industry and Country Growth Tactic

This tactic involves the search for industries or countries that indicate new growth prospects, and the search for stocks or mutual funds that can profit accordingly. What you want to find is an industry or country that is in the early stages of a new wave of growth. Here is a list of the best industry growth opportunities:

➤ New industries in their early growth stages

➤ Mature industries that develop new products

➤ Mature industries going through a financial reorganization

➤ Mature industries going through a mission reorganization

➤ Mature industries going through a management reorganization

An example of the first is certainly the Internet, which has made a lot of people wealthy.

Here is a list of the best country or regional growth opportunities:

➤ Emerging-market countries in their early growth stages

➤ Emerging-market countries adopting capitalism

➤ Developed countries experiencing economic cycle changes

➤ Countries establishing new governments

➤ Countries with falling inflation and economic growth

A great example of the first opportunity is China. Each one of these growth opportunities is also an example of a trend, and you can take advantage of almost every single one of them by using mutual funds. Most of these growth trends are long term, which means you often have plenty of time to take advantage of them.

Economic Cycle Tactic

This tactic is based on the cycle of economic expansion and contraction. It requires you to estimate the economy's current condition and the most likely future condition. You can do this by estimating the growth of the gross domestic product, which is

The Economic or GDP Cycle

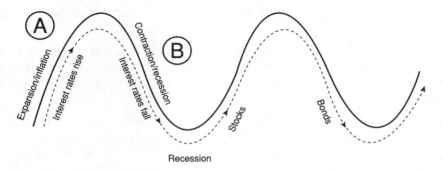

announced monthly in most financial newspapers. The actual growth rate tells you what has happened. You have to guess what you think will happen. This is not an exact science, but you can make estimates using certain economic data. An economic expansion is made up of increased employment, consumer spending, increased corporate borrowing, and corporate earnings growth. An economic contraction (recession) is the opposite. The easiest way to predict economic expansions and contractions is to watch the monthly index of leading indicators. This index is made up of 12 leading economic indicators that move in advance of the business or economic cycle. If the index is rising, you can more than likely expect a growing economy. The opposite is also true.

Once you've made estimates, then you make asset allocation decisions (deciding what percentages of your portfolio to put in which types of investments) based upon where you think we are in the economic cycle. The economic cycle is best illustrated by plotting the growth rate of the gross domestic product (GDP). In the illustration in this section, you can see what this cycle looks like in a somewhat perfect world.

As you can see, at certain points in the cycle bonds perform well; at others, stocks do well. If you know the current position of the economy on this curve and understand how different securities react to certain points in the cycle, you know how to allocate your portfolio.

For example, when the economy expands (Area A), interest rates usually go up and bond prices fall.

Words of the Wealthy

The **gross domestic product (GDP)** is the total value of goods and services produced by a country during a year. The GDP's rate of growth is much more popular in the news than the actual total GDP number. When plotted on a graph, this growth rate illustrates the country's economic cycle.

Therefore, you may not want to own long-term bonds. At a certain point in the expansion, as interest rates on bonds become more attractive, stock investors tend to sell stocks and buy bonds. This may cause the stock market to do poorly. Therefore, at some point you might want to build a position in money-market funds.

When the economy contracts (Area B), interest rates fall and bond prices rise; it's a great time to own long-term bonds. At some point during the contraction, stock investors will anticipate a turnaround in the economy and begin to buy stocks—even as the economy continues to do poorly.

So when is a good time to own stocks? Stocks tend to do very well when a contracting economy is predicted to turn expansionary. They continue to do well until interest rates are predicted to go up. Notice that in both cases, I said "predicted." Investors usually don't wait to see the actual economic change. They make moves in anticipation of these economic changes. Therefore, stocks prices often move well in advance of economic data.

Market Cycle Tactic

At any given point in time, the overall stock market can be considered too high, too low, or just right. There are a lot of ways to measure this specifically. It's not enough to just say the market is up 25 percent in 10 months. Relative to 10 months ago, yes, the market could be too high. However, relative to corporate earnings, the market prices could be low.

How do you measure the market's price relative to corporate earnings? You have to look at the average P/E ratio of the major indexes each week in publications such as *The Globe and Mail's Report on Business* and the *National Post*. A market P/E of 20 or more traditionally was considered high, and meant stock prices could fall. But during the late 1990s, North American Market P/E ratios have climbed past 30, with investors giddily expecting corporate earnings to continue rising strongly.

Words of the Wealthy

The **P/E ratio** is the price of a stock divided by the yearly earnings per share. It is the price of a stock relative to its earnings, which is important to know when you compare one stock to another. It is also important in determining if a stock is under- or overpriced relative to other stocks.

If you consider the market to be overpriced, you might want to be conservative and focus on value-oriented stocks—stocks that have already corrected or fallen in value. This strategy is very conservative—when stock prices fall, value-oriented stocks seem to fall less than the average. You might even begin building a position in a money-market account. Why? If you are right and the market makes a correction, you will have some of your assets protected in the money-market account, and you'll have money to invest at lower prices. If you are wrong and the market doesn't correct, you'll still be participating.

If you consider the market to be underpriced or fairly valued, you want to be fully invested.

There are other ways to measure the market, such as the average market-to-book value and the average dividend yield of the market indexes.

Demographic Tactic

Demographics affect the market more than most people realize. One of the most significant demographics in this century has been the effect of the baby-boom generation on our economy. It is important to understand the ripple effect this wave of births has caused. The baby-boom generation is 80-million strong in North America.

Boom Bust & Echo by David K. Foot looks at the impact of demographics, particularly of the aging baby boomers, on the economy and on society. As the boomers move into their 40s and 50s, the prime investing years, they are having and will continue to have a tremendous impact on financial markets in North America. Foot writes of Canada, "By 2006, the entire 9.8-million-strong baby-boom generation will be in the 40-to-60 group of savers."

As this group moves into retirement, they will have more time and expendable income for leisure and entertainment, such as golf, concerts, and travel. The fitness, health-care, and pharmaceutical industries will also likely be positively affected. But keep in mind that once in retirement, the baby-boomers will likely favour bonds and treasury bills over equities, at least for a substantial portion of their portfolios. Consequently, equity markets could slow down considerably.

Information Gap Tactic

The information gap is the gap in time between a newsworthy event and the time when the public recognizes the event. The wider the gap, the bigger the profit potential. Whether you invest in the market or own a business, you have to make educated assumptions based on information.

Successful investors know the cycle of research:

1. Study information that you gather.
2. Make assumptions about the future.
3. Test your assumptions.
4. Measure results.
5. Gather more information.
6. Make adjustments.
7. Test again.

8. Measure results.

9. Gather more information.

10. Test again.

The quality of information you gather can significantly affect your outcome. Therefore, your goal must be to continually put yourself in front of the best quality information available.

Knowledge of this gap alone gives you several advantages. First, we know that mainstream media enjoys covering blood, guts, and conflict. Stories such as the North American Free Trade Agreement (NAFTA), the Turkish stock market hitting over 200 percent in 1993, and post-health-care reform in 1995 were all given a much lower priority.

Second, we know that the public tends to focus its attention on poor quality media—usually sensational journalism. People seem more interested in the two-headed Martian baby than in the economic events taking place in Singapore. Only a fraction of the public reads high quality publications such as *The Economist,* The *National Post*, or *Forbes*. They are the only ones who get to take advantage of this knowledge. The reality, in my opinion, is that even fewer people take the time or have the imagination to project this knowledge into the future.

The goal, therefore, is to narrow your gap by being an avid reader of high quality information. Narrowing your information gap is all about getting the information first, before the rest of the public sees it. To profit from narrowing the gap, you must act. Remember that *not* acting can sometimes be a good idea, too.

Technology Gap Tactic

The technology gap is the gap between the best technology *available* today and the technology currently *in use* today. The bigger the gap, the bigger the profit potential. The technology gap can be applied to countries, industries, and individual companies. Technology in its simplest definition is the key to efficiency and, ultimately, profits. The profitability of most companies today has a lot to do with the level of technological sophistication in place. If a company, industry, or country installs or incorporates a higher level of technology, its efficiency should improve, and increased profitability should follow. Therefore, if you identify companies, industries, or countries that are (for whatever reason) using out-of-date technology, you might find an opportunity.

The key is to invest in entities that can benefit the most from improved technology. Small improvements in technology can exponentially increase productivity and efficiency. This is the name of the game in the '90s. Where are the biggest gaps right now? They could be in the following areas:

➤ **Technology industry** Consumers who do not have cable or other high-speed connection to the Internet. The technology is there, but the majority of consumers are still not high-speed connected.

➤ **Health care** New drug therapies. We have the technology to cure so many diseases, yet certain areas of the world, such as the emerging-market countries, are just now getting the benefits of these drugs.

➤ **Entertainment** Surround-sound, virtual reality. We now have the technology to produce theatre-quality sound in every living room, and the price of the equipment is dropping dramatically. Yet the percentage of homes with these systems is still quite low.

➤ **Emerging-market countries** Building infrastructure and basic industries. We have the technology to build extensive infrastructures and basic industries for cities and countries, yet many of the emerging-market countries have yet to do so.

Inefficient Market Gap Tactic

Whether you agree or not, all investment markets, to some degree, are inefficient. The inefficient market gap measures this level of inefficiency. Specifically, the inefficient market gap is the difference between a market's current level of efficiency and its ideal level of efficiency. This is, of course, impossible to measure exactly. I'm referring to a more subjective measurement—certainly quantifiable, I'm sure. But for our purposes here, I want to keep it simple.

The efficiency I'm referring to is the ease with which information upon which investment decisions are made flows to the public. If there were an even distribution of all relative information about a particular market to the entire investing public, you would have a perfectly efficient market.

An efficient market assumes, first, that there is an even distribution of all information to the public. Second, it assumes that the public can make investment decisions based on this information quickly and efficiently. Third, it assumes that these decisions can be made with no restrictions.

As you can probably imagine, a perfectly efficient market is not only hard to profit from, but also quite boring. If it's perfectly efficient, there's no way you can strategically take advantage of it. Therefore, your chance of return is the same as anyone else's. So, you want to look for pockets of inefficiency—where you can strategically take advantage of a market.

There are two basic types of inefficiencies: *natural* and *forced*. Natural inefficiency occurs in the market when information is distributed chaotically. Improper information distribution can include:

➤ Distorted or exaggerated information

➤ Lack of information

➤ Incorrect information

➤ Misunderstood information

The most commonly occurring natural inefficiency I see in the market is obscure and forgotten stocks. These stocks are followed very little by the big multinational brokerage firms and followed even less by the media (at least positively). There are many of these stocks out there, but only a few are worth investing in.

The best way to take advantage of these is to hire the best value-oriented stock pickers in the world. With all the mutual funds available now, this is relatively easy to do.

The second type of inefficiency is forced inefficiency. There are very few examples of this, but I have a feeling that with more government regulation, there will be many forced inefficiencies coming this decade.

Words of the Wealthy

A **junk bond**, also known as a high-yield bond, represents an IOU issued by a company whose ability to repay its interest and principal in a timely manner depends on the economy, and on its ability to sell its products or services. Standard & Poors as well as Moody's Investment services offer corporate bond ratings. A junk bond is any bond with a rating below BBB.

The best example I can give is the junk bond market in the early 1990s. Back in the days of Michael Milken and Drexal Burnam Lambert, (the late '80s) junk bonds were considered evil. Once loved by many insurance companies, these bonds became the enemy of all insurance companies and many institutional investors.

Have you seen the commercial showing a wrecking ball swinging toward a building while a voice says, "Back in the '80s, most insurance companies invested in junk bonds." The ball hits a building and takes an enormous hunk of concrete and steel with it. In the next scene, the same ball is falling toward a similar building while the voice says, "However, we only invested in investment-grade bonds." Then the ball hits the building and explodes—while the building stays intact.

This is an illustration of forced inefficiency. Because of events in the past and the resulting new written policies, most (if not all) insurance companies cannot purchase non-investment-grade corporate bonds, otherwise known as junk bonds. But *you* can! And the minute your junk bond becomes investment grade, insurance companies will trip over themselves to buy it. Therefore, once the junk bond gets a more attractive credit rating, the market for the bond is much more efficient. But until that point, the inefficiency is there.

That Reminds Me...

You don't have to buy individual junk bonds anymore. All you have to do is find a good junk bond (high-yield bond) fund.

The Weekly Top-10 Tactic

I personally believe that a list of the top-performing mutual funds in the past 10 years is useless information. The world economy is completely different from what it was 10 years ago. However, I do keep an eye on the top-10 list for the month. By watching the top-performing funds and stocks list each month, I get an idea of both the leading and laggard industries or sectors in the market. Why is this important?

If a mutual fund or stock from a particular sector is new to the leader's list, it may indicate an opportunity. This is especially true if this same sector has been on the laggard list in the recent past. Likewise, if an industry that was previously growing is new to the laggard list consistently for a few weeks, it might indicate a correction in that industry.

I also use these lists to compare my sector fund's performance to other similar sector funds. If I see a fund in a similar sector hit the laggard list, I immediately begin to watch other similar funds. As other funds in the same sector begin to correct, I tend to sell in anticipation of a correction in that industry. Because the funds with less quality management tend to fall first, you may have a chance to sell before the correction.

You can find a list of the top-performing funds last month in the business pages and on the Internet. Check www.globefund.com for performance data, reports, and charts.

The Least You Need to Know

➤ Keep your eyes on the economic cycle, interest rates, and the market's "feeling" toward inflation.

➤ Look for what most investors are panicking about and consider investing in it.

➤ When you think the market is overpriced, put some money in a money-market fund.

➤ Always keep a core group of broadly diversified funds or stocks that you never plan to sell under any circumstances. Designate a small portion of your portfolio for trading and switching funds.

Chapter 14

The Laws of Successful Portfolio Management

In This Chapter

➤ What 10 years of investment experience can teach you

➤ The investment laws that can make you rich

➤ What it takes to be a successful investor

➤ The secret to wealth

➤ A special note to brokers and advisors

➤ Eliminating all unnecessary fees and commissions

It takes years to learn how to be a successful investor. Some people rely strictly on their own experience. Others read books and learn from others. I've found that the most successful investors do a little of both. By studying the experiences of others, you can save a lot of valuable time.

Learning from others who have gone before you can help speed up the learning process and prevent years of mistakes. I know this from my own experience. I've always said that if you want to be good at anything, go find the people who are the best at it and model after them. I may not be the best investor, but I sure have learned a lot from some of the best investors in the world. This chapter is a list of investment laws I've learned from others, as well as on my own. I've also summarized a few laws I've mentioned in earlier chapters.

Waschka's Laws of Investing

These strategies and philosophies have taken me more than 10 years to find, refine, and develop. I hope they are as profitable for you as they have been for me and my clients.

Know When You're Being Sold

About 90 percent of the investment advice you will hear or read in your lifetime is marketing related. As in most businesses today, most people in the investment industry want to sell you something. It may be a subscription, a security, or an insurance policy. Whatever it is, just be careful to evaluate the facts and disregard the marketing fluff before buying.

Stand on the Shoulders of Giants

I've said this before, but it's so important. Take advantage of other people's talents whenever you can. At the very least, learn from them. Sir Isaac Newton once said, "If I have seen further, it is because I stood on the shoulders of giants." He was giving credit to all the mentors and philosophers that came before him. I do the same thing as an advisor and investor. I first select specific themes that I think will be profitable during the next five years. Then I hire "Orville Redenbachers" (fund managers) to help. Remember Orville Redenbacher's wisdom, "Do one thing and do it better than anyone else." The fund manager who is targeting Hong Kong, Malaysia, and Singapore will know more than you and I will about that region. He travels there, knows the language, and will find opportunities years before we would from here in Canada.

What You Don't Know Can Really Hurt You

If you don't know that the investment you're making will cost you 8.5 percent and that there's no secondary market for it, it's going to hurt. If you don't do your homework, you may not realize it until it's too late.

If It Sounds Too Good to Be True, It Probably Is

This says it all. How many times have you been suckered into something that turned out really bad? I know I've fallen victim more than a few times.

If you want to substantially reduce the chance of getting your financial hide skinned, learn to separate the wheat from the chaff before you invest. Look for all the possible signs of deception: hidden fees, misleading information, absence of disclosure documents, and conflicts of interest.

Accept Risk, but Learn How to Manage It

Risk managed properly can be your key to wealth. Return is what you get for your willingness to assume risk. Learn how to manage it through diversification and market knowledge.

Always Be Prepared for the Stock Market to Go Down

Most investors live in fear of a correction. Some worry about it more than others. The successful investors I know focus on the long term and seem to welcome an occasional correction. They see corrections as buying opportunities.

Be Proactive

Don't just throw your money in a fund. Do some of your own research and make investing your hobby. If you have to, consider getting some help from a fee-based advisor.

Know the Difference between Rumour and Reality

Don't use rumours to invest. Most of them are wrong. If they are even remotely close to factual, it's probably too late to do anything. Do your own research before you invest any money.

Treasure Tip

Avoid going for quick gains. You might be tempted to sell out of a fund that has quickly gone up 25 percent. Don't bother. The big gains are made over long periods of time—years or even decades.

Recognise Conflicts of Interest When You See Them

Find out how your source of advice or information gets paid. Most financial advisors are paid commissions to sell funds by the fund companies, through the funds' MERs.

Wealth Warning

Seek to be your own financial advisor. If you feel you need help, find someone you trust highly, and know how much they make from you.

Focus First on Value, Then on Costs

A great deal of this book has been dedicated to reducing your investment costs. However, it would be a shame for you to know the cost of every investment, yet completely overlook the value each offers. Some funds may have larger than average fees, but may well be worth

Treasure Tip

The Canadian investment industry is changing rapidly. Companies are finally responding to investors' demands for low-MER, no-load funds. The cost of maintaining a self-directed RRSP and other invest-ments accounts is a fraction of what it used to be, or nothing at all. Take advantage of these changes!

the extra expense due to the fund's focus on areas where do-it-yourself or index investing is difficult, such as small-cap stocks or emerging-market stocks.

Focus on What You Can Control

There are two sets of variables in the world of wealth/investing: Those we can control and those we cannot.

We cannot control the price of a stock in our portfolio, but we can control the amount of money we save/invest or spend. Most investors focus on the stock market—which is completely out of our control—while only a few focus on what they can control. The few that focus primarily on controlling their savings/investment and spending dollars tend to be increasingly wealthier.

Don't Sell in a Quick Correction

Selling is the worst thing you can possibly do during a brief stock market correction. A correction is simply an absence of buyers amidst a flood of investors wanting to sell. If you join them, you'll completely miss the market rebound when there's an absence of sellers and a flood of buyers.

That Reminds Me...

Here is some great advice for brokers and advisors, which I always keep in mind: Your clients and prospective clients aren't idiots. They are your parents, your relatives, and your friends and many are sharp investors. At first glance, they may not seem all that experienced, but if you try to feed them a bunch of garbage, they'll know it. Treat them with the respect they deserve. Teach them all you can, and take good care of them. If you do, you'll be reward-ed with success.

Avoid Custodian Fees

A custodian fee is a yearly expense charged to your account by the brokerage firm (or custodian) simply for having the account open. Not all firms charge custodian fees—especially the discount brokerage firms—if you keep a certain minimum balance. The brokerage firms justify the fee by offering services such as cash management accounts. These accounts allow the investor to hold all securities in one account, which can include a money-market account, into which all credit balances (extra cash) are automatically swept into a money-market fund (or interest-bearing account). This usually happens on a weekly, if not daily, basis. This is called the "automated feature" of the account.

The last main feature of the account is margin capability. If your cash management account has securities but no available cash/money-market balance, you can still write a cheque and borrow against (margin) your securities. You'll pay interest on that loan, but the rate is usually reasonable.

Buy Closed-End Funds that Sell at a Discount

Closed-end funds are mutual funds that offer a set amount of shares when they are initially offered, after which they are openly traded like stocks on the stock exchanges. What makes them so unique is the difference between their market price and actual net asset value price (NAV—what they are actually worth per share). If the market price is higher than the actual NAV, then the fund is selling at a premium. If the market price is lower than the actual NAV, the fund is selling at a discount. If you want more information about these funds, look in Chapter 8 under Closed-End Funds.

Any premium you pay on a closed-end mutual fund is like adding another potential expense item to your portfolio. Therefore, only buy them when they offer a discount to their net asset value. Since these mutual funds are traded like stocks on the exchanges, they don't necessarily trade at their actual net asset value. Due to the emotional nature of the stock market, these funds often trade at prices below the actual value of the fund portfolio. They also can trade at prices above their net asset value—that's when you want to avoid them. These funds give the internationally minded investor access to most of the world's individual stock markets, often at bargain basement prices (discounts). For example, the Latin American Discovery Fund (LDF) traded at an average 96 cents on the dollar in 1993, and had a total return of 112 percent for the year. That's *very* nice.

Avoid Limited Partnerships

Stay away from investment products such as limited partnerships or anything not traded on the open market. These are typically illiquid, very expensive, and difficult to accurately price. The successful investors I know avoid these—you should, too.

Avoid Buying on Margin for Extended Periods

Brokerage firms will allow you to borrow money against your securities. The rate of interest you will pay is usually competitive with bank rates. This service can be very handy if you are fully invested and need money on a short-term basis. However, on a long-term basis, it's not a great idea. Borrowing money to invest in the stock and bond markets over a long period is too expensive, and just not worth the risk.

Never, Never, Never Invest Just for the Tax Savings

If you doubt my wisdom, just ask any wealthy individual over the age of 45 about tax-sheltered investing and limited partnerships. Your first and second priorities of investing should be profit and proper management of risk (or capital preservation). My first long-run priority has to be not to lose my client's money. My second priority—a very close second—is profit. If you manage your own money, you might reverse the order of these two. However, never make tax savings one of the top two priorities. Until we have absolute zero-tax shelters or loopholes, there will always be a "tax advantaged investment product" that will offer to save you tax dollars. These are usually very expensive and have little or no profit potential. Avoid these!

Don't Buy from Strangers

Never buy an investment over the phone from someone you do not know. If the investment sounds good, ask for references and do your homework.

Wealth Warning

Everything is negotiable. If your brokerage firm wants to charge you fees to keep a certain account open, why not ask them to waive it to keep your business? The worst they can say is 'no.'

Take Advantage of Breakpoints

Focus on larger transactions when possible for breakpoint discounts. Some mutual funds have lower MERs for big investments. For example, the Royal Bank U.S. Index Fund has a maximum MER of 0.5 percent for most investors, but only 0.3 percent for investments of $250,000 or more.

Other Investment Laws Revisited

The second section of this chapter is designed to summarize other key investment laws presented earlier in the book. These are vital to the wealth-building process and I thought you might benefit from having them listed again for review.

There's Always a Bull Market Somewhere

There are too many investments doing well to stay in something that's going down.

The Market Is Full of Inefficiency

Where there's inefficiency, there is profit potential.

Be an Unreasonable Investor

Try to think differently, with more imagination and creativity than do other investors.

Your First Investment Must Do It All

If you are investing less than $5,000, can accept some volatility, and can do without the money for at least four years, you should start with a mutual fund that invests all over the world. Choose the one investment that meets all your criteria.

Understand No-Load Mutual Funds vs. Load Funds

There are two kinds of open-end mutual funds—those that have commissions or "loads" and those that do not. All mutual funds have management fees (average is about 2.3 percent), but only load funds have extra commission charges to pay the broker or pay for advertising. By doing a little more of the legwork yourself, you can save as much as 8.5 percent on your purchase. Avoiding a commission means more of your dollars are actually invested. Avoiding high MER funds enhances long-term returns.

Consolidate Accounts

If you like buying no-load funds, but you don't like multiple statements, multiple phone numbers, and doing business by mail, you may want to contact a discount brokerage firm.

Treasure Tip

After every market correction, there's an opportunity to buy an investment at an undervalued price. And vice versa: after every major market rally, there is an opportunity to sell and take a profit. Most investors overreact as much in a negative direction as they do in a positive direction. For example, what is hated the most often seems to be quite popular later. Inefficiency breeds opportunity.

Start an RRSP

Especially if you are self-employed, this is certainly the least expensive qualified retirement plan to start and maintain. The sooner you start, the better. Self-directed RRSPs give you great flexibility.

Never Use Life Insurance for Investment

Life insurance policies were never intended for investment.

Be Careful Purchasing Mutual Funds in December

Most mutual funds issue capital gains distributions in December. If you own the fund on the day of record (the official day the shareholder is given the dividend), you are given the capital gain—which means you pay the tax on a gain from which you might not have benefited. This doesn't apply to funds held inside your RRSP, since the gains aren't taxed.

Check Twice for All Fees and Commissions

When you purchase anything from a full-service broker, investment advisor, insurance agent, or anyone in the financial industry, ask at least twice about all the costs and fees you will be charged.

Educate Yourself with Free or Low-Cost Resources

Attend local investment workshops and seminars. Call your local community college and ask if there are any noncredit investment courses offered.

If Interest Rates Are Rising, Don't Buy Long-Term Bonds

Remember, when interest rates rise, bond prices fall. Therefore, avoid intermediate- and long-term bond funds when interest rates are rising. The best time to be in these bonds is when rates are falling. You can do this directly by investing in individual bonds or use a mutual fund.

Don't Buy Proprietary Products

Avoid loaded proprietary mutual funds, annuities, and packaged products such as unit trusts.

Don't Be a Trader

You don't have to trade often to make money in the market, especially if you are using mutual funds.

Use "No Transaction Fee" Programs (NTF)

When you can, take advantage of the NTF programs available at discount brokerage firms.

Don't Buy Individual Foreign Stocks or Bonds

If you are a do-it-yourselfer, don't buy individual foreign stocks and bonds—instead use foreign mutual funds.

Ask for a Discount

It's all negotiable, so ask your broker or advisor how you can get breaks on commissions and fees.

Eliminate as Many Barriers or Limitations as You Can

Make certain you can purchase any type of investment you want from your brokerage firm, including no-load mutual funds.

Demand Liquidity

Stick with marketable securities that have available secondary markets.

Make Portfolio Management Your Passion

If portfolio management is your passion, you'll work at it harder, smarter, and longer than most people. The result will be wisdom and profits. If your passion lies somewhere else, find someone to help you who *has* a passion for portfolio management.

My hope is that these ideas will help you achieve investment excellence—the cost-efficient balancing of risk and return.

That Reminds Me...

The happiest wealthy people I know focused on having fun at work. Most people don't enjoy their work. That's why most people don't get rich. Their attitude prevents them from ever getting anywhere in life. So many of them hate their job, their boss, and their coworkers. They bring this frustration home and it can result in divorce and even abuse. This is a cycle of misery that eventually affects every aspect of a person's life. The only way out is by change of attitude—away from selfishness and toward helping others and getting along with others, including the boss.

The Least You Need to Know

➤ You must be able to identify the difference between real unbiased investment advice and marketing related advice.

➤ If an investment sounds too good to be true, it probably is.

➤ Profits are your reward for accepting risk and learning how to manage it properly.

➤ Focus on the things you can control, like the amount of money you spend and save.

➤ Always study the costs of doing business before you invest in anything.

Chapter 15

The Most Common Mistakes Made by Investors

In This Chapter

➤ The crazy things investors do

➤ What makes investors procrastinate?

➤ The investment traps people put themselves in

➤ The weird reasons people buy bad investments

➤ How to prevent the most common investment mistakes

If you plan on reaching Wealth Level 3 or above, you're more than likely going to make some serious mistakes along the way. This chapter is designed to prevent most of them. But the best way to learn anything is by trial and error, and even the most successful investors make mistakes. In fact, investment management could also be called "the management of mistakes." If you are an investor, it's not a question of if you're going to be wrong, it's a question of *when*. The key to the investment game is to try to be right more than you are wrong.

The good news is that you can learn just as much from the mistakes of others as you can from your own. Learning from your own mistakes takes a lot of time and money. Learning from other people's mistakes saves you time and money, and can catapult you far ahead of your natural learning process. That's what this chapter is all about. You'll recognize some of these mistakes because they are the opposite of what I've suggested in other chapters.

Wealth Warning

How far could you get in your car (in a forward direction) if you had to look in your rearview mirror 95 percent of the time? The same theory applies to using long-term past performance of mutual funds to make investment decisions. If markets repeated themselves, past performance would give you an indication of future returns. Unfortunately, the market changes daily.

Treasure Tip

Unless you know exactly when you are going to pass away, you don't know how much time you have or exactly how much money you'll need. The perfect financial life would consist of exactly enough money to live on until the day you die. Unfortunately, because of all the variables, you have to plan for an uncertain future. How do you do it? Start saving now!

Common Mistakes Made by Beginning Investors

If you are a beginner at investing, this section will help you prevent some mistakes. There are certainly many more possibilities—this is just a list of the most common ones I've seen (or experienced first hand).

➤ **I just met a broker over the phone, and he's great.** Brokers still make cold-calls every day. Some day this practice will be against the law. Until then, be careful.

➤ **I bought the fund because it had a great year last year.** The most common mistake investors make is investing where the market hockey puck has been. No matter how well a fund did last year, it is a new year now and everyone (including the fund manager) is faced with completely different circumstances and completely different markets. Investing is a forward-thinking game. You place a series of diversified bets on your best judgment of the future, watch your bets, make changes when necessary, and maintain a watch on the world for more new bets.

➤ **I'm not willing to take any risk.** Many investors don't understand that risk is something you accept and manage. If you avoid it, your assets will be subject to inflation risk (meaning, you'll make interest, but that interest won't help your investment grow faster than inflation). Most people unwilling to take risk become lenders. They lend money to banks and the government in exchange for interest payments on their GICs and bonds. What they don't realize is that to build wealth, you have to be an owner. You have to buy stocks or start your own company.

➤ **I've got plenty of time to start saving money.** This is definitely one of the most common mistakes Canadians make today. They put off saving money until some arbitrary date in the future when their ship is supposed to come in. They honestly believe that to make it worthwhile, they have to save big amounts. But that's not true. It's the *habit* of saving that's important, and the little amounts add up over time.

➤ **It's too late to start saving money.** This is the opposite of the last mistake. People wait until they have enough money to save (which to them is never), and wind up believing that they don't have enough time to save the amount of money they need. This is double jeopardy. They feel like they're stuck between a rock and a hard place. However, it's never too late to start saving money.

Common Mistakes Made by Intermediate Investors

An intermediate investor is someone who has been managing her own portfolio for more than a year. As your wealth grows and you become more aware of the basics of investing, you'll begin to make subtle errors that you might not realize for years. Here is a list of a few.

➤ **I picked a good mutual fund family.** Since discount brokerage firms began offering hundreds of no-load mutual funds to their clients, it makes absolutely no sense to do business with one mutual fund family. Buying exclusively from one mutual fund family is like saying all the funds that start with "P" are the best. You're destined for mediocrity with one fund family. Why limit yourself? Give yourself the opportunity to invest in hundreds of different funds by using the discount brokerage firms I mentioned in Chapter 10.

➤ **It's OK to have this much money in one stock.** Too much money in one stock is a typical problem for those who work or who have worked for a publicly traded company. Granted, an employee might know a great deal more about that company than do most other investors. But if one small thing goes wrong with the company and the stock price plummets, his portfolio will also plummet. It's not worth the risk. Do what it takes to diversify your portfolio. If you have a huge capital gain and you hesitate because of taxes, sell off some of your stock each year and spread out the tax. Consider gifts to charities.

➤ **My account's so big, I need five brokerage firms to do business.** Many investors get spread out among several different brokerage firms. They get so many statements each month that they have to add up and recalculate their portfolio allocation. They get several tax statements at the end of the year. If they want to make a trade and they have only a little money in each account, they have to write several cheques, or transfer money from one account into another. To check their account between statements, they have to call each firm and get the numbers. Basically, they live in a busy nightmare. Why not keep it simple? I have yet to see why anyone needs more than two brokerage firms.

➤ **Look at this great yield in the newspaper!** Don't be fooled by what I call "yield bait." An ad in the paper once read, "Free conversion of your low-interest RRSP to our eight-percent RRSP. No equity risk. Call our help desk without obligation." GIC and treasury bill rates at the time were well below eight percent on all maturities. With interest rates as low as they are, how can this company offer "eight percent," "no equity risk," and give you "free conversion"? Answer: They are selling an annuity with a one-year guaranteed rate only. The penalty if you sell the annuity the first year is approximately six percent, and it declines to zero after six years. The annuity company will take the money invested and, more than likely, purchase corporate and long-term government bonds. If unsuspecting investors buy this RRSP and keep it for a year, one of three things is likely to happen:

1. They will be happy with the new yield declared each year and keep the annuity.

2. They will be unhappy with the yield and will want out.

3. They will find a better opportunity and will want out.

Yield bait is a term I came up with to describe the many different tools (i.e., annuities, bond funds, and proprietary investment products) commission-based firms use to attract unsuspecting investors who need income. These investments are normally advertised as high-paying investments with little or no risk. Most of the time, investors purchase these investments without any idea of the expenses and possible penalties involved. The moment they try to sell or get out, *BOOM!* Reality sets in. They immediately see how expensive the investment actually is, but the withdrawal penalty will probably prevent any change. In the case above regarding the annuity, the real question is, "Why do you want to limit your alternatives when you don't have to?" Why not purchase individual bonds or a no-load bond fund that costs little or nothing to sell next year if you want out?

Remember, both fixed and variable annuities have sharp hooks with barbs. Once you get in, you're limited to whatever the annuity company offers you, regardless of other possible opportunities. They may attract you with the yield as bait, but the consequences can be heavy commission charges or fees. The most dangerous yield bait today is the long-term (10- to 30-year) government bond fund. If rates continue to go up, the fund's price will fall. Most of these government bond funds are bought with safety of principal in mind. "Full faith of the Canadian Government" means little to someone who loses 15 percent of principal on their government bond fund after only a one-percent rise in rates. Remember, not all funds are bad. Just be smart: do your homework before buying any bond fund. This is especially important when buying any fixed-income security from a commissioned broker or insurance salesperson. If you buy, they can make commission income of 8.5 percent from your money. It's what you *don't* know that will hurt you.

➤ **I heard a rumour.** Using rumours for investment research is like playing Russian roulette. One might be good every now and then, but the odds are against you making money. Typically, if the rumour has any truth to it at all, by the time you hear it, it's much too late.

➤ **The fund's up 10 percent this month—I think I'll take some profits.** Regardless of whether you use stocks or mutual funds, you don't have to trade very often to make money. In fact, most of the wealthy investors I know maintain a long-term outlook. They hold most of their securities over the long term in good times and bad. For the most part, they don't try to time the market. They consistently add money to their portfolio, or at least let some of the gains be reinvested, knowing that in the long run they will be rewarded for their patience. However, when they feel an investment is no longer worth keeping, they sell it. So they do some trading, but not a lot.

That Reminds Me...

Where do rumours start? I have a theory. There are many people in the world who have entirely too much free time on their hands. Free time can often result in insecurity. Victims of insecurity spend a lot of time talking, trying to prove to others and themselves that their insecurities don't exist. One way these people disguise financial insecurity is to talk about everything they've heard—most of which is insignificant, yet easy to sensationalize. Abraham Lincoln once said, "It's better to keep one's mouth shut and be thought a fool, than to open it and resolve all doubt."

➤ **I'm waiting for the market to go down.** Many investors try to time the market. Many wait to buy or sell in anticipation of a market drop. But no one knows when the market will correct. It's a guessing game that I guarantee you'll lose if you play it short term. You can only play long term and even then it's very difficult. If you really are convinced that the market is too high, divide your portfolio into four pieces. Invest each piece at a different time. You could invest once each month for four months, or once each quarter over a period of a year. Either way, you win. If the market does correct, you will be purchasing at lower prices. If the market continues higher, you are participating.

That Reminds Me...

A client recently hired me to manage a piece of his portfolio. He had been waiting for a correction since 1990 to invest. For almost six years, his $5–million portfolio has been sitting in GICs and money-market funds. This is a long time to wait, especially if you consider that the market is up over 70 percent since 1990. As you can imagine, he's spent a lot of time beating himself up over this. He kept thinking about all the money he could have made if he had invested in the market back in 1990.

➤ **I can't sell yet, I've got a loss and I'm waiting for the fund (or stock) to break even.** This is one of the craziest statements I've ever heard. What difference does it make whether the stock goes back up to the price at which it was purchased? While you're waiting, your money could've been in another investment—making money. What's important is whether or not you would be willing to buy the stock today if you had your money in cash. If not, sell it, even if you do so at a loss.

➤ **I can't sell now; my capital gain is too big.** So many people forget that this is a profit game, not a tax game. If you base your decisions on how much tax you're going to pay, you will lose. Zero-based thinking, again, should be used to make this kind of decision. No matter how much tax you have to pay, if the investment is bad, sell it or give it away to charity.

Common Mistakes Made by Advanced Investors

An advanced investor is someone who has been managing his own money for more than five years. Even he makes mistakes.

➤ **My bond allocation should match my age.** I've covered this before, but it's worth repeating. I don't know who started this garbage, but it sure is a common theory. Just because you're 50 years old doesn't mean that your portfolio should be 50 percent in bonds. The percentage of money you put in bonds should be based upon two variables: your risk tolerance, and what you think interest rates will do in the future. If you are a very conservative investor, you might want to keep a large portion of your portfolio in short-term bonds. When you do retire, it's prudent to keep at least some of your money in short- or mid-term bonds, just in case the stock market turns down for a long period of time.

➤ **I know what I'm doing.** Many investors think they know too much. They get a "big head" because they follow all the market data and think that quantitative measurements win the investment game. I can certainly tell you from experience, they don't. If they did, everyone who could operate a computer would consistently beat the market. Quantitative measurement is important, but the market moves more on the basis of emotion than anything else. Learn all you can; then listen to your gut and go with your instincts.

➤ **If you need income, you must have mutual funds and stocks that produce big dividends.** Income and dividends are fine, but some people overdo it, putting all of their retirement savings in GICs and funds and stocks that pay dividends. The advantage of dividends from Canadian companies is that they're taxed at a lower rate than income. It's good to have a steady stream of dividends, but don't go overboard. You can sell parts of your funds or stocks to supplement your income.

➤ **I've made too much money, and I've got to stop paying so much in taxes.** I've actually had clients who told me that I made them too much money. No kidding! Two years ago, I called one of my favourite clients. She is retired, single, and lives in a small town. She lives a very simple life, yet she loves to travel. I explained to her that her account performed very well this year. For the 12 months in 1993, her account grew 25.5 percent (total weighted average). Remember what should follow any statement like this—"past performance is not indicative of future results." She made $104,844 on a beginning balance of

Treasure Tip

An irrational investor might say that the stock market moves with expected earnings, inflation, and interest rates. An irrational man might say that the stock market moves with the whims of human emotion. The irony is that they are both correct.

Words of the Wealthy

Financial quantitative analysis involves the study of numerical information as the basis of decision-making. Under quantitative theory, everything is expressed in measurable form and is, therefore, predictable. Investors who subscribe to this theory believe that by studying specific market data, they can accurately predict the market's movements.

$433,707. During the year, she wrote cheques totalling $42,149, which still left her $62,695. To anyone else on the planet, this would have been music to their ears. However, this was not the case. Her reply was, "Larry, you made me too much money!"

I told her, "You know, I don't think any client has ever told me that." She said, "You might have put me in a higher tax bracket." This was probably true, considering the fact that she also received income that year from timber sold on her farm. I said, "You may be right, but I also made you enough money to pay the additional taxes. I also made you an additional $25,000 that was reinvested into your account." She paused a minute and said, "Well, I guess I should be happy." To which I replied, "Yes ma'am."

This client worries too much about taxes. When I met her, her account was 90 percent bonds with maturities beyond 15 years. Her goal in working with me was to diversify and increase her return. She wanted a 10-percent return with minimal fluctuation on the downside. I exceeded her return goal without coming close to her downside limit. But all she could think about was the tax she would have to pay. Don't be blind to profits when you're faced with taxes.

The Least You Need to Know

➤ Don't buy an investment from a stranger over the phone or in person.

➤ Don't just settle for a good track record. Do some homework and ask yourself what could happen in the future with the investment.

➤ Keep your investment life simple, get some help, diversify your portfolio, learn how to invest with your gut and instinct, and be a little irrational.

➤ It's never too late to start saving money. Do it now and make it a habit for life.

Part 3

Achieving Wealth Levels 4 and 5 with Your Own Business

You can achieve Wealth Level 3 easily if you use the practices I've shared with you so far in Parts 1 and 2. However, achieving Wealth Levels 4 and 5 may require some extra work. Many of the people I know made it to this level using their own businesses. They used the same principles of saving monthly and investing, but their businesses gave them an extra boost, both in terms of additional income and growing equity value. These are the two keys to building wealth with your own business: salary or dividend income, and equity value. If you build a business that can be sold in the future, you have the potential to build your wealth as fast as the business grows. Small businesses have the potential to grow very fast because they are nimble, flexible, and easily modified to meet customers' needs. Therefore, a fast-growing small business could be just the ticket to getting you to the upper wealth levels. This part will teach you the basics of getting started on your venture.

Chapter 16

Can You Supplement Your Income with Your Hobby?

In This Chapter

➤ Why start a business?

➤ Designing your dream business

➤ Writing a business plan that works

➤ The best business plan software

Can you imagine starting your own business with one of your favourite hobbies? It's a dream that only a very few people realize. Why? First of all, most people don't even think it's possible. They think you have to be extremely talented, rich, or famous to start a business. Second, they think that making money should be hard. One of my employees loves to do research and after spending days at the library, she said that she feels guilty because she doesn't feel like she's working. She thinks work must be hard. It's simply not true. Your work should be enjoyable. It's okay to have fun at work. The third reason most people don't start a business doing what they enjoy is because they haven't taken the time to figure out what they enjoy doing, much less to make a plan to implement it. This chapter begins to explore how your own business can be part of a plan to achieve the wealth level you want to achieve using a hobby or career that you enjoy.

If your target is Wealth Level 4, you're going to have to accumulate enough assets to produce a total return sufficient to substantially increase your desired lifestyle, and keep up with inflation. That may seem overwhelming at first—it was for me.

However, once I started my own business and saw the dividends and equity growth, I realized just how fast a business can build wealth. And, if you want to achieve Wealth Level 5, starting your own business is almost a requirement.

Why Do People Start Their Own Businesses?

Here is a list of the most common reasons why people want to start their own business:

➤ To pursue their dream job doing what they enjoy.

➤ To achieve financial independence.

➤ To escape corporate bureaucracy.

➤ To achieve creative independence.

➤ To achieve a more flexible schedule.

➤ To build wealth.

Do any of these apply to you? Have you ever asked yourself why you want to start your own business? Now is a good time to do it. Ask yourself these questions, and if the answers are positive, you should definitely explore business opportunities:

➤ Why do you want to start your own business?

➤ Would you enjoy working for yourself? Why?

Businesses Can Reduce Taxes

Another reason to start a small business is to reduce taxation. When you start your business, even if you don't incorporate, you can start deducting its expenses from your income even before it's generating sales or profits. According to Revenue Canada's rules, as long as your business has a reasonable chance of turning a profit in the future, you are allowed to deduct expenses directly related to running your business. That can include anything from paper clips and pencils to consulting fees and business lunches, and costs for marketing, travel, software, and other items and services related to your business. It also includes the cost of operating your home office, such as a portion of your rent or mortgage, utility bills, and other such costs.

These deductions can add up to a substantial sum of money and save you big dollars on your tax return. It is a powerful incentive for you to start up even a very small business as a sideline to your job. As long as you are legitimately seeking to earn a profit with your business, you can make all kinds of deductions. Of course, the idea isn't to make a bunch of expenditures just because you can deduct them from your income. The idea is to earn profits from your business. There are many good books about small businesses and taxation.

What Business Will You Start?

This is the hardest question for some people to answer, once they've decided that they do want to start a business. Unless you have had a burning desire to start a particular type of business, you may get stuck here. But I'm going to coach you through this process and make it a lot easier for you.

The first step is to review your answers to the three questions in Chapter 5 under the subheading A Passion for What You Do. Here they are:

1. Your doctor calls you and tells you that in exactly six months, you will die a peaceful death due to a weird virus. What would you do during this six-month period? Who would you spend time with? What activities would you spend time doing? What would be important to you? (List at least 20 answers.)

2. An unknown relative died and left you a portfolio of cash totalling $2 million. What would you do? Who would you spend time with? What activities would you spend time doing? What would be important to you? Would you quit work? How would you spend your money? (List at least 20 answers.)

3. What three great endeavours would you dare to attempt if you were guaranteed you could not fail?

If you have not answered those questions, do it now. This simple exercise may just change your life for the better. Remember the rules:

➤ Sit in solitude.

➤ Find a quiet place outside in a natural setting.

➤ There's no such thing as a stupid answer.

➤ Anything is possible—don't judge your answers yet.

➤ Complete at least 20 answers to the first two questions.

➤ Complete at least three answers to the last question.

Wealth Warning

Most people think that to start a business they need some incredible new invention or product that will change the world. It would certainly help if you did have such a product, but it is not a requirement. All you need is a passion for producing a product or service, and a customer who will buy it from you.

Treasure Tip

The key to success in your own business is to be passionate about what you are doing. Passion creates tenacity, and if you're tenacious enough to give it everything you've got, success usually follows.

Please do not read any further until you have completed this exercise. The answers to these questions should give you a clear picture of your goals and values in life. Basically, you have just listed your passions and dreams. Use them to find and design the business of your dreams.

If you don't see a business idea coming right off the page, you might want to take some time and use the answers to at least design the parameters of the business you're going to start. For example, if you enjoy spending time at home, you might declare this as one of your business parameters. If you know and enjoy working with computers, this might be a key parameter also. If you will continue listing your desired parameters, it will be much easier to select the perfect business for you.

After you have a list of parameters, your next step is to screen every business idea you have. The perfect business might not meet every parameter for you, but it should satisfy at least your top three. Therefore, it is necessary to prioritize your parameters. Which one is the most important to you? Which is second? Third?

If you are still having trouble finding the perfect business, here are some extra questions that might help you:

➤ What do you enjoy doing in your free time?

➤ What do you like to read in your free time?

➤ What do you excel in? What are you good at?

➤ What do others say you are good at?

Whatever you decided to do, make sure your business enables you to achieve at least your top three priorities. If not, you might not be able to maintain the necessary passion you'll need to be successful. If this is the case, redesign the business concept to meet your goals.

That Reminds Me...

Everyone's parameters are different. I wanted to be able to manage money for people, live anywhere, hire others to run the company for me and manage them, focus on what I enjoy (money management), take vacations, build a source of residual income, keep clients for life, work even if I was physically disabled, and continue working until I was 80 years old if I wanted to. Once I decided upon these parameters, it was very easy to make a decision.

Once you have decided upon the business idea(s) that fit your parameters, you need to focus your market (potential customers). Who will buy your product or service? Do some research to find a market willing to buy from you. Here are some questions to ask yourself about your market:

➤ Will your business fill a need (of your customers)?

➤ Who is your competition?

➤ What is your strategic advantage over your competition?

➤ What makes your product or service better?

➤ How can you create a demand for your product or service?

How to Write a Winning Business Plan

Before you get started building your wealth further with your business, make sure to take time out to design and plan exactly what you're going to do. Some people hate business plans. I'm crazy about them. I did more than 15 different business plans before I found my dream business—a money management firm. Planning is the most important part of starting a successful business. Your success will not necessarily depend on whether or not you complete a business plan, but it sure does help. In order to write a good business plan, you'll have to do some research. The following is my business plan outline. This business plan was not only used to help plan and develop my business, it was also used to secure a $100,000 loan from a local bank. I was 31 years old at the time and had very little collateral. I'm convinced the bank gave me the money primarily because of the organization of the plan. Use this outline to help you organize your plan. Record the outline on paper or in your computer and fill in the blanks, adding in the supporting documents where needed.

Every business plan is different, so some of the titles in this plan may not apply to you. This is just an example of a plan that worked. Where necessary, I have inserted optional items that you might consider. The bottom-line question is: Will your company make money?

My business plan filled a three-ring binder. I explained every assumption and added all the necessary supporting documents. It was (and still is) a blueprint of my business. Some of my friends told me that my plan was too long—it was overkill. After I got my $100,000 loan and my net income grew by 1,000 percent the next year, I knew that the plan was just right!

If the task of writing your business plan and doing your financial statements seems overwhelming, buy one of the many business plan software packages available.

Part I: The Proposal

What is Waschka Capital Investments or WCI?

Loan Request and Purpose (Estimated Start-up Costs)

Method and Terms of Repayment

Part II: History Of WCI And the Investment Advisory Business

History of WCI and Larry Waschka

Mission Statement and Investment Philosophy

Ownership and Corporate Structure

Description of Services

The Investment Industry

What Makes WCI Different from the Competition?

Part III: Marketing Plan—How We Build Our Business

Who Is Our Market?

Marketing and Advertising Strategy

Pricing Strategy

The Competition

Economic Overview

Part IV: Management

Principals and Key Associates

Organizational Chart

Research and Development

Part V: Financials (This is a view of the beginning.)

(pro-forma) Balance Sheets

(pro-forma) Income Statements (Profit & Loss Statement)

(pro-forma) Statements of Cash Flow

Ratio Analysis (If you are an existing business)

Part VI: Financial Projections—Short Range (First Year)

Assumptions

Projected Income Statements (Profit & Loss Statement)

Projected Cash Flow Statements

Projected Balance Sheets

Projected Ratio Analysis

Part VII: Financial Projections—Long Range (Three Years)

Assumptions

Projected Income Statements (Profit & Loss Statement)

Projected Cash Flow Statements

Projected Balance Sheets

Projected Ratio Analysis

Part VIII: Supporting Documents

Gross Income Projections on a Worst-Case Scenario

Related Estimates for Expenses, Payroll, and Net Income

Graphs & Data

Gross Income Projections on a Best-Case Scenario

Related Estimates for Expenses, Payroll, and Net Income

Graphs & Data

Gross Income Projections on an Outrageous Case Scenario

Related Estimates for Expenses, Payroll, and Net Income

Graphs & Data

Part IX: Appendix

Principal Resumes

Job Descriptions for All Associates

Business Advisors and References

Client References

New Office Lease

New Office Improvement List

Automobile, Equipment, and Furniture List

Results of Recent Client Survey

Larry Waschka's Personal Financial Statement

Personal Budget

Copy of Life Insurance Policy on Larry Waschka

Business Plan Software

There are several business plan software packages available that can make this a whole lot easier for you. Make sure your package will do what you want it to. If you need good pro-forma financial statements, make sure the software will provide them for you. If not, a good accountant will help you. Remember that no single software package will ever completely personalize your plan. Automation is great, but if you take it too far, especially in building your business plan, the results may disappoint you. Make sure you do all you can to personalize your end product. Get your accountant or a friend to read it before you go to the bank with it.

Pro-Forma Financial Statements

If you plan to achieve Wealth Level 4 or 5 using your own business, you're going to have to understand financial statements. They are the key measuring tool of your business efficiency and profitability. The first critical element in your financial statements is your return on investment. Before you start a business, you need to make sure your business passes the *return on investment* (ROI) test. Many business owners don't understand this test. They jump into a business without even considering (or knowing) what their ROI will be. To pass the ROI test, you must prove to yourself that your return on investment can exceed the historical returns of the stock market (which have been more than 10 percent for the last several years). Your ROI can be calculated by dividing your net income by the amount of capital you've invested in your company. The obvious goal of your business should be to maximize ROI, and this can be done in two ways: reducing expenses or increasing gross income.

Wealth Warning

Pro-forma financial statements are used to project the estimated financial results of a new company. They consist of an income statement, balance sheet, and cash flow statement.

Why is ROI so important? If you can't beat the stock market's return, why start a business when you can invest your money in the stock market? Why work so hard in your own business when you can invest money in the stock market from the comforts of your own home—and without any employees?

How do you know what your ROI will be? You'll need to prepare pro-forma financial statements using accurate or best judgment data. Pro-forma statements are simply estimated financial statements based on several assumptions. They enable you to answer important questions. For example, given a certain amount of estimated sales and expenses, how much profit can your business produce? The easiest way to complete these statements is with software, or by relying on a good accountant. Understanding how these statements work can make or break you in the first few years. Take some time

That Reminds Me...

A 61-year-old business owner told me one day that he wasn't in business to make money. He was trying to say that his focus was more on the welfare of his employees and customers. I couldn't believe his statement. This guy was either joking or had his priorities completely backwards. I quickly responded, "The very best thing you can do for your employees and customers is to make money. If you don't, there will be no business, no salary for your employees, and no service for your customers."

to learn the basics of how these statements work and how to read them. You may hate accounting, but I promise, you'll hate failure and bankruptcy much more.

A critical element of your pro-forma statements is cash flow management, which is measured using a "statement of cash flow" or "cash flow statement." This statement measures the actual beginning and ending balance of cash within a company. If you've never owned your own company, you may not realize how important cash flow can be. I know businesses that grew more than 100 percent per year in sales, but then went bankrupt because of poor cash flow management. Since their clients

Treasure Tip

In a cash crunch, ask your suppliers and vendors to let you push payments back. Big companies do this all the time. Your supplier would rather be paid late than never.

didn't have to pay for the goods for 30 days, the businesses found themselves with great sales growth, but no cash to continue operating. The key is to plan in advance with estimated monthly cash flow statements, and know exactly how big your line of credit at the bank should be. I'll discuss bankers and how to get an adequate line of credit in Chapter 20. You and your banker will want to know where your break-even point will be. If you want to ensure success in business the first few years, take the time to learn all you can about cash flow management. Buy a book or take a class if you have to. There are many tricks to the trade that can help you when you get into a crunch.

Words of the Wealthy

Outsource is a new term that simply means to pay someone outside your firm to do a job for you. It's an alternative to putting someone on your payroll.

Treasure Tip

A great way to test your compatibility with future partners is to go on a short vacation together. Don't bring the entire family. Just the two (or three) of you should go. You'll know in three days whether or not you can work together.

Taking on a Partner

If you want to achieve Wealth Level 4 or 5, don't take on a partner unless you have to. Though not insurmountable, the potential problems are extensive. The fight for control is the biggest problem. The second-biggest is trust and support. If one partner does most of the work, the other becomes resentful and loses trust in the other. The third biggest problem seems to be the inability to keep a single vision. If the two partners are both strong willed, they will often want to go in different directions.

Try your best to hire or outsource everything you need to start your business. Only if you can't hire or outsource should you consider a partner. If it's money you lack and someone's offering you money for a partnership or equity, try every other angle before you accept. If at all possible, don't trade control for money. You should always try to maintain control over your business. A partnership may diminish your control. However, there are exceptions; not all partnerships are bad. Before considering one, get to know the person well. Ask yourself if you can work together in good times and bad.

A Last-Minute Checklist

The following is a list of other items you might want to think about:

> ➤ Where will your business be located?
> ➤ What will be your legal structure? (See an accountant or lawyer.)

➤ What insurance coverage will you need?

➤ How will you compensate yourself? What is the minimum amount of salary you need each month?

➤ Will this business help you do more than make a decent living?

➤ Can you do this without a partner?

➤ Can you sell this business later?

Supplement Your Existing Income

If you want to achieve Wealth Level 4 using your own business, don't quit your existing job until you know that your venture can eventually produce an equal or higher income for you. Make sure you have adequate capital or income for the first year of living expenses. Be sure to finish your business plan, and then test your theory on a small scale before you jump out on your own. Test market your product and your production idea, then learn from those tests. Don't go into a full-scale business until you know your idea will work. I know from experience that this can save you time and thousands of dollars.

Treasure Tip

I spent more than three months setting up my company before I left my employer. After giving my final notice, I walked into my own office ready to do business on the first day.

How Do You Know When You've Made It?

You've made it when you reach the point where you can afford to spend a week every quarter on vacation somewhere in Europe or the Caribbean, but you don't because you're having too much fun at work! In 1995, my goal was to take a week of vacation every month. I did it for about four months and actually found myself missing my work. When you reach this mindset, achieving Wealth Level 4 is much easier to do.

You also know you've made it when someone calls you on the phone and asks if you might be interested in selling your business. This just happened to me recently. This wasn't an accident. I built the business so that I could sell it later if I ever want to retire. I have no plans to do this, but the concept of building my wealth through the equity value of my company was done by design. It needs to be part of your plan, too. Make sure you can sell your business one day. Find a way to build equity. Even if you offer a service, teach someone else how to do it. Hire an intern or apprentice who can take over later. I've hired five capable people in my firm who someday will be able to run my company without me. That's the ultimate dream. What will I do? I see myself being like Sam Walton, who continued to support his employees by helping them achieve their personal and business goals. He was like a cheerleader for his team. What a great job!

The Least You Need to Know

➤ Make sure your business allows you to achieve your wealth and personal goals, and to do what you love to do.

➤ Have a passion for your work and a market for your product or service. That's all you need to start a business and achieve Wealth Level 4 or 5.

➤ Plan. It's the most important part of starting a successful business. And a good business plan is the key to that planning process.

➤ Don't take on a partner unless you know you can't start the business without one.

Chapter 17

Working for the Perfect Boss— Yourself!

In This Chapter

➤ Managing all the overwhelming responsibilities

➤ Building your Business Planning Notebook

➤ Designing the systems and procedures of your business

➤ Focusing on marketing

➤ What to do when things go wrong

➤ Why business owners fail

The key to wealth is ownership of something unique and attractive that either produces income and capital gains, or has the potential to do so in the future. A successful business can do this for you faster than any other strategy because of the extraordinary growth rates possible.

There is a price to pay if you want to be your own boss. However, if you took my advice in Chapter 16 and you love what you do, the price will be easy to pay. When I started my money management firm in 1990, I didn't expect to take many vacations. I knew it would take a lot of work to be successful, but I didn't realize how much more *time* and money it would take. This chapter reviews the sweat equity you'll have to invest to build wealth through your own business.

Wearing All the Hats

With your own business, you are now your own boss, and you're faced with more responsibility than ever. But you love it because you are building your wealth doing what you love to do. To be profitable, you have to be able to single-mindedly focus on each area of your business. If you're not organized, you'll be stretched to the maximum every day of your business life. You're going to be overwhelmed with responsibility—some of which you haven't planned on. Many business owners get in this cycle of overwhelming frustration and are never able to grow their business. They're too busy sawing the log to stop and sharpen the saw.

Therefore, you need a tool to help keep you on track. The best way to manage your business effectively is to build what I call a Business Planning Notebook. This is just an extension or working model of your business plan. Simply take a large three-ring notebook and divide your business plan into separate segments using titled dividers. Your business plan should already have identified these segments, but you may want to modify them a bit. Here is a list of the most common areas:

Words of the Wealthy

Sweat equity is the hard work you pour into your business, which results in equity value. It's just like buying a home and doing some of the remodeling yourself. The work you do actually increases the value of your business.

That Reminds Me...

A few years ago, I spent some time with a business consultant in San Diego. His name was Roger Lane and he taught me a lot about planning and goal setting for my business. Most of my friends know I'm a goal-setting and planning nut. They thought I was crazy for spending the time and money that I did with this guy. But the results were incredible and worth every penny. He said that to have a successful business, I had to achieve two goals. First, I had to achieve a 50 percent or better profit margin with a payroll that didn't exceed 20 percent of my operating income. Second, I had to develop a set of procedures and a staff that could run the business without me. These are good goals to start with. Once you achieve them, they are easy to maintain.

➤ Product/Service Development

➤ Marketing

➤ Management/Personnel

➤ Administration

➤ Financial

➤ Competition

Every business is different, and your segments will be different from mine. Just make sure you cover what's important to you. Within each segment, include the business plan copy that corresponds to that segment. You can even use different coloured tabs to break down each area's heading into smaller segments. Marketing could be further divided into pricing, target market, publicity, and advertising. Each segment should include at least these four basic items:

➤ Corresponding business plan copy

➤ Goals in process

➤ Future goals (ideas to consider in the future)

➤ The procedures to follow as the goal becomes a system

If you take the time to maintain this working business plan, you will keep your business and your life more on track. You'll also escape the inevitable overwhelming feeling that keeps most business owners running in circles.

Treasure Tip

Maintaining your business planner on your computer will enable you to update and modify your plan more conveniently.

Design Systems and Written Procedures

After you have designed your business planning notebook, you need to take time each month to build the assembly lines or systems that make your business run successfully. If you take the time to do this, your business will not only run more efficiently, but it will be better positioned to expand and grow. This, in turn, will help you build your wealth much faster.

Every business is different, but each has some type of assembly line. My assembly line produces diversified portfolios for my clients, along with quarterly statements, monthly newsletters, and audio tapes. Each of these products is assembled using a separate assembly process. My responsibility is making sure my assembly lines run as efficiently and effectively as possible. One way to do this is to make sure my employees fully understand their roles. These assembly lines are also called "systems" and they are the basic framework upon which all businesses are built.

Your first job as a business owner is to identify and build your own systems. These systems must be designed and written in the form of a procedures manual. This is a working manual that must coincide with your business planning notebook. Every segment of your business has certain procedures that make up the assembly line of your business. These procedures are initially developed out of goals that have been set. Here are the steps to developing a procedure:

➤ Goal-setting

➤ Brainstorming the tasks necessary to achieve the goal

➤ Listing tasks necessary

➤ Prioritizing the tasks—developing the procedure

➤ Implementing/testing the procedure

➤ Measuring results

➤ Improving the procedures

➤ Implementing/testing the tasks again

➤ Measuring results

➤ Improving the procedures

This process goes on forever. Any business not dedicated to constant improvement is doomed. Eventually someone smarter will come along with a concept that is just a little improvement on your basic product or service. She will kick your rear end right out of the game with some simple idea that you should have come up with in the first place.

That Reminds Me...

Why do you think a little local hamburger franchise like a McDonald's can sell for $1 million or more? Sure, the profit margins are great. But I think the main reason is that the systems and procedures are so efficient and well maintained that anyone could manage the franchise. Every task in that franchise, from pouring a drink to turning off the light at closing, is written down and delegated to an employee. That's what your goal should be. You should develop a procedures manual within your business planning notebook that everyone in your company can see and improve upon every day. That's what it takes to build a successful, profitable, and sellable business.

How do you prevent this from happening? Develop a procedure for constant product/service improvement, and dedicate yourself to enforcing it regularly.

Written procedures do more than help you to run your business. They will enable you to

➤ Develop new products and services

➤ Train new and promoted employees

➤ Find procedures you can outsource

➤ Find ways to automate your business

➤ See inefficiencies in your business

➤ Have your employees cross-train each other

➤ Make your business more attractive to potential buyers someday

Once the procedures are built, you must focus your efforts on making them as efficient and effective as possible. You can't do this alone. This is best done *with* your employees. If you have no employees, get a friend, spouse, or supplier to help you. You can also call on other business people in your industry.

The next step is delegating all the procedures you can, so that you can focus on the most important ones. The key is to find the right employees who are responsible enough to take the ball and run with it. You don't want employees who just do the task; you want associates who are eager to help you improve your mousetrap. One way to do this is to reward them with little bonuses. This can be done individually, but it's best if you reward your whole employee team. Any innovation or new idea that you implement can help your business for years to come. It's worth the expense.

Focus on Marketing

If you don't sell anything, you don't make any money. If you don't make any money, you can't save any money. Plus, the value of your business will decline, as will your wealth. Therefore, the most important segment or procedure of your business is marketing. Your business must have a marketing plan or procedure that you know will bring in business. How do you develop one? You follow the steps to building a procedure that were listed earlier.

The whole idea of marketing is to identify your target market and find the most cost-effective way to sell to it. This is done by testing your approach or advertising. Continue testing until you find an approach or ad that works. Once you find one that works, use it. But don't stop trying to improve it. If you stop improving, your market will change and you'll miss out.

10 Marketing Questions You Need to Ask Yourself

Your marketing efforts are vital to the value of your business and, therefore, your wealth. The following is a list of marketing questions for you to think about. They will enable you to develop your marketing procedure.

1. Can you explain and identify the demand for your product/service?
2. Who is your competition?
3. What are the distinct characteristics of your product or service?
4. Who exactly is your target market?
5. Where does your target market live?
6. How will you determine the price?
7. How will you advertise and get the message out?
8. How will you test your advertising on a small scale?
9. Can you describe in detail your advertising budget for the first year?
10. How will you deliver your product to your customer?

What If Things Go Wrong?

The wealthiest people I know seem to expect occasional mistakes to happen. They learn from every mistake they make and do whatever they can to avoid letting it happen again. You're going to have to accept the fact that you will have failures in your business. No matter how much you plan, things are going to go wrong. If you're not experiencing some failure on a regular basis, you're probably not trying very hard to succeed. As a business owner, you are under the constant threat of sudden changes in the economy, competition, customer needs, and employee needs. You can take some preventative measures, but you'll still have to be ready for surprises.

How do you prepare in case things go wrong? First, imagine the worst things that could happen in your business. Sit down and design measures that could prevent these things from happening. Second, develop a damage control plan. The following is a damage control plan I designed. Every problem is unique and not every question will apply—but it's a start.

➤ Separate the symptoms from the true problem.
➤ Describe in detail the exact underlying problem.

➤ What are the true obstacles?

➤ What elements can/cannot be controlled?

➤ How will you change the things you can control?

➤ What are the possible solutions? (list at least 10)

➤ Prioritize the best solutions and implement the best.

➤ How can you prevent this from happening again?

If you want some creative ways to solve your problem, get your employees involved. They may come up with ideas that you haven't even considered. If you don't have any employees, get a group of your friends, or even your best customers if you have to. Don't give up without getting some ideas from other people.

If you have a cash flow problem, then you'll want to immediately preserve all cash. This can be done by pushing back payables, postponing expenses, expanding your line of credit, and giving customers discounts for early payment. Visit your banker immediately if necessary. If your banker is smart, he'll help you get through your problem. If the problem continues, examine all your expenses and cut back where you can. If you have to sell off assets to survive, do so. You could also ask your employees to help by allowing you to postpone payroll. They might be willing if the alternative is a layoff. You could also offer equity in your business as a partial substitute for salary.

Treasure Tip

My employees are fantastic problem solvers. They always come up with some of the best ideas. Why? Because each of them is unique and each sees the business in a different light. I encourage them to think creatively, and try not to be judgmental. The results have been outstanding.

Taking Time Off

The wealth-building process requires lots of motivation and creativity. The richest man in the world on his deathbed would trade all his wealth for another pain-free and peaceful week of life. The cemeteries are full of wealthy businessmen and businesswomen who worked themselves to death. To maintain your motivation and creativity, you have to take time out from your business. When I started my business, I lived across the street from my office in a 500-square-foot apartment. For four years, I spent days, nights, and weekends working at my office. My friends almost forgot about me. If it hadn't been for my desire to eat, sleep, and work out, I would never have left my office. Looking back, I realize I could have been more productive if I had taken a little time out to relax. But I simply felt guilty for not working. I had made a commitment to myself to be the best money manager in the region, and I knew that not one of my competitors was willing to work as hard as I was.

Give yourself permission to take some time off occasionally. Spend that time in a relaxing atmosphere where you can rejuvenate yourself. Most business owners think that if you work hard all the time, you'll eventually be successful. This is not true! You have to work smart. This implies a lot of thinking and planning, both of which require time and a peaceful, relaxed mind. Without either of these, your business cannot prosper. Therefore, don't forget to take some time out.

The 22 Most Common Mistakes Business Owners Make—Why Businesses Fail

I've spent a lot of time talking to wealthy business owners about why, statistically, so many businesses fail. You've heard all the pessimism regarding new businesses. They say that more than 90 percent of all new businesses fail. I've also been told that more than 95 percent of new restaurants fail. But the human spirit never ceases to amaze me. Despite these horrible odds, new businesses start up every day.

What you need to understand is that most of the businesses that fail do so for similar reasons. Knowing why they failed is very important to someone who might be considering starting up a new business. Here are the 22 most common reasons why business owners fail:

➤ Don't set clear goals or objectives

➤ Don't dream big enough

➤ Fail to plan or don't know how to plan

➤ Don't have enough discipline to follow the plan

That Reminds Me...

The author and lecturer Stephen Covey told a story in one of his speeches about a man who came upon a lumberjack who was sawing a log with a big handsaw. The lumberjack was sweating, panting, and sawing like crazy, but his saw was dull. He had made some progress, but at the rate he was going, he was more than likely going to be there all night sawing this log. The man asked the lumberjack, "What are you doing?" The lumberjack replied as he caught his breath, "I'm sawing this log." The man then asked, "Why don't you stop and sharpen your saw?" To which the lumberjack replied, "I can't. I'm too busy sawing."

➤ Can't focus their attention

➤ Don't maintain enough cash

➤ Hire bad employees

➤ Forget to test on a small scale

➤ Spend too much money (personally)

➤ Spend too much money on the startup

➤ Start a business just for the money

➤ Don't know how to work with a banker

➤ Refuse to borrow money

➤ Don't test a big-ticket item before buying

➤ Make hasty decisions that could—and should—have been researched

➤ Don't make customer service a top priority

➤ Don't listen to the customer and empathize

➤ Don't listen to employees

➤ Ignore industry trends and new product developments

➤ Start a business in the wrong location

➤ Let the competition steal their market

➤ Fail to or are unable to delegate

The Least You Need to Know

➤ Using your business plan, build a Business Planning Notebook, with dividers for each segment or department of your business, that can be used for goal planning.

➤ Use the goals you set and achieve to build a set of systems and procedures that will allow you to run your business more efficiently.

➤ Use these written procedures to delegate tasks to your employees so you can focus on the most important aspects of your business.

➤ Identify your target market and find the most cost-effective way to sell to them. Constantly test new ads and different approaches.

➤ Plan on things going wrong. Have a damage control plan that will help you to identify the problem, solve it quickly, and prevent it from happening again.

➤ Learn from the mistakes of business owners who went before you and blazed a trail.

Chapter 18

Your Accountant Is Your Friend

In This Chapter

➤ Why you must have an accountant

➤ Who's going to help you when the government audits you?

➤ What a good accountant can do for you

➤ The importance of financial statements

➤ How to get the most out of your accountant

Almost without exception, every wealthy individual I've ever met had a good accountant. But many business people still don't understand the value of a good accountant. I think it's because most people don't understand the value of measurement and accountability, which are vital to the success of a business. Most people think an accountant is someone who will fill out your income tax forms. However, good accountants can do so much more than your taxes. They can help you solve problems, plan for your future, maintain financial statements, set goals, set up a financial plan, offer second opinions, and refer you to other professionals when necessary. They are, in essence, the coach and statistician in the wealth game. Best of all, they can be like a silent partner in your business venture, assisting you with difficult financial decisions. I just don't know how to run a business without one.

Finding the Perfect Accountant

The best way to find the perfect accountant is to get references from friends or business owners like yourself. If you don't own a business, you should still work with an accountant who can help you start one if you decide to later. If you are just starting your business, ask someone who has a small, growing, non-competing business that's only a few years old. Other sources of accountant references include family, friends, successful individuals, and the *Yellow Pages*.

Don't hire the first accountant you meet. Interview at least three in person before you make your decision. Here are some questions you might want to ask them.

> ➤ **Are you a licensed accountant?** If you want an expert in accounting, make sure your accountant is a Chartered Accountant, Certified General Accountant, or Certified Management Accountant. You might even ask to see his licence. You might also ask if the individual has an undergraduate or Master's degree.

Wealth Warning

If at all possible, I would suggest not doing business with your competitor's accountant.

Treasure Tip

You may want to call your Institute of Chartered Accountants, who can tell you if your prospective accountant is certified and has a permit to practise. You might also want to ask if there have been any complaints filed on her.

> ➤ **What type of tax work do you specialize in?** You need an accountant who specializes in small businesses and tax work. You also need an accountant who understands the basics of corporations, partnerships, and investments.

> ➤ **How do you charge your fees? What is your hourly rate?** Every accountant is different. Most charge by the hour, but there are also flat fees as well as fees based on a percentage of your return. I prefer an hourly fee for corporate work such as monthly financial statements and advising, but a flat fee for my tax returns.

> ➤ **If I hire you, would you—or someone else— prepare my tax return?** If you are hiring an accountant, you want *that accountant* doing your work. At least have your accountant review the work if it's done by others.

> ➤ **How long have you been in business?** Make sure your accountant has been a practising accountant for at least five years and has experience in start-up and fast-growing businesses.

> ➤ How many employees do you have? Accountants? It's nice to know how much depth your accountant's firm has. Does she have a qualified support team? Are there any other accountants working at the firm?

➤ **How accessible will you be?**
Unfortunately, this might have to be a judgment call. You may never know how accessible your accountant is until you need her. Ask her what she'll do to make herself available.

➤ **What percentage of your clients had to file extensions last year?** If the answer is more than 20 percent, the accountant probably has too much going on to take care of you. There may be a legitimate reason, so ask why. Her clients might have procrastinated and not sent their information in time.

➤ **How can you help me reduce my tax burden?** This may seem like a silly question, but it's a great way to see exactly how the accountant thinks. You might even ask about how he's helped his other clients reduce their taxes.

➤ **Will you furnish me with a letter of engagement?** This will list in detail all the services that will be performed for you, as well as the fees that will be charged.

➤ **Ask *yourself* if this person is a good listener.** It really bugs me when people don't listen to me. What I really enjoy is someone who not only listens, but also empathizes with me. I want my accountant to do just that. I want her to put herself in my shoes for a minute so she can better understand my situation. Will your accountant do that? If not, find someone who will.

➤ **Will you furnish me with a list of client references?** If the accountant is unwilling to furnish you with a list of client references, scratch her off your list. Once you do get references, call them and ask them what they like and dislike about the accountant. Ask them how accessible she's been.

Treasure Tip

Ask the prospective accountant for a list of client references. Call each one and ask how accessible the accountant has been for them.

Words of the Wealthy

A **letter of engagement** is a document prepared by the accountant that outlines in detail what he will do for you. The letter should also illustrate how the accountant will be compensated and at what rate.

Treasure Tip

There's a reason why God gave us one mouth and two ears.

Measuring Your Way to Wealth

I've learned that whatever is systematically measured seems to improve. Whenever I pay close attention to my financial statements, I see my weaknesses and I begin to focus on ways to improve my company. It's a natural tendency. If you don't get a chance to see your company financial statements on a monthly basis, you may be burying your head in the sand. If you want to run a successful company, you must measure your success at least every month. You can do this yourself with financial software, have someone in your office do it for you, or hire an accountant.

I chose the latter. Why? First, accountants are "Orville Redenbachers." They do one thing and (I hope) they do it better than anybody—at least they do it better than me! I want someone who single-mindedly focuses on tax planning and financial statements. Second, there are too many tax code changes to keep up with myself. Third, it's better to have someone outside my firm measuring my success. I think he will be more objective and unbiased. Fourth, if I pay an accountant to do what he does best while I continue to do what I do best, we'll both make more money in the long run. Fifth, most creditors require audited financial statements prepared by an accountant. A basic set of financial statements should include:

➤ Income statement (profit and loss statement)

➤ Balance sheet (assets, liabilities, and equity)

➤ Cash flow statement

That Reminds Me...

If you expect to build your wealth through your business, you need to understand the basics of financial statements. Take advantage of classes available at your local university. Some banks also offer similar classes on cash management. If you can't find a class, go to the bookstore for help. This might seem to be a boring subject, but it is vital to your business success. If you can't read a financial statement, you won't know how well your company is performing.

A full-service accountant can also help you with additional services and measurements such as:

➤ Pro-forma financial statements

➤ Financial ratio analysis

➤ Personal financial statements

➤ Financial statement forecasting

➤ Depreciation schedules

➤ Payroll management

➤ Business valuation

If you have a good understanding of financial statements, you can do your own financial statement forecasting using one of several software packages that are available.

If you don't understand financial statements, or just hate working with them, it might be better to ask your accountant to do your financial statement forecasting for you. It's worth the money each year to have this done. This kind of forecasting involves three steps. First, you make a few key assumptions regarding future sales growth and expenses for the next several years. Second, using financial statement forecasting software, you enter your assumptions as well as your last several years' financial statements. Third, you let the computer calculate the expected effect of the assumptions on your future financial statements. If you don't like the desired effect, you can make certain changes in your assumptions. This kind of business forecasting not only allows you to find the optimal amount of sales growth for your company, but also gives you the opportunity to project your company's profitability. Therefore, if you can do this successfully, you are also able to measure, project, and keep track of your wealth.

Having Someone Who Knows You When Revenue Canada Calls

When Revenue Canada calls you to set up an audit, the first thing you're going to want is some help. You're going to need someone who knows your business as well or better than you do. Who's going to know you better financially than your accountant?

Call your accountant and have her go over with you what you can expect from a tax audit. Discuss what you two can do together to make an audit less likely to happen, and easier to handle if it does.

Wealth Warning

How do you prepare for a tax audit? The best tool you have before, during, and after your audit is a good accountant who's been with you for years.

Accountants cannot do everything. If you need additional help in an audit, you may want to seek the council of a tax lawyer with a lot of audit experience. Find a firm that has a good track record. Make certain that it has defended clients successfully against Revenue Canada.

Treasure Tip

A business can report net income, but at the same time may have a negative cash flow. Without positive cash flow, your business will more than likely go bankrupt over time. That's why I always remember the phrase, "Cash is king."

Treasure Tip

Be sure to review your financial goals with your accountant. If he's aware of your goals, he'll be more likely to come up with ideas that can help you achieve them faster.

Problem Solving

The most common problem business owners face in their first five years of business is cash flow. One of the single best solutions can be a good accountant. First, accountants can measure your cash flow each month for you. Second, they can identify your problem faster using your company financial statements. Third, they can recommend ways to solve the problem quickly and show you ways to prevent further problems.

The second most common problem business owners face is maximizing the profit margin (the profits of the business divided by the revenues, which is the key measurement of profitability). Business owners and investors have a similar problem. Most investors don't know their portfolio's yearly return and, believe it or not, many business owners don't even know their profit margin. If they don't know their margin, they don't know if they've maximized it, either.

Goal Setting

Many business owners don't think about using their accountants when it comes to setting goals. They don't understand the value the accountant can add to the goal-setting process. Not only do accountants prepare your financial statements, but they see things that you don't. They have the capability of forecasting your financial success for you. Your accountant can help brainstorm and plan financial goals for your business. She can also help you achieve those goals by helping you monitor your progress each month.

Basic Personal Financial Planning

Your accountant can also be a great source of basic personal financial planning. If you are ever going to achieve Wealth Level 3, 4, or 5, you must spend time maintaining your personal financial plan. The two obvious aspects of financial planning with which an accountant can help you are retirement planning and personal budgeting. Not all accountants are good at this, but if you take the time to find a good accountant, he can be instrumental in your wealth-building process, which must include budgeting and retirement planning.

Retirement planning is key to the wealth-building process and is simply a matter of planning to save and setting up the vehicle in which to save. Your accountant can help you in deciding what plan is best for you and your company. If you don't have a retirement plan established, stop and do it now. Wealth Levels 3, 4, and 5 are almost impossible without one. It is, without a doubt, the most common denominator among the wealthy people I've met.

Budgeting is something most people naturally dread, but it can make you rich. A good accountant will help you budget your business expenses, as well as your personal expenses. Once he sets you up, you can monitor yourself or use the accountant for accountability. If you know someone is monitoring your actions, you may be more inclined to make improvements.

Treasure Tip

Your accountant could be a key ingredient in your wealth-building recipe. Be sure to ask her for help when you set up a budget or retirement plan. She may have some valuable ideas that you might have overlooked.

Second Opinions

A good accountant is someone who knows you and your business and is willing to give you advice whenever you ask. During your wealth-building journey, you are going to be faced with many decisions. Some will be quite easy, and some will be very difficult. A good accountant who knows your situation is like a partner. Use this partner whenever you can to help you with the big decisions. My clients use their accountants to help them with many different decisions, including:

➤ Business expansion

➤ Mergers and acquisitions

➤ Business deals with others

➤ Lease vs. buy decisions

➤ Investment ideas and tax consequences

➤ Investment professionals

➤ Investment performance evaluation

Referrals to Other Professionals

If you are serious about reaching Wealth Levels 4 and 5, you're definitely going to need help from other professionals. Your accountant works with many other clients who have similar needs and problems. This can make him a great source of referrals. Be sure to ask for at least three referrals. Here is a list of different types of professionals your accountant should know:

➤ Investment advisors

➤ Investment brokers

➤ Financial planners (fee-only)

➤ Tax lawyers

➤ Insurance agents

➤ Bankers

Treasure Tip

Your accountant may even be a good source of information regarding prospective employees. Since he works with other businesses, he may know of an employee who might be looking for a promotion or other employment.

Treasure Tip

If you decide to sell your business to retire, or when you've achieved the wealth level you'd like, your accountant may know a potential buyer.

Helping You with Your Banker

Wealthy people have strong relationships with their bankers. Why? Because bankers are an excellent source of inexpensive capital that can be used to start or expand a business. Most business owners don't think of their accountants when it comes to banking. However, the banker does. Anyone who's ever borrowed money from a banker knows that good, accurate accounting is very important to a banker. Before you visit your bank looking for a loan, visit your accountant. Make sure your personal financial statement is up to date. Ask him to help you with your loan proposal. Get your financial statements in order, and consider bringing your accountant with you when your banker wants to discuss your loan proposal.

After you have started your business, you might also want to send copies of your financial statements each quarter to your banker—even if they're not required. This makes a banker feel good about you as a client.

Setting Up Your Corporate Documents

An accountant can do most of the initial work involved in helping you decide how you want to legally set up your company. However, you may want to get additional assistance from a lawyer who is experienced with all the different types of ways to incorporate.

Getting the Most from Your Accountant

One of the best ways to minimize the cost involved in hiring a good accountant is to provide him with accurate and organized records. I know people who show up on their accountant's doorstep with a box of unorganized invoices and cancelled cheques. This is no way to run a business and no way to build wealth. Wealthy people keep their records organized and automate their accounting. Try to automate your business accounting from the beginning by using one of the many accounting software packages available.

The Least You Need to Know

➤ A good accountant is someone who will single-mindedly watch over your company's finances, keep up with tax laws, give you an objective opinion, and, most important, give you the opportunity to focus on what you're the best at so you can build wealth faster.

➤ If you'll take the time to get to know your accountant and help him learn more about your business, you'll have an inexpensive partner who can help you solve problems, plan for your company's future, and build wealth to your desired level.

➤ Use your accountant to help improve your relationship with your banker by systematically offering copies of your financial statements, even if they're not required.

➤ Wealthy business owners automate the basics of their business accounting using one of the many accounting software packages available.

Your Banker Is Your Friend

In This Chapter

➤ Establishing good credit

➤ Building the perfect loan proposal

➤ Knowing the right questions to ask your banker

➤ What if your loan is denied?

➤ What if you can't pay your loan off?

To reach Wealth Levels 4 and 5, you have to have a good relationship with your banker. Eventually you're going to need money to invest in your business, and bankers are the key to inexpensive money. All you have to do is pay yearly interest, which is usually offered at the most competitive rate available. If you go anywhere else for a loan, you're almost guaranteed to pay a higher rate. Therefore, you must make a habit of getting to know your banker. The wealthy people I know take their banker to lunch, play golf with her, and invite her and her spouse to dinner parties.

Two things never seem to change in the business world: businesses need to borrow money to survive and be profitable, and banks need to lend money to survive and be profitable. If it's that simple, why are so many people turned down for loans? Because they don't understand how to borrow money from a bank. Bankers look for very specific documentation before they can lend money. If you have the qualifications and know the documentation needed and how to present it, you should be able to borrow all the money you need.

A professor at my college taught me one thing I will never forget. He said, "There will always be more money chasing good ideas than good ideas chasing money." I consequently found out that he was right. There are many different sources of capital or money for your business venture. There are banks, venture capital firms, investment bankers, pension funds, insurance companies, and private placement firms. What you must understand is that some are more expensive than others. The least expensive is a bank loan. Banks don't usually ask for equity positions (ownership) in your company. All they want is interest paid on the loan and the principal paid back on a timely basis. Plus, the rate of interest they ask for is usually the lowest of all the sources. Therefore, a bank loan is the most efficient and cost-effective source of capital.

A good relationship with a banker who understands your company and your needs is key to your wealth-building success. A good relationship must include both financial and personal character. Your financial character is measured by your net worth as well as your proven ability to produce a cash flow from your business. A good personality isn't enough to satisfy a banker. You must develop a track record of cash flow (actual profitability from your work). A large net worth also helps, but cash flow can be just as important. Fortunately, you can do this in your existing job before you start your business. Start keeping records of your own success and ability to produce results. Illustrate this for your banker before you start your company, and your chances of landing a loan will be much greater.

Establishing Good Credit

The first thing you must have before you approach a bank is good credit. Establishing good credit is vital to the wealth-building process. How do you do it? Borrow money and pay it back on time. It's as simple as that! Make this a habit and never be late on a payment. The very first thing a banker will want to know is how well you've done this in the past. He finds out using a report called your *credit history*. This report will tell you (and your banker) all about most of the loans you've had, as well as any late payments on bills or loans. Considering how important this report is, I suggest you get a copy before your banker does.

When you call a credit agency, don't get frustrated with the automated answering service. Stay on the phone until you get what you need. You can also write the agency and request your report. Be sure to give your complete legal name and social insurance number.

When your credit report arrives, go over it carefully and look for anything that might be detrimental to your credit. If you see any discrepancies that might disturb your banker, sit down and write an explanation of your side of the story. Include all the facts, names, and dates. By law, you can insert up to 100 words into your file at the credit agency. When your banker sees the discrepancy, he'll also see the explanation. This might calm his fears.

You can obtain your own credit history by contacting the bureaus directly. Usually you'll need photocopies of two pieces of identification, along with proof of your current address taken from a utility bill or credit card invoice. Mail this information to Equifax Canada Inc., Box 190, Jean-Talon Station, Montreal, Quebec H1S 2Z2 (1-800-465-7166) or Trans Union Consumer Relations Department, P.O. Box 338-LCD1, Hamilton, Ontario L8L 7W2 (416-291-7032). They will mail the appropriate information to you in about two weeks.

How to Find the Right Banker for You

The right banker can help you reach Wealth Levels 4 and 5. Notice I said "banker" and not "bank." I prefer someone who can make a decision. That means a person with authority, usually in a business-banking centre of one of the major banks. Most large banks delegate smaller loans to junior lending officers whose inexperience can be a problem.

The best way to find a good banker is to get recommendations from other successful small businesses in your area. Find at least three bankers. Stop by and introduce yourself. Tell them you are looking for a banker and that you will have a proposal soon to present to them. Get to know a little about them personally. Do they seem easy to talk to? Are they interested in you and your company?

Treasure Tip

You can also ask your accountant for a bank reference. Ask him for names of three bankers he knows and recommends.

That Reminds Me...

My company was recently nominated for Arkansas' Small Business of the Year by the *Arkansas Business Magazine*. I was amazed at how many different banks called on me once the nominees were listed in the paper. What infuriates me is that they didn't call on me until after my business was five years old. When my company and average deposits were much smaller, banks didn't care much about me. I had to find a banker who could empathize with me and understand my needs as a small business owner.

The Perfect Loan Proposal

You need money to start and maintain your business in order to expand and achieve Wealth Levels 4 and 5. Your banker needs to lend money, and all she wants is a client who can borrow money and pay it back on time. The best way to prove you can do so is to prepare a proper loan proposal. Your business plan should double as a loan proposal. Some of the segments will be more important than others to your banker. What will she be looking for? Here is a list of the five most important items:

➤ Your credit history

➤ The collateral you have to back the loan

➤ Your personal and business cash flow

➤ The amount of liquid assets you have available

➤ Your own personal character

These items can be presented several ways. It's best to include them in your loan proposal. Follow these up with several additional documents listed below and you'll have the perfect loan proposal. First, it must cover your corporate history. This explains your company's mission and direction.

Second, the proposal must include a summary of the loan request, which can be a simple sentence. My proposal read, "WCI is requesting a loan of $100,000 for new office equipment, furniture, and additional working capital."

Next, the proposal must include a cash flow statement. This should be included in the financial statements of the proposal. This statement shows exactly how much cash your business generates, as well as a projection of future cash flow over the next three years.

Words of the Wealthy

Collateral is something of value that is pledged against a loan in case of default. When you list collateral such as furniture, equipment, property, or accounts receivable, you should also include documents that will evidence the value of these items.

Fourth, the proposal should list all the possible sources of collateral that can be used to back the loan. This includes furniture, equipment, property, stocks, bonds, GICs, and anything of value. The bank will want you to personally guarantee the loan, which means you must be willing to pledge everything you have to pay it off.

Fifth, the proposal must have detailed financial statements including at least a balance sheet and income statement. These statements should include the past three years as well as projected statements for the next three years. Your banker will pay particular attention to the effect of your business operations on your corporate equity. This figure is calculated by subtracting your company's liabilities from its assets. She will also look at how you have balanced your assets and liabilities.

Sixth, the proposal should include copies of your personal and business credit reports. Call the credit agencies listed earlier in this chapter and request both.

Seventh, the proposal should include a list of more than one source of repayment. Your banker will want to know if there is any source of income, other than your business, that can be applied to payments if you have trouble.

Your business plan or loan proposal should also be considered a wealth plan. It is your ticket to the capital you'll need to build your business and ultimately achieve your desired wealth level. Be sure to do the best job you can and always maintain it as a working plan.

Finally, the proposal must include a personal financial statement that summarizes your own personal assets, liabilities, and sources of income.

Your banker will also be looking for several other documents:

➤ Personal (and business) tax returns for the past three years

➤ Articles of incorporation, bylaws, corporate resolutions, and partnership agreements

➤ A detailed expense budget (a personal budget will also help)

➤ A detailed marketing plan including a list of your top three customers or prospective customers. If applicable, be sure to ask for your customer's permission.

➤ Your competition and what makes you better

➤ A personal resume on you and any partners you may have

➤ Letters of recommendation (clients, previous employers, and so on)

➤ Proof of life insurance

That Reminds Me...

When bankers take care of you, don't forget them. They make money from deposits, as well as loans. Be sure to maintain a significant amount of your company's deposits in an interest-bearing chequing account with that bank. You could go to a brokerage firm money-market account for a higher rate, but the marginal interest rate you'll make isn't worth spoiling your relationship with your banker. You might need to borrow more money later.

➤ Copies of your property titles

➤ Copies of all your current bank and brokerage account statements

This is a lot of work, but it will increase your chances of getting the loan you want under the terms you ask for. The less information a lender must ask for, the more credibility you'll earn. If you skimp on information, the banker might think you are trying to hide a negative aspect of your business or personal history. Loans are more likely to be made on a marginal transaction if the lender believes in the customer. Make certain your proposal is completely free of spelling errors and grammatical mistakes. These just might kill your chances of getting a loan. Hire an editor if you need one.

That Reminds Me...

Many of the major banks provide help with loan applications via their Web sites. Royal Bank, for example, provides a wealth of information about starting and running a small business on its Web site at www.royalbank.com. The Canadian Bankers Association also provides booklets, brochures, and CD-ROMs for entrepreneurs. You can reach the association by phone in Toronto at 416-362-6092.

Questions to Ask When Interviewing Bankers

The banker you select will be a vital part of your wealth-building journey. Don't just settle for the first one that says "yes." Spend some time getting to know them. You're about to start a long-term relationship that could be very beneficial to both of you.

Once you have your loan proposal ready, set appointments with at least three bankers. Before you give them the proposal, get to know them as people. What are their interests? What do they enjoy about being a banker? Then ask the following questions:

➤ **What is your loan approval limit?** This is the amount of money your banker can approve without having to present your loan to a superior. I prefer to deal with bankers who can approve my loan. If you need a great deal of money, you may have no choice. You at least want to deal with a banker who can approve a significant amount of money.

➤ **Do you have areas of emphasis or expertise?** Some bankers specialize in consumer loans and some focus on business loans. Some banks do a lot of business with a particular industry such as real estate. Knowing this about your prospective banker might give you some insight into how well the banker can serve your credit needs.

➤ **Can you give me a list of client references?** This might completely blow your banker's mind, but you need to know what other people think about him and the bank. Even if you were referred to this bank by a friend, you might want to do some of your own research. Ask for clients who also have small businesses, who can relate to your needs and concerns. When you call the references, be sure to have some specific questions ready. Use the questions in Chapter 9 as a guide. If the banker refuses to call any of his clients to ask if they would mind providing a reference, go to another bank.

What If Your Loan Is Denied?

The wealthy people I know didn't build their wealth being timid or shy. They were tenacious in their efforts and when they were faced with a "no," they continued to look for a "yes." If you get turned down by a banker, ask why and try to correct the problem. Then resubmit the proposal. Make sure the problem isn't bank-related. If he gives you a vague answer, ask him to be more specific. If he continues to be vague, don't do business with him. The bank might be having some problems of its own.

Don't give up. Go to several other banks and present your proposal. After my own bank turned me down in 1994, I presented a proposal to four other banks—and got four offers.

Treasure Tip

Be sure to dress professionally when you go to meet and interview your prospective banker. Be candid, be honest, and be yourself. They want to do business with people with good character and integrity.

Words of the Wealthy

A bank's **capital ratio** is calculated by dividing the bank's capital by its total assets. This ratio measures the bank's availability of capital, as well as its financial strength.

Treasure Tip

Be sure to ask your prospective banker if she and her bank are accustomed to working with small companies. Prove it to yourself: ask for a small company client reference and call them.

What If You Can't Make Your Payments?

Wealthy people do whatever it takes to make their loan payments. However, occasionally there can be unexpected problems. Fortunately, bankers understand this. They're human, too. If you see a potential problem with your cash flow and you don't think you can make a payment, immediately sit down with your banker, explain the problem to him, and tell him you want to pay the loan off as soon as you can. Ask him to work with you on a new payment plan. Your banker doesn't want to foreclose on your loan. It might completely blow his chances of your paying the money back. Therefore, he may be willing to do all he can to help you. Ask for an extended payment plan or a lower interest rate. Do whatever it takes to pay the loan off. Bankruptcy should not be an option. If you file for bankruptcy, it will haunt you for the rest of your life. No bank or lending institution will ever look at you in the same way again.

That Reminds Me...

In my fourth year in business, my banker made the mistake of telling me over the phone that she wouldn't even consider helping me structure a $100,000 bank loan to expand my business. This was a complete surprise to me. It just didn't make any sense. I had been with this bank for several years and had, in a timely manner, paid off all my loans except for my company car loan, for which I was still making payments. Well, I took it personally, which was wrong of me, but it sure motivated me to shop around at other banks. I presented my loan proposal to four other banks and all four wanted to lend me the money (structured the way I wanted). But this is not the end of the story.

Three months after the first bank refused to consider my loan request, I called to draw on my $20,000 line of credit, which was still at the first bank and had been in force for the previous two years. When I called, the teller said that my line of credit had been cancelled. I called the loans officer who had turned me down for the loan and said, "Can you explain why my line of credit has been cancelled?" This is what she had to say: "Well, I assumed that you were going to another bank. So I cancelled it." The bank cancelled my line of credit without even sending me a notice. But good things come from bad, and this story does have a happy ending. I called my new banker and told him I needed a $40,000 line of credit. He said, "Come by now and we'll have the paperwork ready for you." I just love these guys and they love my company. Don't be discouraged if the bank initially tells you "no." Find one that wants your business.

The Least You Need to Know

➤ A good banker can be your key to unlocking the door to Wealth Levels 4 and 5, but before you go to a banker, check out your credit by calling one of the "big three" credit agencies and requesting a copy of your credit report.

➤ The perfect loan proposal will tell the banker about your credit history, collateral backing the loan, cash flow, amount of liquid assets, and personal character.

➤ The key to finding the right banker is asking the right questions, getting the right answers, and talking to some of her other clients.

➤ If your loan is denied, do what other wealthy people do and don't give up—find out why, solve the problem, apply again, and consider other bankers.

Chapter 20

Hire the Best and Delegate

In This Chapter

➤ Before you hire, consider outsourcing

➤ Manage payroll and you'll improve your margins

➤ Hire the best by attracting the best

➤ Why pay your new employee more than they expect?

➤ The power of a net bonus program

This chapter has the single greatest potential for catapulting your business forward into profitability. That means this chapter also has the greatest potential of getting you to Wealth Levels 4 and 5. I know this from experience. My employees have empowered me and my business to grow faster and more profitably than almost all of the money management firms in the U.S. My profit margins currently exceed 60 percent. The original goal was to exceed 50 percent. How did we get to 60 percent? This chapter will give you the answer. It wasn't just one strategy that got us there, it was a combination of tactics that my employees and I implemented together along the way. I could not have done it without them.

Getting Help—Don't Be So Quick to Hire

Before you run out and hire someone, ask yourself first if you can outsource the work. Outsourcing allows you to hire the best without having to take them on your payroll. For example, unless you are an accountant, you're going to need accounting work done for your business. Instead of hiring an accountant and putting him on your payroll, you can outsource your accounting work by paying an independent accountant to do the job for you. Look at every procedure of your business and ask yourself if it can be outsourced. Then find someone willing to do the work. You can find help from:

➤ Temporary services

➤ Employee leasing companies

➤ Vendors who offer help

Keeping Payroll at 25 Percent

One other thing you need to be aware of before you hire is your total payroll costs. If you can get payroll costs under control, you are well on your way to being more profitable and more wealthy. Many business owners go out and hire what they think they need well before they look at their budget for payroll. The inevitable result is a poor profit margin or a layoff. Establish a goal to keep your payroll costs at or below 25 percent. My definition of payroll costs includes salaries, payroll taxes, and insurance costs for all employees (excluding you). I've let my payroll exceed 25 percent temporarily when I hire someone new, but within six months, returned it to the 25-percent mark.

How to Find and Attract the Best Employees

Your business's wealth-building potential is directly tied to the capacity of work your employees can handle. The amount of work they can handle is directly tied to their desire to achieve company goals. The level of desire they have will depend upon their passion for the business and their belief that if they work hard in your company, they can achieve their own personal goals.

How do you find the right employees for your business? First, you have to decide exactly what you are looking for in an employee. Using great detail, describe the best employee you could hire. Write this down before you begin your search. This will help you keep on track.

Second, look at your competitors and suppliers for possible employees. These people know your industry better than anyone walking in off the street. Their experience will greatly reduce the amount of training they will need. Plus, if they are really good at what they do, they'll be known by all the primary business people in your industry. This means that you can ask others (in confidence) about these people before you hire them.

Ask Key People You Know in Your Industry

If you don't know anyone specifically in your industry that you can hire, ask key people you know for referrals. Explain exactly what you are looking for. Ask them who the best candidate would be.

That Reminds Me...

After one year in business, I asked around in my industry and found out that the best support person in the state was unhappy with her employer. Her name was Linda and I had worked with her before. I called her and asked her to come in for an interview. She later accepted my job offer and has been working with me ever since.

Look for Those Who Are Disgruntled or Seem to Want More

If you have to, visit other similar companies—or get your friends to—and ask around. Find out who might be unhappy with his current position. Look for someone who wants a bigger challenge and more responsibility.

Pay Employees a Little More than They Expect

Wealthy business owners know the value of paying employees a little more than they expect. It's a great way of telling your new employees that they are worth the extra money. This builds not only self-confidence in the employee, but also loyalty and trust. Show me a company with loyal, trustworthy, and confident employees, and I'll show you a wealth-building machine. First, find out how much you can afford to pay them. Then ask exactly what they need. You want to find the smallest amount of salary they need to feel comfortable coming to work for you. If they are really excited about working for you, they should, more than likely, give you a relatively low figure to begin with. Once you've established this amount and you're ready to hire them, offer them a little extra and tell them it's because they're worth it. If you've really done your homework and you're face to face with a great potential employee, it will be worth the extra salary to get the talent. The little extra could be a net bonus program.

That Reminds Me...

When I need a new employee, I ask a few key people to "bird dog" for me. In fact, I myself become a bird dog. What do I mean by a bird dog? A bird dog is a dog on a mission. He has one thing on his mind and nothing else. Birds, birds, birds. He can't think of anything better. He'll go without food, without water, and without sleep just to get a chance at seeing a bird. If you've ever seen these dogs in action, you know exactly what I'm talking about. Not every business owner can do this. But if you're looking for a key employee (which all of mine are), you stand a better chance of getting a good quality person by doing some sniffing around. It may take some time, so you may have to be patient. Great employees don't grow on trees. The best ones are loyal, and therefore slow to leave their current employers.

Establish a Net Bonus Program

A *net bonus program* is an incentive pay program based on a certain percentage of the net income from your business. It is the key to motivating your employees to help achieve your company (and therefore your wealth-building) goals.

The first bonus program I installed was based on gross income. This motivated my employees to grow, but they had no incentive to spend money efficiently. During our weekly meetings, they had little interest in working on saving money. All they could think about was growth. The day I changed the bonus program to one based on net income, *the entire company changed!* My employees instantly became interested in reducing overhead expenses. It was like magic. Suddenly they thought like I did. They became interested in reducing every expense they could find. They also began to take more of an interest in planning for the company's future.

It's imperative for you to understand how powerful this concept of a net bonus is for your business. I will never run a business again without it. Overnight it can change your business forever. Try it.

Treasure Tip

I give my employees 15 percent of my company's net income. This lump of money is then divided and distributed according to each employee's percentage of payroll.

The easiest way to calculate net bonuses every month or quarter is to build a computer spreadsheet that can calculate it for you. Once your monthly financial statements are produced, all you have to do is enter the data and, presto, everything is done.

The net bonus program is designed to allow your employees to share a predetermined percentage of your net income. Once you have decided on the percentage and have calculated the net bonus total, you divide the bonus dollars according to each employee's percentage of payroll. Half is paid immediately and half is placed in a pool to be distributed at the end of the year. However, an employee must still be employed by the end of the year in order to receive the other half.

You should include all employees in your bonus program. However, there should be an initiation period for new employees. Mine is currently six months: all new employees must wait six months before they are placed in the bonus program. Here's how I calculate my bonuses:

	Operating income
Subtract	**Overhead expenses** (minus depreciation)
Subtract	**Loan payments** (for capital expenditures)
Subtract	**Money for cash reserves** ($2,000, for example)
	Net income
	x 15 percent
	Net bonus amount
	x 1/2
	Immediate Bonus
	x Percentage of payroll = Employee's bonus

You Have to Delegate

Most wealthy people will tell you that delegating is initially very difficult. However, if you can do it successfully, you dramatically increase your chances of achieving Wealth Levels 4 and 5. It took me several years to understand this concept. It wasn't a natural transition for me. During the first few years of my business, I had to do just about everything myself. Slowly, I recognized the need for help, and began looking at all the options. I could hire someone without experience for very little money, but I would

Treasure Tip

Do all you can to make your company an exciting and fun place to work. The results will amaze you. Your employees will be more efficient, effective, and much more loyal.

have to train them. This would take time. Therefore, I decided to spend more money and get someone with experience—someone who could walk right in and go to work. I hired the best person in the state and began delegating all my administrative work to her. This woman turned my business around. The day I hired the best employee in the state and began to delegate work to her is the day my company's growth took a turn upwards.

The lesson I learned is that you can't do it alone; you need help. In the early years of starting a business, you are a manager of activities. Soon you have to hire help, and you become a manager of activities and people. Eventually you become a manager of people. If you want to increase your business to any significant size, you must become a manager of people. If this is the natural evolution of a business, wouldn't it be smart in the early years to focus your efforts on hiring the best employees? I say it's absolutely imperative.

That Reminds Me...

One day I decided to start a newsletter for my clients. I asked my newest employee, Angie, if she would take on the project, and she gladly accepted. She had absolutely no experience and very little guidance from me. I explained the concept, bought her software and training, and then got out of the way. The result was incredible. Now she is producing two newsletters at the same time. These are her babies, and she's proud of them—so am I. When you delegate a task, step back and let your employee figure it out.

Match Responsibilities with Personality

When you hire, make sure the responsibilities you want taken care of properly match the personality of the prospective employee. Ask your prospective employee what he really enjoys doing. Ask him about his strengths and weaknesses. Find out what he does best and make sure that it matches what you are looking for. If the person you need to hire is going to be in sales, find someone with excellent people skills. If you need an administrative person, make sure he enjoys working with numbers. This is an ongoing process, too. You have to stay abreast of your employees as they develop over time. People do change sometimes, so be sure to meet individually with each employee on a regular basis.

Meet with Your Employees Individually

If you really want to build wealth through the growth of your business, you need to know each of your employees' personal goals and aspirations. If you care enough to help them achieve these goals, they'll be much more loyal and dedicated to your vision. Help them, and they'll help you. I don't believe in the traditional employee review meeting. Instead, I get to know the employee's own personal goals and I help them accomplish those goals through the success of my company. If I can show my employee how she can accomplish her personal goal by accomplishing the company's goal, we have both won. Plus, there's no need for me to be a motivator. If my employee sees how her personal goal can be accomplished through the success of the company, then she'll naturally be motivated to produce. It's a very simple concept.

Conduct Regular Team Meetings

To be a successful and profitable business that can be sold later, you must hold weekly, monthly, and yearly meetings. Team meetings are vital to the success of a business. They hold together the people and the responsibilities of an organization, and they develop and maintain a team spirit that is necessary for success. Weekly meetings should be for monitoring the progress of goals set each month. They shouldn't be any longer than one hour. The primary purpose of monthly meetings is to discuss the results of each goal in progress and to set new goals. Monthly meetings should be an all-day event. Yearly meetings should be at least two days and should be held outside the office. The primary purpose of a yearly meeting is to set goals for the upcoming year.

The basic weekly and monthly meeting agendas should at least include:

➤ **Old Business** Review items from last week that need attention.

➤ **Goal Review** Review the status and results of current goals.

➤ **New Business** Discuss new goals and any other items.

➤ **Calendar Planning** Go over everyone's calendar.

Wealth Warning

My last boss literally "met" us to death. Almost every day there was a meeting. What made it worse is that he would lecture all of us for the mistakes of a few. We didn't deserve to be treated like that. I learned both the value of a weekly meeting, as well as the value of one-on-one employee counselling sessions.

Treasure Tip

One of my mottos in the office is, "If you're not making mistakes, you're not trying."

The great thing about meetings in my firm is the Old Business section. This is a great way to keep everyone (including me) accountable for the projects that should be in process. If they are in process too long, they should be eliminated, delegated, or tabled to later dates.

You must also encourage an open and flexible meeting where anything can be discussed. If your employees are intimidated or afraid to give their opinions, you may have problems for years before you ever see them. Your employees should be your greatest asset. Most employers don't realize their employees' full potential.

Develop Your Vision and Let Your Employees Help

The key to long-term business success and the wealth-building process is getting employees involved in developing your vision, and then letting them run with it. Your role should be to manage these people and support them. If you have a big vision, chances are you're not going to be able to do it all yourself.

Consider an ESOP Plan

An ESOP plan is an *employee stock ownership plan*. It is used to give employees of private and publicly traded companies the opportunity to buy stock in a company over time. The employees become owners, which makes them feel part of the company. The owner gets motivated employees and an opportunity to sell his stock and raise cash. ESOP plans have made many business owners very wealthy, and it could be your ticket to Wealth Levels 4 and 5.

All ESOPs require a legal document setting up the plan and a trustee. A certain percentage of each employee's salary is expensed as a profit-sharing plan deduction and put into the plan to buy company stock.

Before you do anything, take some time to decide exactly what you want to accomplish with your ESOP. This should be your first step. Communicate these goals to your lawyer before he begins designing the plan. There may be another way to accomplish your objectives without starting an ESOP.

Second, sit down with your employees and discuss what an ESOP can do for them. Get a lawyer to help explain it if you have to.

Third, the ESOP plan must be written and designed properly by a lawyer who specializes in these plans.

Fourth, begin the plan and let it work for you. As things change, your lawyer can help you.

The Least You Need to Know

➤ Before you run out and hire that perfect employee, examine the responsibilities of the job and decide whether you can outsource the work.

➤ If you'll pay your new employees a little more than they expect, you'll be rewarded with happy, loyal employees, a much more profitable company, and a faster ride to Wealth Levels 4 and 5.

➤ Pay all your employees a bonus based on a percentage of net profits, and watch your company and net worth grow like a weed.

➤ If you really expect to grow your business significantly and reach Wealth Levels 4 and 5, you must become more a manager of people than a manager of tasks.

➤ If you really want to build your business and your net worth, hire the best, match their work with their personality, give them responsibility, and get out of the way.

Chapter 21

Maximizing Profits and Selling Your Business

In This Chapter

➤ Leaping over the competition

➤ Determining the value of your business

➤ Finding a buyer

➤ Negotiating the sale of your business

➤ Taking your company public

As you know from Chapter 3, you have achieved Wealth Level 4 if the market value of your business would produce (after capital gains taxes) enough proceeds to build a portfolio sufficient to support and substantially increase your desired lifestyle, while at the same time keeping up with inflation. Regardless of whether or not you plan to sell your business someday, if you plan to achieve Wealth Level 4 using your own business, you need to understand the theory of preparing your company for a sale.

One of the benefits of owning your own business is the opportunity to build wealth at a much faster pace relative to the traditional method of monthly investments in the stock market. Since the equity value of your business is tied to its growth and profitability, the key to building wealth is maximizing earnings growth. This not only makes you money, it also makes your business worth more to a buyer. What I've learned is that what makes your business worth more to a buyer also makes you money in the process. Therefore, you should run your company as if you were going to sell it sometime in the near future. Whether you can sell your business or not, you can at least save part of your earnings. If you actually sell your business someday, your efforts will be further rewarded at the time of the sale.

This chapter will teach you how to build a company that will not only make you a lot of money, but will make a buyer salivate.

23 Business Strategies that Will Make You Rich

Are you ready to learn how to get to Wealth Levels 4 and 5? These are all common-sense measures to help you increase profits, build your equity value, and make your company more attractive to buyers. Every business is different, which means that a few of these might not apply to your situation. Therefore, use what you can and leave the rest.

1. **Maximize your profit margin.** Take steps to improve your earnings enough to produce a profit margin that exceeds industry standards. Your trade organization should have some data on this. This can be done two ways: cut overhead expenses and maximize sales or gross income. Many business owners try to minimize taxes so much that they inevitably forget about profits. If you plan to sell your business, you need to focus on maximizing profits because that's what the new owner is looking for. Eliminate anything that hides profits.

2. **Get audited financial statements.** Have your financial statements audited by a reputable accounting firm. The first thing a potential buyer will want from you is your company's financial statement. Accurate financial statements will build trust between you and your potential buyer. Plus, the buyer will want to have your statements audited anyway. Having them done in advance will save you a lot of time.

3. **Maximize sales and earnings growth.** Focus on maximizing your company's sales and earnings growth. Your goal should be to achieve a growth rate that exceeds industry standards. Call your trade organization and ask about the average sales and earnings growth rates in your industry. You might also ask who the most successful firms are in your industry. Call the firms and ask if you can visit to share ideas.

4. **Show the potential for more growth.** Build a case that illustrates for the new buyer more potential for growth in sales and market share. If your company dominates the market with a 60-percent market share, the buyer will be worried about the prospects for further growth. Show him how your market may be growing. Illustrate for him how he can achieve a 70-percent market share. Make it easy for him to visualize success.

5. **Design written systems and procedures.** If you and your employees will take the time to design and maintain written systems and procedures, not only will

your company run more smoothly and efficiently, but your prospects for a sale will greatly improve. Empathise with a potential buyer and imagine yourself trying to make a buying decision between two businesses. If everything else were held constant, except that one had a written procedures manual for all operations and all employee positions in the company, which one would you choose? You'd choose the company that can operate the best with the least supervision—the one with written systems and procedures that anyone can follow. That's every business person's dream.

6. **Clean house.** Do you find yourself cleaning your house before company comes over? Well, you need to do the same thing when prospective buyers start to visit. Implement a procedure to keep your facility as neat and tidy as possible. You might even want to consider painting or other improvements that might be more attractive to a buyer. If this were your house, what would you do?

7. **Keep your staff smiling and happy.** If you want to really impress your prospective buyer, show her a group of happy, enthusiastic, team-oriented employees. If you haven't taken the steps to create this, I suggest you do it now. You can't do it overnight, but you can at least get started.

8. **Keep it confidential.** You may not want to tell your employees about your interest in selling. It could create unwanted confusion and fear. If your employees think they might lose their jobs as a result of a sale, they will immediately begin to look elsewhere.

9. **Always take time to plan.** So few people take time out to plan. They get so caught up in their work that they never have time to plan. It's like the lumberjack who was so busy sawing that he didn't have time to sharpen the saw. Every six months, my friend Ted and I escape to the wilderness and spend a day planning. What I enjoy the most is his enthusiasm in the planning process. This makes it easier and a lot more fun. I'll share more on this with you in Chapter 24.

10. **Find the best at your business.** If you want to leap completely over your competition and experience exponential growth, find the best people in your business today and model after them. Some people are reluctant to help, especially if you are in the same town. Therefore, focus on those who are outside your geographic area. Ask them if you can visit and talk about their business.

Treasure Tip

One thing my father taught me by example is that a clean and organized place of business is more attractive to the customer and more enjoyable for the employee. It also cuts down on injuries and the resulting insurance costs. Thanks, Dad.

11. **Do what you love to do, and delegate everything else.** I covered this in Chapters 17 and 22, but it's important enough to repeat.

12. **Always have a big vision.** In order to build a better business, you have to have a vision of what you want to build. This vision must be big enough to drive you and challenge you. I have found that if my vision is too small, it eventually bores me. However, if it's big and wonderful, I become naturally motivated. The only way you'll know if your vision is big enough is to try to achieve it first. Remember to expect setbacks and to use the tools in Chapter 18 to get you back on track.

13. **Focus on what you're good at.** What are you better at than most people? What do others say you're good at? If you'll identify your strengths and use them, you might find yourself with a natural competitive advantage that will speed you on to success. If you're really good at something now, just imagine how competitive you'd be if you focused on improving that skill even more. Use your natural strengths to build your business and beat your competition.

That Reminds Me...

I remember when I was young, I built a tree house with my friend Brandon. We would spend weeks building what we thought was the best tree house in the world, and in our little world, it was the best! We'd play with great pride in that tree house. It was our escape. However, within a week, we got bored. We thought of all the things we'd do differently, and all the things that needed improvement. We knew we wanted a bigger, better house, so we built another. We got bored again and built another. It took me many years to understand the moral of that adventure. I had learned that you have to have a dream big enough to challenge you all your life. Otherwise, you'll end up building one tree house after another.

14. **Eliminate the fear of failure.** Fear of failure will kill your business. You should always ask yourself, "What is the worst thing that can happen?" Next, you should ask yourself, "Can I handle the worst thing?" If the answer is "yes," then don't worry about it anymore. Make plans to handle the worst thing, and then eliminate the fear.

15. **Work hard.** The average executive workweek is about 60 hours. However, if you have an exciting vision and a plan to achieve it, you might find yourself wanting to work more than 60 hours.

16. **Avoid negative people.** If you want to ruin your vision, spend time with problem-oriented, negative, and jealous people. If you want to build a better business, focus your social efforts on associating yourself with positive people who are also success-oriented. Successful business owners associate themselves with others who appreciate win-win relationships. They celebrate each others' victories and are eager to help in times of defeat.

    The same is true with business relationships. If you know that a potential or existing client is going to be a problem in the future, you might want to give him to your competitor. Just explain that you really feel that their objectives will be better served by the other company.

17. **Be an information sponge.** In today's world of computers, the Internet, and fast-paced business transactions, you have to keep track of many changes. If you want to learn new ways to improve your business, you must become a *Curious George* and ask a lot of questions. You also need to be able to read a lot of information in a short time. What should you focus your attention on? The following list gives the most common fast-paced changes that will affect your business:

    ➤ Improved computer systems that improve your efficiency

    ➤ Internet software that can connect you to your customer

    ➤ Changes in your industry and the economy

    ➤ Changes in the needs of the customer

    ➤ Changes in your competition

18. **Maintain a good attitude.** If you want to build a better business, you must develop an air of confidence, enthusiasm, and humility. For example, if you try to make a sale with a

Treasure Tip

Trade shows and conventions held for your industry are by far one of the greatest learning tools available to you. Few people understand their value.

Wealth Warning

If you want to be an efficient information sponge, subscribe to Audio-Tech Business Book Summaries (800-776-1910). This company will provide you with written and audiocassette summaries of business books each month. A one-year subscription is US$135 and worth every penny.

fearful or hungry attitude, the prospective buyer will more than likely run away. You have to be confident in yourself, your product, and your business. You also have to be optimistic and see an opportunity in every problem you encounter.

19. **Focus on helping others.** Customer service is simply the art of helping others and exceeding their expectations. The most successful companies in the world don't try to just meet their customers' needs, they try to exceed them. This should be one of your company's core policies. One way to start this process is to examine your marketing efforts. If you exceed the expectations of a prospective buyer, you increase the odds of her becoming a client. For example, after my first 12 months in business, I changed my marketing focus from selling to teaching. The rewards have been outstanding. During the following three years, my company grew more than 100 percent each year. Why? Because I changed my marketing focus to helping others learn how to invest. The more I helped other people learn, the more my business grew. If every company understood this single principle, the world would be a better place.

20. **Develop your genius.** Genius is not knowledge. My definition of a genius is someone who can single-mindedly focus on one thing at a time. This may sound easy to you, but with all the hats you're going to have to wear as a business owner, it ain't easy! Make it easy on yourself and don't try to do more than one thing at a time. If you have to leave the office to think, do so!

21. **You must be a decision-maker.** First, ask yourself this question: "Am I a decision-maker?" If your answer is "yes," then proceed. If your answer is "no," ask yourself this question again until your answer is "yes." To be a good decision-maker, you must understand two things. The first is the principle of the worst-case scenario. As I said earlier in this chapter, if you can handle it, then don't worry about it. The second is the pros and cons of the decision. List these and weigh each alternative; then select the best alternative. Accept the fact that you'll be wrong some of the time.

22. **Make sure you need it before you buy it.** Within six months of starting my own business, I spent more than $10,000 on software that I never used.

Treasure Tip

Selling is a lot like dating. If you need the client badly, he'll run away. If you don't need the client, he'll never leave.

Treasure Tip

I learned a valuable lesson in customer service from the man who takes care of my laundry. Raymond is, by far, the most customer-service-oriented person I know. What's his secret? When I asked him, he replied, "Basically, what I do all day is try not to say 'no' to any of my customers." This says it all.

I honestly thought I needed it, but when I narrowed my focus from financial planning to money management, the software became obsolete. This was an expensive lesson in planning. That money could have been spent on so many other things. It still drives me crazy to know that I spent that much money on something that wasn't needed, during a time when every penny counted. You can learn from my mistake. Before you buy anything—especially a big-ticket item—think about it for a while and make sure you need it.

Treasure Tip

Any software package worth buying will offer you a trial period. If the software offers no trial period, I suggest you shop around for one that does.

23. **Establish some barrier to entry.** Do whatever it takes to set up as many barriers to entry as you can. A barrier to entry is simply something that deters or prevents other people from competing against you. The best barriers are licences, patents, copyrights, and professional degrees. If none of these apply to your business, then consider other tactics:

➤ Advertise and dominate your market.

➤ Be willing to do what others won't do.

➤ Establish yourself as an expert in the local media.

➤ Establish an outrageous customer-service program.

Why Sell?

Everyone is different and every business owner has her own reasons for selling. Your reason might be to build a liquid portfolio that would provide more than enough income for you to live—Wealth Level 4. The most common reasons business owners sell their businesses (or a part of their businesses) include the following:

➤ Retirement

➤ Desire to diversify into other businesses

➤ Need for additional capital to continue growth

➤ Strategic alliance with a larger company that allows economies of scale and new markets

What's Your Business Worth?

In order for you to know when you've reached Wealth Levels 4 or 5, you need to know how your business is valued. Putting a price on a closely held business is a difficult process. To put it bluntly, the value of a business is equal to the most amount of money anyone is willing to pay for it. It's not like selling a house for which you have comparable sales transactions within the same neighbourhood. In contrast, sale prices of closely held companies aren't usually public information, and that makes the valuation process quite difficult. Therefore, you often have to calculate an estimate of fair market value based on very vague criteria. The fair market value is only an estimate. In the end, the real value is whatever price the buyer and seller agree upon at the time of the sale.

Some business owners jump to the conclusion that their company is worth 16 times their earnings, just like some companies traded on the Toronto Stock Exchange. They fail to recognize that publicly traded companies have several advantages over most closely held companies:

➤ Easier access to capital

➤ Ability to use stock for acquisitions

➤ Highly scrutinized financial reporting to the Securities Commission

➤ Diversified group of management and directors

➤ Company success that doesn't rely on one person

The most common methods of valuation involve mathematical models that take into account the company's assets, past and future earnings, industry outlook, strength of management, and uniqueness of the product/service. The three most common valuation methods are described next.

The Asset Method

The easiest valuation method is the *asset method*. The asset method simply sums up the fair market value of the company's underlying assets minus the liabilities. This approach is considered best when valuing a company with significant tangible assets such as real estate and commodities. It would not be a good valuation method for a service business with very few tangible assets.

The Market Comparison Method

The most common method of valuation is the *market comparison method*, which is quite similar to the methods used today in valuing real estate. Using this method, the company's financial performance and operations are compared to other similar companies recently involved in a sale transaction. It is imperative that the companies chosen for comparison are in the same business and similar in size. Factors are used to compare each business with yours, to come up with a price that's fair to both parties. These factors are ratios that divide the price of the company's stock by other financial numbers. The most common factor is the P/E ratio or *price to pre-tax earnings ratio*. If you knew the average P/E ratio of the last five companies sold recently in your industry, you could easily multiply that average factor by your own pre-tax earnings to produce a good estimated fair market price. You can do the same thing with these other common factors if you have the following information about other companies that have recently been sold:

➤ Price/pre-tax earnings

➤ Price/cash flow

➤ Price/book value

Unfortunately, since privately held business transactions are not disclosed to the public, the financial information you need to make these comparable measurements is difficult, if not impossible, to find. However, you may find that your industry's trade organization keeps up with these factors. Maybe it can give you a rule of thumb. The alternative is to do the research yourself by calling the new owners of companies that have been recently purchased. Explain to the new owner that you don't necessarily need to know how much she paid for the business; you just want to get some relative measurements such as the ratios listed above. You might even promise to share your ratios after you sell your company at a later date. Some business owners will cooperate, and others will not.

The Discount Method

The third way to value a company is called the *discount method* or *income capitalization method*. This method is based on the theory of estimating the current worth of the future financial benefits your company can offer the new owner. More specifically, this method calculates the current value of a company's expected future earnings over a certain period of time using a discount or current value factor. The calculation is complicated, which is another reason you may want to get some help from a business broker or intermediary.

Industry-Specific Method

You'll also find that every industry has its own unique pricing methods. These are specific valuation measurements that others in your industry have used in past transactions. For example, the beer and soft drink industries both typically use the number of cases sold in a year to come up with an estimated value. They call this the *price-per-case method*. If a distributorship sold 500,000 cases last year and the price-per-case factor is $1.25, the distributorship is worth approximately $625,000.

One final note on valuing your business. You can spend time valuing your own business if you like that sort of thing. However, a good accountant would be happy to do it for you.

Finding a Buyer

Before you can sell your business and get to Wealth Level 4 or 5, you must find a buyer for your business. Buyers can be hard to find if you don't know who the market players are. Even if you do know the players, will you know how to conduct the sale? Selling a business involves complex valuation methods, tax considerations, and strategic negotiations. Can you do all that alone?

➤ **There are people who can help you.** Depending upon the size of your business, there are basically three types of people who can help you find a buyer and walk you through the sales process. They will also help you negotiate the sale. If you own a small business with less than $1 million in sales, you can hire a business broker. You can find business brokers listed in the *Yellow Pages* of most major cities.

If your business has $2 million to $50 million in sales, you're considered a middle-market business, in which case you would want to hire what is known as an intermediary. Intermediaries are similar to business brokers, but are accustomed to dealing with much larger businesses and more sophisticated negotiations. Intermediaries are hard to find unless you live in a major metropolitan city. If your business grows to more than $50 million in sales, you may want to consider hiring an investment banking company. These companies are easy to find in the phone book.

Be sure to do your research before you hire one of these people. At the very least, ask for references and call them with questions. If you know of a company in your industry that's been sold recently, ask the seller and buyer who helped them. Most trade organizations also keep track of intermediaries that specialize in their industry.

➤ **Maximize your company's exposure to buyers.** Make sure your company is in all the local chamber of commerce listings. Confirm the way they categorize your company, who they list as president, and all other pertinent information. This includes the membership list, as well as other directories that might apply, such as the book of local manufacturers.

Ask your provincial industrial development office for its guide to businesses in your province. Are you listed? Is the information up to date? Think of all the different services your company offers and make sure you are properly listed in the phone book under these services.

➤ **Talk to local accountants, lawyers, and bankers.** These people know others who might be looking for a business to buy.

➤ **Offer a reward.** You might want to offer a reward for the person who can bring you a referral that results in a sale.

➤ **Don't list your business in the local newspaper.** You may not want everyone to know you're selling. Plus, you'll have all kinds of people calling you, most of whom will not be qualified. If you do list locally, be anonymous and let your business broker or intermediary help you.

Building a Business Profile

A business profile is similar to a business plan. It will be used by your prospective buyers as they begin their research on your company. This profile could make you a very rich person if you design it carefully. Given the right amount of profitability, it might be your ticket to Wealth Level 5. Be sure to be accurate and honest. An outline of a typical business profile follows:

I. Introduction
  A. Summary of operations
  B. Financial summary
  C. History of company
  D. Ownership
  E. Reasons for sale
  F. Company strengths and opportunities

II. Description of Business
  A. General business description
  B. Description of market and current market share
  C. Future growth potential
  D. Sales and marketing
  E. Competition
  F. Management and employees
  G. Current customers
  H. Suppliers and contracts

III. Business Facilities
  A. Location and facilities
  B. Equipment

IV. List of Exhibits
  A. Audited financial statements
  B. Marketing material and brochures
  C. Listing of major equipment and furniture
  D. Resumes and job descriptions of all key employees
  E. Results of recent client survey
  F. Business advisors and references

Treasure Tip

Before you sell your business, make sure you're ready. Spend some time imagining what you'll be doing after the sale. What will your goals be? What will you want to do next? Do you want to continue working with the new owner?

Making the Sale

Most of the clients I know who have achieved Wealth Levels 4 and 5 have sold their businesses. They knew what their company was worth, they negotiated with the buyer to agree upon a win-win deal, and they had help all along the way.

What Do You Want from the Sale?

The following list of questions should help you decide exactly what you want out of the sale:

➤ Would you be willing to finance the sale?

➤ Do you want to continue to work with the company after it's sold?

➤ If you were required to work for another year or two as part of the negotiation, would you be willing to do so? For how long?

➤ If you did work, what hours would you want to keep? Do you need to continue your health insurance? What responsibilities would you want to focus on?

➤ How will you structure the deal to achieve your financial goals?

➤ Do you have key employees, or your children, in your business who want to continue working? Will the new owners keep them?

➤ What would your employees do if they knew you were thinking about selling? Should you keep it confidential?

Once you know what you want out of the transaction, prioritize each item by its level of importance to you. This will make the negotiation much easier because you'll know what you can and cannot compromise. Be sure to let your attorney know your priorities and make sure he keeps the win-win concept in mind. Many attorneys will fight tooth and nail without compromising anything. Don't let this happen. You must be willing to compromise some things.

How to Negotiate the Right Way

The negotiation process takes time and, therefore, a lot of patience. You and the buyer must both be willing to work hard to make the transaction go smoothly. Here are several tips that will make the process a little easier and less time consuming:

➤ Know exactly what you are and are not willing to compromise.

➤ Know your goals, but be flexible regarding their accomplishment.

➤ Don't insist on winning every argument.

➤ Empathise with the buyer and his needs.

➤ Don't get too excited if you get a better deal than you expected.

➤ Never hesitate to walk away from a sale that doesn't meet your goals.

➤ Never *threaten* to walk away unless you are serious about it.

➤ Listen for the buyer's goals.

➤ Listen and find out what exactly the buyer is willing to compromise.

➤ Be honest and strive for a win-win outcome.

How to Make the Sale Go Smoothly

Make sure you understand, in advance, the tax liabilities of selling your company. Hire a tax lawyer who can help you structure the sale to minimize taxes.

Don't procrastinate or be unprofessional in the transaction. Be patient and understand that this is a difficult process. However, don't allow your buyer to stall for no reason.

The personality of the buyer is very important, especially if you plan to continue working with the company. If you have more than one attractive offer, be sure to give a lot of consideration to the nature of the person or people with whom you'll be working. Spend some social time with the buyer and get to know him personally. This can improve the level of trust and rapport necessary for a good transaction.

Allow the new buyer to get to know your employees on a social level. If your employees are happy with the new owner, things will run much more smoothly for both you and the buyer.

Make sure the buyer has enough money after the sale for working capital and emergencies. You might get your business back if he runs out of money. If the buyer says he plans to make up for the lack of cash through net earnings from the business, make sure your company is profitable enough to accomplish this. You also want to make sure you get enough money up front to cover two things: any commission you

Treasure Tip

Strive for a win-win deal where both you and the buyer are happy.

Treasure Tip

Be sure to do your research on your buyer. Make sure you know whom you're dealing with. Does she have adequate capital? Is she capable of running the company? Make the research process easy for the buyer. Try to do the homework for her in advance. Be honest and don't try to hide anything that can surprise your buyer later.

might have to pay to your broker or intermediary, and any expenses you might encounter if you happen to get the business back.

Make sure your company is profitable enough to cover the debt payments for the buyer. If your buyer can't pay the debt on the business, he'll have to give it back to you.

Words of the Wealthy

An **underwriter** is a brokerage firm that handles the process of offering a company's stock to the public through an **initial public offering**.

Taking Your Company Public— The Initial Public Offering

If your heart is set on achieving Wealth Level 5, you must understand how to take your company public. When you make an *initial public offering* (IPO), you sell a certain percentage of your company's stock to the public for money. You usually sell only a minimal amount of stock so that you can still maintain control. The underwriter helps the company decide upon the price of the new shares and the timing of the IPO.

Taking your company public gives you the opportunity to cash in on your company's success without having to give up control or sell your majority interest of the shares. Here are some of the benefits of taking your company public:

➤ You only sell part of your company.

➤ You can still be the largest shareholder and maintain some control.

➤ The value of your company is much higher.

➤ Your stock is much more liquid.

➤ Publicly held stock can more easily be used as collateral.

All these benefits come with a price:

➤ You have to give up some future profits.

➤ You have to fully disclose financial information on your company.

➤ Your company will be highly regulated by the Securities Commission.

➤ You must answer to shareholders.

➤ You must answer to your board of directors.

Other Books that Can Help

If you decide to start your own business, be sure to check out *The Complete Idiot's Guide to Being an Entrepreneur in Canada*. It is filled with great tips and all the ideas you need to get started. Your library and local bookstore will have other titles that will help.

The Least You Need to Know

➤ Maximize the profit margin of your business. It will not only help you get to Wealth Levels 4 and 5, but will make your business more attractive to a buyer.

➤ Find the most successful businesses in your industry and model after them. It's the best way to grow exponentially, dominate your competition, and achieve Wealth Levels 4 and 5.

➤ Don't try to sell your business without a business broker or intermediary.

➤ Take time to reflect on what you expect from the sale and what it will take to reach Wealth Levels 4 or 5, *before* you begin to negotiate the sale.

Part 4

Rich People Have Rich Habits

One thing I've noticed about most, if not all, wealthy people I know is that they have certain habits that help them to maintain their wealth for themselves as well as for their heirs. I've covered many of these habits in the earlier parts of the book, but this part will cover a few more you should be aware of as you approach Wealth Levels 3, 4, and 5.

First, wealthy people pay close attention to the amount of taxes they pay. Second, they live their lives according to certain rules or paradigms that seem to prolong their wealth. And third, they use planning methods that allow them to achieve extraordinary goals. The last three chapters in this book will teach you these habits so that you can maintain wealth for yourself and generations to come.

Chapter 22

Reducing Your Tax Bite

In This Chapter

➤ The only tax shelters left

➤ Silly mistakes people make that cost them big

➤ Estate planning made simple

➤ Why you will need a tax attorney

The importance of minimizing taxes is directly related to the size of your wealth and the amount of taxes you pay. My accountant estimated the amount of taxes I would have to pay by April of next year, and I nearly had a heart attack. Suddenly, I'm motivated to do everything I can to fight taxes. However, I know from experience that certain tools and strategies work and others do not. This chapter focuses on the habits and strategies that do help, as well as the habits that don't. There are not a lot of tax shelters or loopholes left anymore. However, this chapter does cover several strategies you can still use.

What about your heirs? If you died today, would your assets be distributed to the right people? Who would be your executor? This chapter will help you understand the basics of estate planning, as well as get you started on your own plan.

Words of the Wealthy

A **retirement savings plan** is an account into which pre-tax dollar contributions are made, to be used later during retirement. The primary benefit is that all assets within the plan grow tax-deferred until taken out at a later date.

Wealth Warning

Don't let an insurance salesman talk you into using a life insurance policy for the purpose of accumulating cash value during your lifetime for investment and retirement income. It's way too expensive and far too complex for these purposes.

The Last of the Great Tax Shelters

Back in the late 1970s, limited partnerships were the hottest tax shelters around. They lured billions of dollars from investors who were looking for tax breaks. What the majority of these investors got instead was a big loss. They thought saving tax was more important than making money.

Things are different now and the real tax shelters, for the most part, no longer exist. What remain now are RRSPs. I've mentioned them before, but here they are again.

Contribute to an RRSP

You can contribute up to 18 percent of your earned income from the previous year, to a maximum of $13,500. You deduct the contribution from your taxable income, and the interest, dividends, and capital gains compound themselves tax-free, as long they remain in the RRSP. You can move the money, within an RRSP, into all sorts of investments—from guaranteed investment certificates to mutual funds to stocks and bonds.

The contribution limit applies to all contributions to a registered pension fund, whether we make them ourselves or whether they are made on our behalf (with our money, don't forget) by our employer. Many of us work full time for an employer, who deposits a portion of our earnings into a company pension plan. That means we have to subtract our pension contributions from our total maximum RRSP contribution—18 percent of last year's earned income—to determine the amount that we can contribute ourselves.

Because they have to pay tax on the money when they remove it from an RRSP, many people wonder why they should bother investing in an RRSP at all.

Here's why: even after you pay the tax when you remove your money from an RRSP, you still end up with substantially more than you would have if you had invested it outside an RRSP.

The Most Common Tax–Related Mistakes

One of the most common characteristics I see among wealthy people is their knowledge of taxes and their tenacity in eliminating tax-related mistakes. They hate mistakes, especially when it means paying more taxes than they should. They do everything in their power to pay the least amount of taxes. A large part of this effort is not making the silly mistakes most other people make.

Believing Tax Savings Are Priority Number One

For people who make building wealth a priority, the most common tax-related mistake is the belief that saving taxes is more important than making money. Don't let this happen to you. Remember your first goal is to build wealth.
Saving taxes must be, at best, your second goal.

Making Silly Mathematical Errors

One of the best ways to reduce your tax is to reduce mistakes. In fact, a number of accountants I spoke to all said that the most common mistake was simple mathematical error. These mathematical errors can continue to affect your numbers, especially if you've designed your own spreadsheets for estimating your taxes and financial statement projections. I know this from the silly mistakes I've made in the mathematical formulas I use while doing my own financial statement projections. Once the mistake is made, it can continue to be a problem until it's detected.

Treasure Tip

When you do your own tax work or financial statement projections, remember the carpenters' rule: measure twice, cut once. That *is*, double-check your work!

Keeping Poor Records

Failing to keep good records of expenses will cost you a lot of money, but it is easy to correct. If you can't correct it, hire someone who will. Set up a system of records and maintain it well. Keep track of all contributions to charity, cost bases of investments, confirmations of buys and sells from your brokerage firm, and all cheque registers. Otherwise, you are going to overlook deductions, lose important records, and pay your accountant and Revenue Canada more money than you should.

Wealth Warning

A classic example of poor record-keeping is the mutual fund buyer who purchased a mutual fund years ago, but has no statements or records of all the dividends that have been reinvested. Every rein-vestment of dividends creates a new cost basis for the purchased shares.

Treasure Tip

Don't be afraid to question your accountant's work, ideas, or actions. Remember, he's human and can certainly make mistakes, too.

Trying to Do It All Yourself

I see this all the time—people trying to do their own taxes and financial statements just to save a dime. Why not hire a specialist who can do all this for you? Here's a list of reasons why:

➤ An accountant is a specialist who knows the tax code

➤ One person *dedicated* to this will do a better job

➤ Other people may be more objective than you are

➤ Hiring help eliminates any procrastination

➤ The cost is nothing compared to the potential mistakes and sleepless nights of worry

Overlooking Deductions

The following is a list of some of the most overlooked deductions:

➤ Fees for tax preparation services and Revenue Canada audits

➤ Amortization of taxable bond premiums

➤ Appreciation on property donated to charities

➤ Business gifts of $25 or less

➤ Cellular telephones and charges used for your business

➤ Cleaning and laundering services when travelling

➤ Commissions on sales of property

➤ Contact lenses

➤ Depreciation of home computers

➤ Fees for a safety-deposit box to hold investments

Withholding Too Much or Too Little

If your tax refund is large, you are withholding too much money, and consequently, Revenue Canada is getting a tax-free loan from you. Don't let this happen too long. You'll lose out on the power of compounding over time that's so important to building wealth. However, be careful not to withhold too little money. Have your accountant calculate your estimated quarterly taxes for you each year, and adjust your withholding or quarterly tax payment accordingly. A penalty for underpaying your taxes would be a total waste of money.

Not Taking Advantage of a Registered Retirement Plan

As I said earlier in this chapter, a registered retirement plan is one of the best tax shelters available today.

Not Realizing You Can't Take It with You

It is important to recognize the fact that at your death, you can't take any of your wealth with you. Therefore, it is imperative that you plan for the distribution of your wealth well in advance. This brings us to one of the most important habits of the rich—estate planning.

What Exactly Is Estate Planning?

Estate planning involves the accumulation and disposition of property (or the estate) for the owner and his family or other heirs. The term "planning" implies the existence of goals. The goals in the case of estate planning can include one or more of the following:

➤ To provide security for the direct surviving family

➤ To make sure your assets go where you want them to go

➤ To minimize the financial cost in the transfer of assets, especially estate taxes

➤ To simplify the transfer of assets at your death

➤ To minimize family conflict, hardship, and emotional stress

➤ To provide for the valuation and transfer of a closely held business

Estate planning is also useful in preventing worst-case scenarios:

➤ Direct family members left with financial insecurity

➤ Improper distribution of assets to beneficiaries

Wealth Warning

Don't fall victim over the phone to a slick bond salesman. I know bond salesmen that can make a bond sound so delicious that you'll have to pry yourself off the phone to keep from buying. Do your homework on the salesperson—and yourself—before you buy one.

Words of the Wealthy

Estate planning is simply the art and study of preserving wealth for family and future generations. It involves planning tools and techniques that cannot only reduce estate taxes, but also make things a lot simpler after your death.

➤ Property transferred to minors who aren't old enough to manage it

➤ Only illiquid assets available to pay high estate taxes

➤ Unnecessarily high administrative expenses

➤ Family bitterness and jealousy

The Tools of Estate Planning

The will is the most important tool in estate planning. It is used primarily to maintain wealth for the next generation. It can:

➤ Designate the primary and secondary beneficiaries

➤ Establish trusts through which assets are transferred

➤ Identify how estate taxes will be paid

➤ Appoint guardians for children

➤ Appoint executors, trustees, and fiduciaries as well as specify how they are to carry out their respective duties

Trusts are also important tools. They are written documents that appoint a trustee and provide beneficiaries the benefit of property ownership without the responsibility of managing that property. They are used in addition to wills to take full advantage of the tax laws regarding estate planning. The typical trust sets up an account in the name of the trust, into which assets are placed for the benefit of the owner or her heirs. There are *inter vivos* trusts created by the estate owner before death, and *testamentary trusts* created in the estate owner's will that go into effect at death.

Wealth Warning

Life insurance commissions are usually equal to at least the first year's premium or at least 7 percent if you pay a lump sum premium. Insurance is important and not all life agents are bad; you just need to be aware of the huge influence the commission creates. Shop around before you buy.

Gifts are common estate planning tools that wealthy people habitually use to reduce their potential estate tax burden. If you give some of your wealth to your heirs now, tax-free, they won't have to pay probate fees on the money later—when you're gone.

Life insurance can also be important for two reasons. First, if you don't have an estate to leave to your family, life insurance can provide them with one. This, in turn, would help ensure their financial security after your death. Second, life insurance can be used to pay probate fees at your death.

Retirement plans are also a tool for estate planning. All qualified plans require a designated primary and secondary beneficiary. At the account holder's death, the proceeds are paid directly to the primary beneficiary, or, in a case where the account holder and primary beneficiary die at the same time, the secondary beneficiary. Since the proceeds go directly to the beneficiary, they can sometimes provide instant liquidity for the estate, which may be needed for various reasons.

Getting Started

You must first realize that estate planning is not a one-time thing. After you get the basics set up, you must make the maintenance of your estate plan a habit. The first step to estate planning is deciding what you want to happen after your death, where you want your assets to go, and how your heirs will be able to pay any potential estate taxes that might result. Almost all tax lawyers will provide you with an estate planning questionnaire that will make the planning process much smoother.

Treasure Tip

If you need an insurance agent, I suggest you work with an independent Chartered Life Underwriter. This will ensure that you get some experience and objectivity, along with several quotes from different insurance companies.

The second step involves hiring a tax lawyer to help you design the plan, as well as the right tools you'll need to make it all happen. How can you find the best lawyer? Ask other successful business friends who they would recommend. You might also ask your accountant for a referral. Talk to several lawyers before you select one. Ask for client references, and then call them.

The third step is getting the plan in place and maintaining that plan. This involves yearly checkups with your lawyer to make any changes necessary.

Remember, I am neither a tax lawyer nor an accountant, and no book can take the place of either. Therefore, be sure you check with your accountant and tax lawyer before you use any of the tax or estate planning ideas in this book.

The Least You Need to Know

➤ Wealthy people realize that just because an investment product offers tax-free or tax-deferred income doesn't mean it's suitable for them—or worth investing in.

➤ The best place to find the right accountant is through a referral from another business owner whose business is growing and experiencing the same problems yours will be.

➤ Wealthy people make it a habit to eliminate all personal debt and they use mortgage debt only when necessary.

➤ Wealthy people take advantage of all the estate planning tools available by hiring experienced tax lawyers.

The Wealth Paradigms, and Why People Fail to Get Rich

In This Chapter

➤ Why people don't get rich

➤ The definition of a paradigm

➤ Why paradigms are so important

➤ The paradigm of past performance

➤ The paradigm of philanthropy

Your mind is your biggest asset when it comes to building wealth. Unfortunately, it can also be your biggest liability. Most wealthy people understand this concept and use it to their advantage. They understand the mindsets or mental habits necessary for building wealth, which I've discussed in detail throughout this book.

What you need to examine now are your own mindsets or paradigms. First, you have to understand the definition of paradigms. Second, you need to know how they work and how they can affect you in your everyday life. Once you understand them, you can use all the habits and strategies in this book to build your own wealth paradigms.

11 Reasons People Fail to Get Rich

There are hundreds of reasons people fail to build wealth. Take a look at the following list, and if any of them sound familiar, do all you can immediately to correct the problem and change the way you think.

➤ They work hard but are not smart.

➤ They're not willing to delegate.

➤ They accept self-imposed limitations.

➤ They don't live within their means so they don't have enough to save, and are too proud to scale back their lifestyles.

➤ They're waiting for an inheritance.

➤ They're not willing to take risk.

➤ They don't do enough homework to protect themselves from scavengers.

➤ They don't channel their efforts in the direction of their passion.

➤ They lack single-mindedness of thought.

➤ They let pride get in the way.

➤ They expect and accept entitlements (like welfare).

Realistically, this list is endless. However, each of the items has something in common. Every one involves a mental belief or mindset that ultimately prevents the person from building any significant wealth. These are paradigms. If you understand what paradigms are and how they work, maybe you can improve your chances of building your own wealth.

The Study of Paradigms

In my attempt to fully understand the human mind and the tendency to develop mindsets, I was led to the study of paradigms. This single subject has been one of the primary catalysts for my success in business and my achievement of Wealth Level 4. Without the knowledge of paradigms and how they affected my own life, I don't think I would ever have achieved what I have in the last five years. I'm not exaggerating. My business would more than likely have failed, and I would not have had the opportunity to write this book. Paradigms are incredibly powerful. If you're not aware of your own set of paradigms and how they control your life, you're destined to fail. Take my advice: learn all you can about your own paradigms immediately. You'll never make it to Wealth Levels 4 or 5 without this knowledge.

The greatest contemporary book written on paradigms is *Future Edge* by Joel Arthur Barker. It will change forever the way you look at your world—and for the better.

A paradigm is a set of rules that people perceive as their reality. This same set of rules tells you what can and

Words of the Wealthy

The word **paradigm** (pronounced pair-a-dime) originates from the Greek word *paradeigma*, which means model or pattern.

cannot happen. It also defines success and failure. It's like playing cards. Someone years ago decided upon the rules of the game, and, therefore, that's how to play the game. For some unknown reason, no one really ever questions the rules. They just play the game.

Let me illustrate the power of paradigms using an example. Look at the nine-dot diagram shown on the next page, and draw one like it on a piece of paper.

The objective is to connect all nine dots using four straight lines, and without picking up your pen. Take your pen and begin on one dot. You can only draw four straight lines, and remember you cannot take your pen off the paper. Each line must be

Treasure Tip

A paradigm is simply a mindset or way of perceiving the world. It's the smile of the mother to the baby, it's the forest to the deer, it's the water to the fish, and it's the New York Stock Exchange to the broker on the floor as he screams out a trade.

continuous from the last. If you really want to understand how the human mind thinks, you'll try this exercise. Then flip ahead to find one way to solve the puzzle.

This exercise is more than just a puzzle. It's a lesson in life—at least it was for me. Take a look at the completed puzzle. Ask yourself this question: What had to happen for the puzzle to be solved?

After sharing this with thousands of people in my workshops, the most common reply I get is, "You had to get out of the box," or "You had to go out of the boundaries." My reply is simply, "What box? What boundaries? I drew nine dots."

Nine-Dot Diagram

One Possible Answer

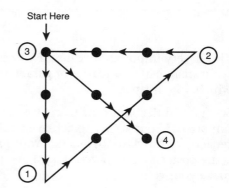

Treasure Tip

One thing that will hold you back from building wealth in your life is a self-imposed limitation. These are usually easy to set up, but often difficult to identify and eliminate.

Did you see a box or boundaries when you first saw the nine-dot diagram? If you drew a box in your mind and limited yourself to its boundaries, you never solved the puzzle. If you did not draw a box in your mind and were open-minded enough not to limit yourself, how many times did you try to solve the puzzle?

There are two things to learn from this exercise. First, your ability to achieve wealth is directly influenced by your ability to identify and control your own personal paradigms. The only way you will be able to do this is through honest reflection and self-examination. Constantly ask yourself these three questions:

➤ Why did I react the way I just did?

➤ What has happened in the past to cause me to react that way?

➤ Do I need to reexamine any of my beliefs (paradigms)?

That Reminds Me...

I saw a T-shirt recently that had a rodeo scene of a cowboy riding a bull. It said, "Guts, cuts, and sore butts." Seems like the same thing I encountered starting my own business on my path to wealth.

This is very important because if you can open your mind and see outside your box (your imagined boundaries or paradigms), you'll be able to achieve all the wealth of which you dream.

Second, think about how many times you tried to solve the puzzle. Why was this important? Your ability to achieve wealth is directly influenced by your own level of tenacity or "stick-to-it-iveness." Your path toward wealth will more than likely involve some obstacles, and if you don't have the passion to stay with the process, you may not make your goal.

How many times will you try? How much faith do you have in your ability? Will you give up and surrender, or will you continue until you achieve your goal? Your creativity, faith, and tenacity are directly related to the level of wealth you are capable of achieving.

When Galileo proved Copernicus's theory correct that the Earth revolved around the sun, he was exiled for years. Why? Simply because the world was not ready for this new idea. Besides, all the books on the subject would have had to be changed. What irony. This guy was exiled for a theory that happened to be correct.

As you develop your plans to build wealth, are you ready to test your willingness to accept new ideas? Are you ready to look at conventional wisdom that you have used for years and accept the fact that it may no longer work? Or will you let conventional wisdom intimidate you?

The Wealth Paradigms

For more than 10 years, I've studied investors who have built their wealth using wealth paradigms. In fact, this entire book is based on these paradigms. Each has been taught in the context of habits, investment selection tactics, and laws. There's no point in repeating them all, but it is important to understand how they work. Therefore, I've selected three paradigms, which you'll recognize from Part 2, that have helped me build the foundation of my investment strategies.

Most of the wealth paradigms I've found usually run counter to conventional wisdom. The ones I'm about to discuss are certainly no exception. Therefore, it is important to understand not only the wealth paradigms, but also the conventional wisdom it goes against—which I call the "anti-wealth" paradigms. In each of the descriptions below, I begin with the anti-wealth paradigm and finish with the wealth paradigm. You'll notice that most of these involve the concept of investing, but each can also be applied to other life situations.

Past Performance versus Hockey Puck Paradigms

What criteria do you use when selecting a mutual fund? Most investors use a one- to 10-year track record. And that's not surprising, considering the fact that almost all the books ever printed on the subject of mutual funds state past performance as the key criteria for selection. Go to any extensive magazine rack in Canada and chances are you will find one, if not two, magazines addressing the issue of "Top Performing Funds" or "The Best Mutual Funds." All of these funds address one primary issue: past performance and its use in selecting a mutual fund. What makes this concept so ironic is the disclaimer you see with each of these ads and articles: "Past performance is no indication of future returns."

A friend of mine once said to me, "Hey, why not use past performance? If you wanted to predict the top passers in the NFL this year, I'd be willing to bet that you would find eight of the top 10 were in the top 15 during the previous season." He might be right about the NFL, but the mutual fund world doesn't work that way. I've studied this stuff for years and it's been proven in many different studies that the top performers last year

That Reminds Me...

If that's not enough to catch your attention, consider this: How far would you get in your car (in a forward direction) if you had to look in your rearview mirror 95 percent of the time? If markets repeated themselves, past performance would give you an indication of future returns. Unfortunately, the market changes exponentially on a daily basis. Therefore, no matter how well a fund did last year, it is a new year now, and everyone (including the fund manager) is faced with completely different circumstances—completely different markets.

(or the past 5, 10, 15 years) are seldom the big performers the next year (or the next 5, 10, 15 years). If what they say is correct and past performance can be used to predict next year's winners, we could put together a quantitative model and build a winning portfolio consistently over time. Unfortunately, the stock market and mutual fund market don't work like the NFL. If that were true, I'd pick the very best players each year and beat everyone else. It's simply not that easy. If you have ever read any of the magazines in your local grocery store, you'd certainly think it was—but it's not. Just about every book ever printed on mutual funds says the same thing my friend did, but I'm telling you it just doesn't work. If it were that easy, everyone would own the best funds every year.

Barker said in his book *Discovering the Future*, "Your past guarantees nothing." He explains that it doesn't matter how good you are at the old paradigm. When the new paradigm begins, everyone starts all over at zero. Barker's statement holds true when investing. The first and most common investment paradigm is what I call the Past Performance Paradigm. This is one of the most devastating and misunderstood of all investment-related paradigms.

When I see a list of last year's best performing funds, I think, "Wow! What a waste of paper!" It reminds me of when I watch a football game and the play-by-play announcer starts talking about last year's game, who won, all the statistics, and then uses the information to comment on the possible outcome of the current night's game. How completely crazy is this? You have totally new teams, maybe even a new coach, new plays, a new quarterback, and probably a whole new field!

The proper paradigm to use is what I call the hockey puck paradigm, which I described earlier in the book using the story of Wayne Gretzky. He said he skates to where he thinks the hockey puck is going to be while everyone else skates to where the hockey puck is (or used to be). The best way to select any investment—whether it be a mutual fund, stock, bond, real estate, or business—is to determine where the market is going, and invest in that direction.

Fear versus Contrarian Paradigms

Another interesting paradigm concerning investment psychology is the reaction most investors have to sudden heavy market declines. One of my clients panicked when Gorbachev was kidnapped and the market dropped suddenly. He wanted to sell everything, and I could not talk him out of it. His paradigms prevented him from seeing any other alternative. Consequently, we sold at the lowest prices that day. Of course, the market suddenly reversed and most funds went back up in price quickly before he changed his mind. His mindset was, "Get out before we lose everything." He fell victim to the fear paradigm.

Words of the Wealthy

The **past performance paradigm** is the mindset and belief that the past performance of an investment should be the primary justification for purchase.

The opposite of the fear paradigm is the contrarian paradigm. A contrarian is someone who invests when everyone is selling. Sudden heavy losses in the market are common and will occur randomly with great intensity. A contrarian views this as an opportunity to purchase investments at lower prices. If you refer to a chart of the stock market over its history, you will notice that all bear markets are followed eventually by a bull market. The contrarian understands this. Stock markets around the world sank like a stone in the fall of 1998, as many panicking investors rushed to sell. A few months later, the losses had been made up. Similarly, market analysts continue to refer to the "crash" of 1987. But if you look at a long-term chart of the U.S. stock market, you'd be hard-pressed to even point out the "crash."

Words of the Wealthy

The **fear paradigm** is the mindset and belief that when everyone is afraid of an investment, it should be avoided. The opposite is the **contrarian paradigm**, based on the belief that if everyone hates an investment, it should definitely be considered.

Greed versus Philanthropic Paradigms

Victims of the greed paradigm focus single-mindedly on building their wealth without any plans for sharing with others or contributing to charity. This is a terrible trap that will inevitably result in loneliness and horrible self-esteem.

The most successful and happiest wealthy people I know contribute regularly to their favourite charities. They find that they ultimately get back more than they give. It may be direct or indirect, but personally I do get back much more than I give away to charities. I call this my philanthropic paradigm. It's not that you should expect anything back, and I think that's important to understand. You must give unconditionally. If you do, you'll be rewarded many times. Call it divine intervention or synchronicity, but it does work. You reap what you sow. Everything goes full circle in the balance of life, and charitable giving is no exception.

I urge you to give this paradigm a chance in your life. Once you experience it, share it with others. Be a role model for giving in your community. Encourage your friends and business associates to contribute to their favourite charities and to become role models for philanthropy. Your contribution doesn't have to be monetary. You could simply offer hands-on volunteer work.

One Final Note on Paradigms

There are too many paradigms to cover. Now that you understand how they work, however, it will be much easier for you to develop your own set. Throughout your journey toward wealth, the most important thing to remember is that some paradigms will help you and some will hurt you. The key is to continue reexamining the paradigms you pick up. Identify them, isolate them, and make sure they are based on beliefs that are true and real.

That Reminds Me...

One of the most philanthropic people I know told me recently that his parents had given to numerous charities anonymously. They had also funded college educations for local children who couldn't afford tuition. They did almost all of their giving on a private basis. This might seem generous, but my friend said the privacy was unfortunate. He wishes now that his parents had been more public with their giving. They could have been excellent role models for the community.

The Least You Need to Know

➤ The reason people don't get rich is their negative mental paradigms related to wealth, finances, and self-imposed limitations.

➤ Once you understand paradigms and how they can affect every aspect of your life, you'll be able to achieve anything you can think of, including Wealth Levels 4 and 5.

➤ As you build your wealth, you must adopt a philanthropic paradigm to ensure your contribution to society and value to your community.

Chapter 24

Planning Secrets That Will Build Wealth Faster

In This Chapter

➤ The most powerful planning tool

➤ The best time-management systems

➤ Brainstorming, mind-mapping, and project planning

➤ Yearly, monthly, weekly, and daily planning

➤ How to make better decisions

If you want to build great wealth, you must learn how to set goals and achieve them. All wealthy people plan regularly. Every great accomplishment of mine has been the direct result of planning skills, which are simple to learn and develop. After using more than 11 different time- and life-management systems, I've developed what I consider to be the best planning system available. Use the ideas in this chapter to design the system that works best for you.

I've learned that whatever you plan for is achievable to the exact degree to which you believe you can achieve it. Therefore, it is imperative that you believe in yourself and your ability to realize the goals you have. The planning secrets in this chapter will help you to do just that. You'll learn both the tools and the strategies necessary to acquire great wealth.

The Power of Your Mind

Before we discuss the actual planning process, you must first understand and appreciate the power of your mind. It is the most important wealth-building tool you have. For example, did you know that your mind doesn't know the difference between reality and imagination? That makes your ability to imagine quite a powerful tool. It allows you to actually live (or practise) every experience in advance. This is called mental imagery.

Mental imagery is the most important tool in the planning process. You can use mental imagery to go through the motions before you actually attempt your task. This will give you the opportunity to capture every step so that you can plan for it and improve it prior to actually executing the plan. You'll be able to know in advance exactly what to expect. You'll know the resources necessary, what needs to be delegated, the possible obstacles to overcome, and the key people you'll need to help you.

Try this exercise. Have someone read the next paragraph to you while you close your eyes. For this exercise to work, you must keep your eyes closed. Ask the helper to carefully read the paragraph aloud at a fairly slow pace.

> *Imagine that you have a nice fresh bright yellow lemon in your hands. Feel the rough, almost oily texture. Bring it up to your nose and smell it. (pause a few seconds) Smell the wonderful lemony scent. It smells clean and fresh. Now take the lemon and slice it in half. Bring one half up to your nose and smell it once again (pause a few seconds). Now take a deep breath and BITE IT! (pause a few seconds). Is your mouth watering?*

Maybe I'm crazy about lemons, but my mouth was watering. I wanted a lemon so badly, I almost had to go out and buy one. It proved to me the power of my imagination.

That Reminds Me...

The world's greatest golfers probably best understand the concept of mental imagery. Before they drive their ball off the tee or take any other shot, they go through every little motion in their mind as if they were actually making the shot. Most of them do this more than once. The mental practice helps them perfect the shot before they even swing the club. You can do this, too, in your own life. It doesn't matter whether you mow lawns or do brain surgery, mental imagery can help improve your performance.

Time- and Life-Planning Tools

I've used more than 11 different time- and life-planning systems. I've concluded that they all have their own strengths and weaknesses. Everybody is different, and what works for me might or might not work for you. In my opinion, here is one of the best systems:

> ➤ **Franklin Planner Organizer** 1-800-265-6655. This system is based on Stephen Covey's book *The Seven Habits Of Highly Effective People*. It comes in different sizes and costs between US$50 and US$200, depending on which package you prefer. It is also available in software form (Franklin Planner Software) that can be used with a Palm Pilot. The software costs US$99.95.

Before you spend money on a system, do a little research. Call potential companies and request information. No matter how good a system is, don't hesitate to customize or improve the system for your needs.

The planning steps in the rest of this chapter are my own personal favourites. They are best implemented using a version of the system listed above. You can certainly design your own system; however, it would take away from the valuable planning time you'll need to accomplish your own goals. My point is that this system costs money, but it is worth every dime.

Yearly Planning

Yearly planning is a key wealth-building habit. This section will describe the most important elements of the yearly planning session. Use these to design your own session.

Mission Statement Work

Have you ever asked yourself this question: Who am I? Take a minute and think. What are the most important values in your life? What do you value the most in life? Look back at your answers to the three questions in Chapter 5. Your answers will help you to start your list. I've listed my value categories below. Yours will be different, but maybe the categories will be similar.

➤ Spiritual well-being   ➤ Financial security

➤ Physical well-being   ➤ Knowledge improvement

➤ Family   ➤ Fun and recreation

➤ Friends   ➤ Career

For each of your value areas, write a mission statement that explains exactly what is important to you, as well as your primary goal regarding that area of your life. Below the mission statement, begin listing your dreams and goals within that particular area. Keep this list handy so you can add more dreams and goals later. It should be considered a working list that will be added to regularly. Anytime you think of something you want to accomplish, write it down and add it to the list. Be sure to check off each goal as you accomplish it.

Conventional Brainstorming

So few people understand how to brainstorm properly, and even fewer appreciate the power that can come from it. To be successful at brainstorming, you need to follow just a few guidelines. If you take the time to follow the guidelines, you will immediately increase your chances of achieving your desired wealth level. The objective of a brainstorming session is to produce the largest number of ideas possible. You're looking for quantity first, and quality second. Here's how it works.

First, start with an open-ended question. For example, your question might be, "How can I reduce my monthly expenses?" Perhaps you want to address a problem or paradigm that's holding you back in your wealth-building activities. Put it in the form of a question: "How can I eliminate this mindset and think more objectively?" Your goal is to write down as many answers to the direct question as you can possibly think of within an hour. Second, write down the first things that come to your mind without concern for grammar or spelling. Just write whatever you think about—no matter how ridiculous or crazy the answer seems. (If you brainstorm in a team setting, make sure no one criticizes any answers.) Third, sit in solitude with no possible interruptions from other people or the phone. Fourth, do this outdoors or be as close to nature as you can. Sit by a house plant if you have to. If you can't get close to nature because it's dark and cold outside and there are no house plants, try to find a quiet place or put on some soothing classical music. Your goal is to create a peaceful atmosphere, free from distraction, that will open your imagination. Fifth, don't stop until you have at least 20 answers.

Go back to the section titled What Business Will You Start? in Chapter 17. The three questions listed are great brainstorming questions. They should also be part of your yearly planning sessions.

Mind-Mapping

My favourite way to brainstorm is called mind-mapping. It was taught to me by my business consultant, Roger Lane, who teaches the Priority Management course. In fact, every chapter in this book was written initially using a mind-map. I'll explain how it works using the mind-map I drew to brainstorm the topics for this chapter.

First, in the centre of a blank piece of paper, I wrote the name of the chapter and circled it. In your case, you would write down the idea or yearly goal you want to brainstorm about. Second, from that circle, I drew a line out to the upper left-hand corner and wrote down the first thing that came to my mind, which was my "communications book." Below this I wrote down the categories within that book. I continued to write down all the ideas that came to mind without any concern for order. You would do the same when creating your own map, getting related thoughts about the question down on paper as they occur to you.

Once you've completed your mind-map, use it to organize and plan your goal—which in my case was to write this chapter. Take your mind-map and identify the main topics or tasks. Then list in chronological order all the steps necessary to accomplish each task. The result should be an organized list of tasks and an organized plan that can actually be used to accomplish a goal. I wrote every chapter in this book using mind-maps. Almost every great goal I've achieved in the last several years began with a mind-map.

A Mind-Map Example

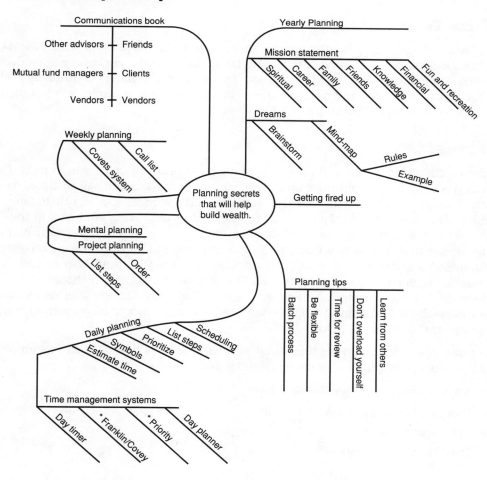

Why is mind-mapping better than conventional brainstorming? According to the research I've studied (as well as my own experiences), the human brain doesn't necessarily work chronologically. It produces thoughts randomly instead of logically. The people who understand this and allow their minds to create ideas in this fashion are much more effective planners. Because mind-mapping gives the brain the opportunity to express ideas naturally, it is the tool of choice for planning and brainstorming.

Monthly Planning

Your personal monthly planning sessions should be conducted mostly in solitude. I often bring a friend just to bounce ideas off, but most of the time I try to sit alone. These sessions allow me to think freely without interruption. This section points out the primary elements of my monthly planning session.

Prioritize Goals

From your categorized list of dreams and goals, decide which goals you want to work on now and which ones you want to save until later. Continue this process until you've prioritized the entire list. Don't be surprised if your priorities change occasionally. Select the most important goal and proceed to project planning. For example, let's assume that your goal is to achieve Wealth Level 3 in 10 years.

Plan Projects

Once you decide on a goal or dream, it has now become a project for you to plan. The first step is to state your objective and expected results as specifically as possible. Write it down: *I want to achieve Wealth Level 3 in 10 years*. Add any more specifics that come to mind. Second, use a mind-map to list all the steps necessary. Write your goal in the middle of the page and begin writing down anything that comes to mind. One part of your mind-map might be to set up a budget. Another might be to go through the steps in Chapter 4 and calculate your target savings goal. Part of this mind-map should include the resources, equipment, and facilities that will be needed. It should also include the key people who can help. Be sure to include possible obstacles, as well as solution ideas. Once the mind-map is completed, the tasks should be prioritized, and a project plan should be written.

This project plan is primarily a prioritized list of all the tasks that need to be completed. Each task should be put in chronological order and include:

➤ Steps necessary for completion

➤ Estimated time each task will require

➤ Estimated starting date

➤ Deadline for completion

The project plan should also include several lists:

➤ Key contacts and phone numbers

➤ Resources, equipment, and facilities needed

➤ Possible obstacles and how each one can be overcome

➤ What tasks can be outsourced

➤ What tasks can be done in-house

➤ Estimated costs

Once you have all the steps and resources listed, use your calendar to identify when you plan to accomplish the tasks. Select the days you plan to focus on each specific task.

Build a Project Notebook

One way to keep up with all your projects is to build a project notebook, which is a three-ring binder with dividers for each project. This tool will help keep your life, as well as your planning sessions, better organized. Use dividers to separate key elements of your project. In the case of achieving Wealth Level 3, you might set up the following dividers: investment account, retirement plan, budgeting, and business ideas. You might want to include your mind-map for future reference.

Reorganize

Each month you may want to take some time to reorganize your tasks if necessary. Things do change and you must be flexible. I guarantee that you're constantly going to

That Reminds Me...

My project notebook is a large three-ring binder with dividers for each project. Under each divider is my project plan, along with all the supporting documents. If a project begins to take up too much space, I make a separate project notebook specifically for that project. This book, for example, became a separate project notebook.

come up with new ideas that will require you to change your path. Therefore, you must review your wealth-building plan at least once a month, and keep it in order, so that you can monitor your progress.

Weekly Planning

Weekly planning is not as important to the wealth-building process as is daily planning, but it is still a great habit. Some people like to plan their week in advance. Others like to plan one day at a time. If you like the idea of weekly planning, Stephen Covey's system (the Franklin Planner Organizer) has a weekly planning sheet that's very handy. It allows you to organize your tasks according to your list of values. The key to any plan is prioritization. First, you should spend most of your time prioritizing the tasks needed to accomplish your monthly goals. Second, you should spend a little time planning the tasks you've selected for this week. What days will be dedicated to these tasks?

I still make a weekly call list that I use each week. For years, I would list people to call for the day, only to recreate more than half of the list the very next day because the people were unavailable and never called me back. Finally, I wised up and began making a weekly list. I keep track of my daily call progress using symbols like "LM," which stands for "left message," or "WCB" for "will call back."

Daily Planning

Daily planning is vital to the wealth-building process. The more you can accomplish in one day, the faster you can build your wealth. The best planned days produce the most results. One of the most powerful planning strategies in the world is planning for tomorrow, one day in advance. Why is this so powerful? It's primarily because your mind is given ample time to imagine accomplishing all that you need to accomplish. Subconsciously, your mind has time to work through all the tasks, as well as identify all the potential conflicts or problems. This enables you to awaken the next day knowing exactly what you are going to accomplish that day. You not only know what you are going to do, but you also know exactly how you're going to do it. The steps to planning your day are simple:

1. Look through your goals for the month (or week) and list the necessary steps you want to accomplish that day. Record any appointments listed in your monthly calendar.

2. Prioritize the list of steps.

3. Identify which steps must be accomplished that day using the letter "A" or number "1."

4. Identify the steps that can wait until tomorrow using the letter "B" or number "2."

5. Estimate the time it takes to accomplish each of these tasks and schedule time to work on them.

Planning Tips

➤ **Stick to your plan, but be flexible.** Things do change unexpectedly, and you might have to find a better way to achieve the wealth level you desire.

➤ **Batch process your work and control your interruptions.** Batch processing just means that you are going to single-mindedly focus on one project at a time for a given period. You can control your interruptions by closing your office door or going to a private place with no phone. Wealthy people understand the power of their own office door.

➤ **Everywhere you go, keep paper and pen ready.** You might want to carry a mini-cassette recorder. It sure makes it easy to record thoughts, especially when driving.

➤ **Don't forget to learn from others and their mistakes.** You don't build wealth by reinventing the wheel. Save some effort, time, and money by finding others who have done what you want to do. Copy and improve their successful actions, habits, etc.

➤ **Don't get overloaded.** This is one of the secrets to great wealth. Do one thing at a time. Don't try to accomplish too many goals at one time. Select the most important one for now, and focus on it. Then go to the next one.

➤ **Take time to review your progress toward building wealth.** Find new ways to accomplish your goals faster. Accountability can be very important in the accomplishment of your goals. You can be accountable to yourself, but you might also want to get a friend to be an "accountability coach." The friend may also be a great source of ideas.

Get Fired Up

If you really want to get fired up about a particular goal or project, take a piece of paper and list all of your greatest accomplishments in life including the year you accomplished them. Spend as much time as it takes to fill at least one page. These accomplishments can include anything that was important to you at that time. You could even include the day you learned how to tie your own shoe! I remember the first time I ever drove a car. Boy, was I excited and proud. I'm an avid water skier and remember vividly the first time I made it through the six buoys of a water ski slalom course. After that, I felt I could accomplish anything, including Wealth Level 5!

Any time you need some inspiration, just pull out this list. Pick one of your accomplishments that you're really proud of, and think back to that time. Close your eyes and relive the excitement and feeling of accomplishment. Now imagine yourself today, accomplishing your current goal or project. Whether it's Wealth Level 1 or 5, imagine feeling the same way as you achieve that next wealth level. Keep that feeling with you and draw power from it.

Make Better Decisions

Building wealth requires an enormous amount of decision-making ability. If you approach every major decision with the same decision-making procedure, you'll find that decisions become a lot easier. Here are the steps I take when making a critical decision:

➤ Describe the primary goal. What am I really trying to accomplish?

➤ Identify all the issues related to this goal.

➤ Gather all the information necessary.

➤ List all the alternatives to choose from. For example, doing nothing may be an alternative.

➤ List the pros and cons of each alternative.

➤ Identify the alternative that best achieves your goal in the least amount of time with the least amount of cost.

➤ Use the answers to prioritize the alternatives and select the best alternative.

If your decision involves another decision made in the past, you might want to consider using the same strategy I mentioned earlier in the book regarding "sell" decisions. It's called zero-based thinking. Ask yourself this question, "Knowing what I know now, would I have made the same decision in the past?" If the answer is no, you may want to reconsider your current situation.

Keep a Communications Book

One of the most powerful tools in my wealth-building arsenal is my communications book. I learned this idea from consultant Roger Lane, and the priority management system he taught me. In this book I have categorized and listed all the names, addresses, and phone numbers of all the people I know and work with. Here are the categories listed in my book:

➤ Friends and family

➤ Clients

➤ Vendors

➤ Other advisors

➤ Mutual fund managers

➤ Business advisors

Each of these people is also listed in a database so that I can sort, list, and send mail to them whenever I need to. The printed copy serves as a backup for the database, and the database copy serves as a backup for the printed copy.

It is important that you keep your communications book near your workplace or home. Every day, I seem to add another person to my list. Mine is more than three inches thick, so I can't very well carry it everywhere I go. If yours is small, you might want to incorporate it into your daily planner.

The Least You Need to Know

➤ The most powerful planning tool for building wealth or anything else is the mind, because it doesn't know the difference between imagination and reality, which means you can use mental imagery to practise accomplishing your goals in advance.

➤ The first step in the planning process is identifying your values: the core of your entire planning process.

➤ To plan efficiently and effectively to accomplish your next wealth level, you must learn how to mind-map and brainstorm properly.

➤ If you really want to achieve the highest wealth levels possible, build a project notebook and communications notebook that can be taken with you on planning sessions outside your office.

Glossary

Words of the Wealthy—The Whole List

Asset   Property with a market value that can be sold for cash. This can include stocks, bonds, real estate, and privately held stock. Liquid assets can be sold quickly, while illiquid assets, such as real estate or a small business, usually take some time to sell.

Capital ratio   Calculated by dividing the bank's capital by its total assets. This ratio measures the bank's availability of capital and financial strength.

Collateral   Something of value that is pledged against a loan in case of default. When you list collateral such as furniture, equipment, property, or accounts receivable, you should also include documents that will evidence the value of these items.

Contrarian   An investor who invests contrary to everyone else, buying when the market is correcting and selling when the market reaches new highs. Contrarians welcome bad news because they know investors can overreact, and, as a result, certain stock prices can fall lower than they should.

Estate planning   Simply the art and study of preserving wealth for family and future generations. It involves planning tools and techniques that can not only reduce estate taxes, but also make things a lot simpler after your death.

Fear paradigm   The mindset and belief that when everyone is afraid of an investment, the investment should be avoided. The opposite is the contrarian paradigm, which is based on the belief that if everyone hates an investment, it should definitely be considered.

Fee-only advisor   A money manager or financial planner who receives a fee for service, usually based on a percentage of assets under management, or on time. Fee-only advisors do not receive any commissions for recommended investments.

Fiduciary An advisor authorized to buy and sell securities on behalf of the client. This authorization is given in the form of a limited power of attorney signed by the client. An advisor has fiduciary responsibility when he is buying and selling securities for the client.

Fixed annuity A contract with a life insurance company through which you give a sum of money, and, based on your age, life expectancy, and current interest rates, you'll eventually receive monthly payments for as long as you live. You decide when you want to receive payments, and, until then, the money grows tax-deferred.

Full-service brokerage firm A firm that offers its clients securities as well as advice. The firm is compensated by commissions, which are paid at the time transactions are made. A discount brokerage firm offers the same selection of securities, but because they do not offer advice, their commissions are usually lower.

Fundamental analysis The study of the basic facts that determine a security's value. A fundamental analysis of a mutual fund includes the study of the securities within the fund, the manager, the philosophy, the expenses, and the average P/E ratio.

Gross domestic product (GDP) The total value of goods and services produced by a country during a year. The GDP's rate of growth is much more popular in the news than is the actual total GDP number. When plotted on a graph, this growth rate illustrates the economic cycle.

Growth A manager who is growth-oriented searches for stocks with high earnings growth. Investors are willing to pay relatively higher prices for these stocks on the chance that they may rise even higher later.

Haggle A word that comes from the Old English term heawan, which meant to beat or cut. Haggling is the process of negotiating the lowest price possible in a purchase transaction. Canada and the U.S. are among the few countries where haggling is not a normal process of everyday shopping.

Harvesting An unconventional way of deriving income from a portfolio that includes not only dividends and interest, but also capital gains.

Hodad People who are generally fake or phoney. Hodads may look and smell as if they're rich, but if you take a close look, they owe lots of money and lease everything they have.

Inflation Most people think that inflation is a simple rise in prices. The technical definition is an increase in the volume of money and credit relative to available goods, which results in a substantial and continuing rise in the general price level. The rate of inflation is measured by the month-to-month percentage change of the Consumer Price Index (CPI).

Junk bond Also known as a high-yield bond, a junk bond represents an IOU issued by a company whose ability to repay its interest and principal in a timely manner depends on the economy and on the company's ability to sell its products or services. Canadian Bond Rating Service as well as Dominion Bond Rating Service offer corporate bond ratings. A junk bond is any bond with a rating below BBB or Baa.

Letter of engagement   A document prepared by an accountant that outlines in detail what he or she will do for you. The letter should also illustrate how the accountant will be compensated and at what rate.

Liquid assets   Includes assets that can be instantly converted into cash. Illiquid assets are the opposite; they are not easily converted into cash.

Micro-delegation   Simply the delegation of micro-view business responsibilities to other professionals. This strategy enables you to focus on the big picture for your business. It also allows you to delegate the details to other people who are often better at them than you are.

Money manager   Another name for a fee-only investment advisor, or simply a person who manages money.

Multi-level portfolio management   A term I use to describe the use of many different mutual funds in a portfolio. These funds add layers of diversification.

Net asset value   The value of each unit of a mutual fund. This is calculated by dividing the total value of the fund by the number of shares outstanding and is reported in the newspapers daily.

No-load funds   Mutual funds that can be purchased, sold, and owned without any commissions. The only charges involved are management fees. Shares are sold at the net asset value price, and no salesperson is paid to sell the shares.

No Transaction Fee (NTF) Program   A program that allows investors to buy hundreds of different no-load funds within the same account, without paying any transaction fees. The program is so popular that even full-service brokerage firms are beginning to follow in its footsteps.

Outsource   A new term that simply means to pay someone outside your firm to do a job for you. It's an alternative to directly putting someone on your payroll.

P/E ratio   The price of a stock divided by the yearly earnings per share. It compares the price of a stock relative to its earnings, which is important when you compare one stock to another. It is also important in determining if a stock is under- or overpriced relative to other stocks.

Paradigm   A word originating from the Greek word *paradeigma*, which means model or pattern.

Past performance paradigm   The belief that the past performance of an investment should be the primary justification for purchase.

Privately held company   A company whose shares are not publicly traded. Privately held stock is issued to a small number of shareholders, and the value or price of the stock is usually determined by comparisons with other similar companies, using factors such as earnings and gross income.

Pro-forma financial statements   Financial statements used to project the estimated financial results of a new company. They consist of an income statement, balance sheet, and cash flow statement.

Qualified plans   RRSPs are the main type of qualified plans into which employees can deposit part of their incomes. The deposit is made pre-tax, and the account grows tax-deferred. An individual can select from a wide number of different investment choices.

Quantitative analysis   The study of numerical information for the basis of decision-making. Under quantitative theory, everything is expressed in measurable form and is therefore predictable. Investors who subscribe to this theory believe that by studying specific market data, they can accurately predict the market's movements.

Relative strength   A graphic illustration of the percentage (or fractional) difference between the price of a security and an index (or any other security). If the security and index rose and fell equally at the same time, the graph would be a straight line.

Return on investment (ROI)   Can be calculated by dividing the net income by the amount of capital invested in the company. There are two ways to increase ROI: reduce expenses or increase sales.

Secondary market   Any market where previously issued securities are traded. The Toronto Stock Exchange (TSE) is the best known example. Through the exchange, investors can buy and sell stocks from each other.

Soft-dollars   An indirect way many advisors are paid a commission for using the services of a particular brokerage firm or mutual fund. The brokerage firm or mutual fund company usually provides the advisor with research, software, or quotation machines that are normally part of the advisor's overhead expenses. Therefore, soft-dollar payments tend to be the equivalent of commissions.

Stock   When you buy shares of stock directly or through a mutual fund, you become part owner of a company. These shares can build your wealth by paying you dividends and by rising in price.

Target savings goal (TSG)   Refers to the amount of money required each year to build a portfolio large enough to support your preferred standard of living at retirement.

Technical analysis   Using charts to read the price history and other statistical patterns of stocks or mutual funds. Many investors and most professionals use these charts to make investment decisions. A technical analyst is also known as a "chartist."

Total return   Also known as portfolio performance, this refers to the percentage return of a portfolio, which includes dividends, interest, and capital gains.

Underwriter   A brokerage firm that handles the process of offering a company's stock to the public through an initial public offering.

Value   A value-oriented manager is one who searches for undervalued stocks that are priced below what the manager actually thinks they're worth. The goal of the value manager is to sell at a profit when the market realizes the stock's true value.

Variable annuity   A variable annuity works the same way as does a fixed annuity, except that its value and payout amount varies in value according to the performance of a portfolio of mutual funds from which the contract holder can select. Typically these policies offer a stock fund, a bond fund, and a money-market fund.

Wealth   Defined by the *Oxford Canadian Dictionary* as "riches; abundant possessions." The word *wealthy* is defined as "having an abundance esp. of money." But the definition of *affluent* sounds even better: "an abundant supply of money, commodities, etc.; wealth." However, you should form your *own* definition.

List of
Web Sites

The American Stock Exchange   http://www.amex.com
This U.S. exchange is where you will find low-fee index stocks (or index shares) that track the S&P 500, S&P 400, Nasdaq 100, Dow Jones Industrial Average, and many other U.S. and international indexes.

Bank of Montreal Investorline   http://www.investorline.com
Bank of Montreal's discount broker. Good rates, plus stock charting, fund, and stock researching.

Bank Rate Monitor   http://www.bankrate.com
A lot of useful news, calculators, and up-to-date interest rate quotes for mortgages, credit cards, auto loans, home equity, and banking.

Canadian MoneySaver   http://www.canadianmoneysaver.ca
This monthly magazine has commentary on saving and investing issues for Canadians.

Charles Schwab Canada   http://www.schwabcanada.com
Good research tools, but higher commissions than other discounters.

CIBC Investors Edge   http://www.investorsedge.cibc.com
The site for CIBC's discount broker offers fund research.

The Dollar Stretcher   http://www.stretcher.com
"Living Better for Less." This site offers helpful suggestions on how to reduce expenses, as well as general tips for financial success. Stories, tips, searchable archives, and a newsletter.

Dow Jones & Co.   http://www.dowjones.com
Good site for researching companies, stocks, and business news.

E*Trade Canada   www.canada.etrade.com
A solid discount broker and a good site for stock and fund research.

Freedgar Database   http://www.freedgar.com
Real-time access to SEC filings at no charge.

The Globe and Mail   http://www.globeinvestor.com
                                http://www.globefund.com
Two handy sites for investors researching Canadian stocks and funds.

Home Path   http://www.homepath.com
This site offers online help in buying or refinancing a home. Interactive calculators and references help users in a wide array of situations.

**Hong Kong Bank of Canada
Investdirect**   http://www.hsbcinvestdirect.com
The bank's discount broker has fund and stock research.

InvestorGuide   http://www.investorguide.com
Research, news, quotes, and a lot of great links.

Investools   http://www.investools.com
Rated in top 10 sites for investors by *Barron's*. Newsletter, quotes and graphs, reports and data, and access to research.

Investor-O-Rama   http://www.investorama.com
One of the best financial sites available for investors. A huge directory of financial Web sites, portfolio tracker, research, company information, charting, market commentary, quotes, and a free electronic newsletter.

Lombard Institutional Brokerage   http://www.lombard.com
Brokerage services, quotes, and graphs.

Microsoft Investor   http://www.investor.com
A huge site offering an online portfolio monitor, MSNBC and Reuter's news offerings, and company information research.

Money Magazine Online   http://www.money.com
News, links, searchable archives, free downloads, tips, and market commentary.

Money Talks   http://www.talks.com
"The daily investment magazine for the serious individual investor." Weekly columns, daily tips, news, related links, and free annual reports.

Morningstar   http://www.morningstar.com
Statistics on more than 6,500 mutual funds, information on more than 8,000 individual stocks, a portfolio analyzer, and lots of commentary.)

Mortgage Net   http://www.mortgage-net.com
Shopping for mortgages made easy. Mortgage reference desk, calculators and tools, and interest rate trends. Economic calendar, forums, and articles.

The Motley Fool   **http://www.fool.com**
News, tips, research, quotes, and graphs. Offers a wealth of general personal finance advice.)

National Bank Discount Brokerage   **www.invesnet.com**
Good low-cost discount broker with some research on the site.

Pawws Financial Network   **http://www.pawws.com**
Brokerage services, news commentary, and market analysis.

Quicken Online   **http://www.networth.galt.com**
Investment news, quotes, book reviews, and columns.

Royal Bank Action Direct   **http://www.actiondirect.com**
A good all-around discount broker. Site allows research on funds and stocks.

Scotia Discount Brokerage   **http://www.sdbi.com**
The Bank of Nova Scotia's discount broker.

Smart Money   **http:// www.smartmoney.com**
Good commentary on U.S. business and investing issues.

Stock Detective   **http://www.stockdetective.com**
Protects investors by listing Web sites and radio and TV programs that are known to carry promotional advertising that is supposedly research. Has a history of pointing out bad investments.

TD Waterhouse   **http://www.tdwaterhouse.ca**
Toronto-Dominion Bank's popular discount broker. Plenty of tools for investing in Canada.

The Wall Street Journal   **http://www.wsj.com**
The Web's most popular subscription-based site is great for keeping up with major companies and U.S. and international business and financial markets.

The Wealthy Way   **http://www.wealthyway.com**
Money-saving and wealth-building techniques and a newsletter.

Yahoo! Finance   **http://quote.yahoo.com**
Provides free service that other sites charge for. Market monitor, an excellent portfolio tracker, and Reuter's news on individual companies.

Zacks Investment Research   **http://www.zacks.com**
Both fee and free services, including investment advice and professional information on 6,000 companies.

Index

A

Accountants, 217–225
Accounting software packages, 225
Actual savings amount, 23
Advisors. *See* Professional advisors
Affluent, 4
AIMR standards, 121, 122
Analyse your current income, 35
Analyse your current spending habits, 37–42
Andreessen, Marc, 4
Antique furniture, 60
Armchair Economist, The (Landsburg), 152
Asset, 16
Asset allocation, 139–142, 190
Asset method, 254
Attitude, 251, 252
Audio-Tech Business Book Summaries, 251
Automobile maintenance, 60
Automobile Protection Association, 59
Automobiles, 52, 58–60
Average income tax rate, 21, 22

B

Balanced funds, 106, 107
Bankers, 224, 227–235
Bankruptcy, 95, 234
Barker, Joel Arthur, 274, 278
Barrier to entry, 253
Basic personal financial planning, 223
Beating the Street (Lynch), 62
Biased investment advice, 83, 84

Bogle on Funds, 62
Bond funds, 107, 108
Bonds, 61, 95, 96
  corporate, 98, 99
  government, 95-98
  interest rates, and, 162–164
  junk, 99, 172
  provincial, 98
  30-year Canada bond, 163
  zeros, 164
Bonuses, 240, 241
Books on investing, 62
Boom Bust & Echo (Foot), 169
Brainstorming, 286
Breakpoint discounts, 180
Brokers
  business, 256
  commission-based salespeople, as, 82, 83
  discount, 86, 109, 134
  full-service, 86, 113
Budgeting, 223
Buffett—The Making of an American Capitalist (Lowenstein), 26
Business broker, 256
Business plan, 199–202
Business planning notebook, 208, 209
Business profile, 257
Business relationships, 251
Buy, when to, 155
Buy-and-hold strategy, 143

C

CAFP, 114
Canada Pension Plan (CPP), 28, 30, 43
Canadian Association of Financial Planners (CAFP), 114
Canadian MoneySaver, 109

Capital gain, 20
Capital ratio, 233
Carpenter's rule, 267
Cars, 52, 58–60
Cash flow, 222
Cash flow statement, 203
Catalysts, 45
CFA designation, 115
Characteristics of wealthy people, 63–65
Chartered financial analyst (CFA), 115
Charting, 153, 154
Chartist, 144
Chrapko, Evan, 4
Closed-end funds, 88, 107, 179
Collateral, 230
Commission-based salespeople, 82, 83
Commission trap, 94
Communications book, 292, 293
Complete Idiot's Guide to Being an Entrepreneur in Canada, 261
Complete Idiot's Guide to Personal Finance for Canadians, 62
Compound growth, 22, 23
Consumer price index (CPI), 21
Consumer Reports, 60
Contrarian, 155
Contrarian paradigm, 279
Corporate bonds, 98, 99
Covey, Stephen, 214
CPI, 21
CPP, 28, 30, 43
Creative thinking, 157, 158
Credit card, 51, 57
Credit history, 228, 229

Custodian fees, 179
Customer service, 252
Cycle of misery, 184

D

Daily planning, 290
Damage control plan, 212, 213
Day planner, 62
Debt, 57
Decision making, 64, 252, 292
Definitions (glossary), 295–299
Delegating, 241, 242
Demographic tactic, 169
Deposit account, 51
Desires, 158
Direct-debit feature, 56, 133
Discipline, 65, 154
Discount brokerage firm, 86, 109, 134
Discount method, 255
Discovering the Future (Barker), 278
Diversification, 108
Domestic stocks, 101

E

Earnings growth, 152,1 53
Economic cycle tactic, 166–168
Economic theory, 151–153
Economist, The, 153
Einstein, Albert, 22, 156
Employee stock ownership plan (ESOP), 244
Employment, 67–77. *See also* Self-employment
  buy stock in your company, 76, 77
  finding the right job, 68–70, 184
  job proposal, 71
  maximize income, 72, 74
  maximize savings, 74
  maximize savings in your investment account, 75, 76
  retirement plans, 75
  role model, 70
  RRSPs, 74, 75
ESOP, 244
Estate planning, 269–271
Expense reduction, 50-52. *See also* Saving money
Expenses, 19

F

Fallacies of wealth, 12
Fear of failure, 250
Fear paradigm, 279
Fee-only advisor, 114, 125, 134
Fiduciary, 113
Financial quantitative analysis, 191
Financial statement forecasting, 221. *See also* Pro-forma financial statements
Financial statements, 220, 248
Financial tools. *See* Portfolio tools
First investment decision, 127–136
Fixed annuity, 91
Fixed expenses, 19
Fixed-income securities, 95–100
Flower portfolio, 146
Foot, David K., 169
Forced inefficiency, 172
Foreign Markets Advisory, 144
Foreign stocks, 101, 102
Four Cs of advisor-client compatibility, 114-124
Franklin Planner Organizer, 285
Frog example, 157
Full-service brokerage firm, 86, 113

Fun, 184
Fundamental analysis, 144
Future Edge (Barker), 274
Future value of annuity factors, 47–49
Futures, 89

G

Gates, Bill, 4
GDP, 167
Genius, 252
GICs, 97
Gifts, 270
Globe and Mail, 62, 85, 109, 148, 155, 168
Glossary, 295–299
Goal setting, 222
Going public, 260
Government bonds, 95–-98
Graham, Ben, 131
Greed paradigm, 279
Gretzky, Wayne, 140
Grey zone, 112
Gross domestic product (GDP), 167
Growth-oriented mutual fund, 134
Guaranteed investment certificates (GICs), 97

H

Haggling, 58
Hands-off investors, 108
Hands-on investors, 108
Harvesting, 20
Hidden commissions/expenses, 85, 94, 112, 117
High-yield (junk) bonds, 98, 99, 172
Hockey puck theory, 140, 278, 279
Hodad, 8
Home energy costs, 52
Home equity loan, 57
Home maintenance, 61

Hot tips, 90
How To Make Money In Stocks (O'Neil), 154
Hybrid fixed-income securities, 99

I

ICFP, 122
Illiquid assets, 16, 17
Imagination, 156
Incentive pay, 240, 241
Income capitalization method, 255
Income tax. *See* Taxes
Index funds, 103–106
Index-tracking stocks, 104, 105
Industry and country growth tactic, 166
Inefficient market gap tactic, 171, 172
Inflation, 21, 42, 43, 152
Information gap tactic, 169, 170
Information sponge, 251
Initial public offering (IPO), 88, 260
Institute of Chartered Financial Analysts (ICFP), 122
Insurance agent, 271
Insurance products, 90. *See also* Life insurance
Inter vivos trusts, 270
Interest rate seesaw, 163
Interest rates, 152, 162–164
Intermediary, 256
International RSP funds, 130
Internet stocks, 141
Internet web sites, 153, 299–301
Inverse, 42
Investment advisors. *See* Professional advisors
Investment company, 102. *See also* Mutual funds

Investment Funds Institute of Canada, 148
Investment laws, 175–184
Investment management cycle, 137–149
   asset allocation, 139–142
   investment selection, 142–147
   maintenance and review, 147–149
Investment objectives, 131
Investment pits, 81
Investment selection, 142–147
IPO, 88, 260

J

Job proposal, 71, 73
Jobs. *See* Employment
Junk bonds, 98, 99, 172

K

Knowledge, 161

L

Lalli, Frank, 5
Landsburg, Steven, 152
Lane, Roger, 208, 286, 292
Laws of successful portfolio management, 175–184
Letter of engagement, 219
Levels of wealth, 25–31
Life insurance, 50, 90, 91, 270
Limited partnerships, 87, 179
Lincoln, Abraham, 189
Liquid assets, 16, 17
Loan proposal, 230-232
Lottery tickets, 50
Lottery winners, 33, 34
Lynch, Peter, 131

M

Macro view, 148
Maintenance (take care of what you own), 60, 61

Maintenance and review, 147–149
Management expense ratio (MER), 86, 106
Margin, 180
Market comparison method, 254, 255
Market cycle tactic, 168
Market indices, 121
Market timing, 143, 144
Marketing, 211, 212
Meetings, 243, 244
Mental imagery, 284
Mental mindset. *See* Portfolio management tactics, Wealth paradigms
MER, 86, 106
Micro-delegation, 148
Micro view, 148
Mind-mapping, 286–288
Misconceptions of wealth, 12
Mission statement, 285, 286
Mistakes
   investors, by, 185–192
   taxes, 267–269
Money market funds, 96
Monthly expense sheet, 40, 41
Monthly planning, 288–290
Morgan Stanley World Market Index, 102
Muller, Dave, 144
Multi-fund portfolio management, 138
Mutual funds, 102–108, 132
   actively managed funds, 106
   advantages/disadvantages, 102, 103
   balanced funds, 106, 107
   bond funds, 107, 108
   buying multiple funds, 134, 135
   closed-end funds, 88, 107, 179
   cost (loads), 86, 87, 108, 181

307

direct-debit feature, 56, 133
growth-oriented vs. value-oriented managers, 134
guides, 134
index funds, 103-106
international funds, 130
management committee, 145
micro-delegation, 148
minimum investment amount, 129
money-market funds, 96
rankings/assessments, 148
sector funds, 147
selection strategies, 142–147

N

National Post, 62, 85, 109, 155, 168
Natural inefficiency, 171
Negative mental paradigms, 274
Negative people, 251
Net asset value, 88
Net bonus program, 240, 241
Net worth statement, 26
Nine-dot diagram, 275
No-load funds, 6, 181
NTF programs, 183

O

O'Neil, William, 154
One Up on Wall Street (Lynch), 62
Optimal wealth-building portfolio, 109
Options, 89
Own your own business. *See* Self-employment
P/E ratio, 100, 101, 168
Panic cycle pendulum, 165
Panic cycle tactic, 164–166
Pape, Gordon, 134
Paradigm barriers, 45

Paradigms, 273–277. *See also* Wealth paradigms
Partnerships, 204
Passion, 63, 64, 158, 183, 197
Past performance, 186, 277, 278
Past performance paradigm, 277–279
Patience, 65
Penny stocks, 89, 80
Philanthropic paradigm, 280
Planning, 283–293
communications book, 292, 293
daily, 290
decision making, 292
get fired up, 291, 292
monthly, 288-290
time- and life-planning systems, 285
tips, 291
values, 285
weekly, 290
yearly, 285-288
Portfolio, 16
Portfolio management cycle. *See* Investment management cycle
Portfolio management tactics, 161–174
demographic tactic, 169
economic cycle tactic, 166–168
industry and country growth tactic, 166
inefficient market gap tactic, 171, 172
information gap tactic, 169, 170
interest rate tactic, 162–164
market cycle tactic, 168
panic cycle tactic, 164–166
technology gap tactic, 170, 171
weekly top-10 tactic, 173
Portfolio performance, 20, 28

Portfolio tools, 81–110
equities, 99-102. *See also* Stocks
fixed-income securities, 95–100
mutual funds, 102-108. *See also* Mutual funds
optimal portfolio, 109
publications, 109
self-employment, 108. *See also* Self-employment
tools to avoid, 81–92
Post, William, 34
Price/earnings (P/E) ratio, 100, 101, 168
Privately held company, 16
Pro-forma financial statements, 202, 203
Procrastinating, 127
Professional advisors, 111–125
accountants, 217–225
background check, 124
bankers, 227–235
CAFP designation, 114
characteristics, 118, 119
client references, 123, 124
compensation, 116–118
credentials, 116, 117
customer service, 119–123
full-service broker, 113
Profit margin, 248
Program cars, 59
Project notebook, 289
Project plan, 288, 289
Proprietary investment products, 85, 86
Prospectus, 84, 102
Psychology of Achievement, The (Tracy), 10, 155

Q

Quarterly tax instalments, 268

R

Rags-to-riches stories, 5

Random Walk Down Wall Street, A (Malkiel), 62
Real estate, 132
Recordkeeping, 225, 267
Redenbacher, Orville, 176
Reengineering, 156, 157
Refinance the mortgage, 57
Registered retirement savings plan (RRSP), 56, 74, 75, 266
Relative strength, 154
Restaurants (eating out), 51
Retirement plans, 270
Retirement planning, 223
Return expectations, 131
Return on investment (ROI) test, 202
Risk, 20, 186
Risk tolerance, 21, 130
ROI test, 202
Role model, 70
RRSP, 56, 74, 75, 266
Rule of, 72, 22
Rumours, 90, 189

S

S&P/TSE 60, 101
Saving money, 56. *See also* Expense reduction
Scheiver, Anne, 5
Scrap yard, 87
Secondary market, 82, 84, 94
Sector funds, 147
Sector rotation, 144–146
Selection strategies, 142–147
Self-employment, 195–261
    accountants, 217–225
    bankers, 227–235
    business plan, 199–202
    business planning notebook, 208, 209
    damage control plan, 212, 213
    delegating, 241, 242
    employees, 213, 237–245
    ESOP plan, 244
    going public, 260

incentive pay program, 240, 241
    last-minute checklist, 204
    marketing, 211, 212
    maximize profits, 247–253
    meetings, 243, 244
    partnerships, 204
    payroll costs, 238
    pro-forma financial statements, 202, 203
    reasons why businesses fail, 214, 215
    selling the business, 253–260
    starting up, 196–199, 205
    systems and procedures, 209–211, 249, 250
    vacation time, 213, 214
    valuation of business, 253–255
Self-made wealthy people, 4, 5
Sell, when to, 155
Selling covered calls, 89
Selling your business, 253–260
Shaw, George Bernard, 156, 157
Shopping, 57, 58
Speed of car example, 158
Spending habits, 37–42
Standard of living, 19
Start early, 17-19
Statement of cash flow, 203
Step-by-step plan (wealth level 1), 33–53
Stockbrokers. *See* Brokers
Stock exchanges, 90
Stock market correction, 130, 131, 178
Stock underwriting, 88
Stocks, 99–102
    bonds, compared, 96
    books on stock picking, 62
    defined, 61
    domestic, 101
    foreign, 101, 102

index-tracking, 104, 105
Internet, 141
market corrections, 130, 131, 178
market value, 100
penny, 89, 80
Strip bonds, 97, 164
Sweat equity, 208
Systems and procedures, 209–211, 249, 250
T
T-bills, 97
Tactics. *See* Portfolio management tactics
Target savings goal (TSG), 23, 26
Tax advantage investment product, 180
Tax audit, 221, 222
Taxes, 265–272
    average income tax rate, 21, 22
    mistakes, 267–269
    RRSP, 266
    withholding, 268
    worrying too much about, 192, 193
Technical analysis, 143, 144
Technology gap tactic, 170, 171
Templeton, Sir John, 155
Testamentary trusts, 270
"Ticket To Trouble", 33
Time, 17
Time commitment, 154
Time management, 62
Time- and life-planning systems, 285
Tortoise-and-the-hare story, 133
Total return, 20, 28
Tracy, Brian, 10, 155
Trade shows and conventions, 251
Treasury bills, 97
Trends, 140–142
Trusts, 270

TSE 300 index, 101
TSG, 23, 26

U

Underwriter, 260
Underwriting fee, 117
Unreasonable thinking, 156, 157
Unsuitable investments, 85–91
Used cars, 58–60

V

Vacation time, 213, 214
Valuation of business, 253–255
Value Investing (Graham), 62
Value investor, 100
Value-oriented mutual fund, 134

Variable annuity, 91
Variable expenses, 19
Variable life insurance policy, 90, 91

W

Wall Street Journal, 109
Walton, Sam, 7
Warehouse clubs, 58
Wealth, 4
Wealth builder worksheet, 36
Wealth deception, 12
Wealth paradigms
    fear vs. contrarian, 279
    greed vs. philanthropic, 279, 280
    past performance vs. hockey puck, 277–279
Wealth test, 8–11
Wealthy, 4

Web sites, 153, 299–301
WEBS, 105
Weekly expense worksheet, 38, 39
Weekly planning, 290
Weekly top-10 tactic, 173
Will, 270
Working for others. *See* Employment

Y

Yearly planning, 285–288
Yield bait, 188
Young, Robert, 4

Z

Zero-based thinking, 85, 149, 190
Zero-coupon treasury bonds, 164

MARK HEINZL is a reporter in the Toronto bureau of *The Wall Street Journal*, and has covered a wide variety of Canadian business and finance topics, including high-tech, mining, manufacturing, and the stock and bond markets. He is the author of the best-selling book *Stop Buying Mutual Funds: Easy Ways To Beat The Pros Investing On Your Own*.

LARRY WASCHKA is a registered investment advisor and owner of Waschka Capital Investments.